A NEW HOME, WHO'LL FOLLOW?

AMERICAN WOMEN WRITERS SERIES

Joanne Dobson, Judith Fetterley, and Elaine Showalter, series editors

ALTERNATIVE ALCOTT
Louisa May Alcott
Elaine Showalter, editor

STORIES FROM THE COUNTRY OF
LOST BORDERS
Mary Austin
Marjorie Pryse, editor

CLOVERNOOK SKETCHES AND
OTHER STORIES
Alice Cary
Judith Fetterley, editor

HOBOMOK AND OTHER WRITINGS
ON INDIANS
Lydia Maria Child
Carolyn L. Karcher, editor

"HOW CELIA CHANGED HER MIND"
AND SELECTED STORIES
Rose Terry Cooke
Elizabeth Ammons, editor

THE LAMPLIGHTER
Maria Susanna Cummins
Nina Baym, editor

RUTH HALL AND OTHER
WRITINGS
Fanny Fern
Joyce Warren, editor

A NEW HOME, WHO'LL
FOLLOW?
Caroline M. Kirkland
Sandra A. Zagarell, editor

QUICKSAND AND PASSING
Nella Larsen
Deborah E. McDowell, editor

OLDTOWN FOLKS
Harriet Beecher Stowe
Dorothy Berkson, editor

HOPE LESLIE
Catharine Maria Sedgwick
Mary Kelley, editor

THE HIDDEN HAND
E.D.E.N. Southworth
Joanne Dobson, editor

"THE AMBER GODS" AND
OTHER STORIES
Harriet Prescott Spofford
Alfred Bendixen, editor

WOMEN ARTISTS, WOMEN
EXILES
"Miss Grief" and Other Stories
Constance Fenimore Woolson
Joan Myers Weimer, editor

A NEW HOME, WHO'LL FOLLOW?

OR

GLIMPSES OF WESTERN LIFE

CAROLINE M. KIRKLAND

Edited and with an Introduction by

SANDRA A. ZAGARELL

RUTGERS UNIVERSITY PRESS

New Brunswick and London

Library of Congress Cataloging-in-Publication Data

Kirkland, Caroline M. (Caroline Matilda), 1801–1864.
    A new home, who'll follow? or, Glimpses of Western life / Caroline M.
Kirkland ; edited with an introduction by Sandra A. Zagarell.
        p.   cm. — (American women writers series)
    Includes bibliographical references.
    ISBN 0-8135-1541-6 (cloth) — ISBN 0-8135-1542-4 (pbk.)
        1. Michigan—History—To 1837—Fiction.   2. Women and literature—
Michigan—History—19th century.   I. Zagarell, Sandra A.
II. Title.   III. Series.
PS2191.N4   1990
813'.3—dc20   89-70088
                                                                                CIP

British Cataloging-in-Publication information available

Copyright © 1990 by Rutgers, The State University
Manufactured in the United States of America

To my family

CONTENTS

ACKNOWLEDGMENTS

I wish to thank Jan Cooper, Pat Matthews, Paula Richman, and Janet A. Seiz for commenting on the introduction at various stages in its composition. A conversation with Carol S. Tufts was very illuminating at a point when I was trying to make sense of some of the shifts in Kirkland's published writing. Thanks also to several people associated with the Rutgers University Press American Women Writers series: to Leslie Mitchner for her interest and enthusiasm; to Jane Dieckmann for superb copyediting; to Joanne Dobson for reading my introduction with knowledge and care, and for asking me hard questions about it. The Oberlin College Library reference staff was most helpful as well, and I thank Cynthia Comer, Alison Gould, and Kathy Hines in particular. I owe special thanks to Valerie MacGowan-Doyle for her patience and her resourcefulness in speeding up the process of interlibrary loan. I also wish to thank several people who helped identify material from which Kirkland quotes: Beth Freeman, Nelson de Jesus, Justine di Fiore, Crispin Spaeth, and Carol S. Tufts. For generous permission to quote from Kirkland's unpublished correspondence and related unpublished materials, I thank the Collection of American Literature, Beinecke Rare Book and Manuscript Library, Yale University; Archives and Manuscripts Department, Chicago Historical Society Hill-Kirkland Papers; Otto Fisher Papers, Burton Historical Collection, Detroit Public Library; Department of Rare Books, Cornell University Library; Houghton Library of Harvard University; the Massachusetts Historical Society. Finally, I am grateful to Oberlin College and the Charles A. Dana Foundation for providing me with funds for a research assistant. To Anne Reid, who proved to be the ideal research assistant, I am most indebted of all.

Caroline Kirkland began her literary life as an innovator. Edgar Allan Poe explains that the success of her first book, *A New Home, Who'll Follow? or, Glimpses of Western Life* (1839), lay in its originality: it "wrought an un- *truth* doubted sensation [because of its] *truth* and novelty." For Poe, Kirkland's *&* significance resided in what later commentators have termed her pioneer *novelty* realism. He noted that while "[t]he west at that time was a field com- paratively untrodden by the sketcher or the novelists . . . to Mrs. Kirkland . . . we were indebted for our acquaintance with the *home* and home-life of the backwoodsman" and complimented the complexity and "life-like" quality of her character sketches (Poe 1181).

Poe's praise is typical of the contemporary antebellum reception of *A New Home,* a satiric, keenly observant narrative based on Kirkland's life as a settler in the wilds of Michigan in the 1830s. When *A New Home* appeared, both American magazines and newspapers—the *Knickerbocker,* the *North American Review,* the *Mirror*—and British journals—*The Antheneum,* the London *Literary Gazette*—praised Kirkland's presentation of western ma- terials for its freshness and realism. Recently, after more than a century of critical silence—during which time Kirkland's work, like that of virtually every other antebellum American woman writer, was labeled "sentimen- tal" and consigned to the literary rubbish heap—her realism has once more begun to command attention.[1]

Still, Kirkland has yet to receive her full due. In addition to being a fledgling realist, she was a sophisticated cultural critic who engaged in *&* wide-ranging, often satiric commentary on the sociocultural conventions

realist & cultural critic

and codes prevailing in both the eastern and the western United States. Further, her lengthy career as a professional literary woman has much to tell us about literary women in antebellum America. Like the majority of such women, she wrote specifically, and enthusiastically, for the burgeoning market that the newly developing publishing industry was helping to create in the decades before the Civil War. Much of her later writing took the form of literary journalism. She wrote educational pieces, sketches, journalistic essays—all genres that have not as yet received sufficient attention from scholars of this period in American literature. As a magazine writer she always had an eye on the public, but she was also a woman of strong convictions—she was a liberal who came to believe that there was considerable progressive potential within the existing social order—and she wrote reflectively on a range of topics, from women's education and dress to prison reform and class divisions within the United States.

Thus Kirkland's writing differs interestingly from most of the output of women writers of the period, for they specialized in fiction—the novels by and about women which Nina Baym, their major theorizer, terms *woman's fiction*. In addition, the pattern that emerges when we consider Kirkland's history as a writer casts light on the kinds of shifts that could occur in a professional literary woman's career during this time period. The freewheeling satire of *A New Home* angered many of Kirkland's Michigan neighbors, and she apparently modulated her public voice in response to that anger. Most of her subsequent work, though polished and thoughtful, does not engage in full-scale social critique; rather, it concentrates on bringing out the potential for improvement within current social and cultural arrangements. Yet toward the end of her career, her writing took another turn: she returned to a broader canvas and a more direct confrontation with conventions, questioning Victorian American constructions of what she and her contemporaries saw as the bedrock of all conventions, gender itself.

Whereas most literary women of the era were writers, moreover, Kirkland worked as a magazine editor as well: she edited the *Union Magazine* (later *Sartain's Union Magazine*) from 1847 to 1851. At a time when women were rarely involved in the business end of publishing, and women writers and their male publishers often drew on traditional gender roles to mediate their relationships,[2] she devised ways of maintaining her status as a "lady" while establishing relations with male entrepreneurs which were often markedly forthright and collegial. Her reasons for moving away from the full-scale cultural critique of *A New Home,* the ways in which she came to work within existing literary conventions while stretching those conventions to accommodate progressive ideas, and the factors in her becoming an adroit participant in the literary world of her day, are all part of a story that is intriguing in its own right. Because gender and economics play shaping roles in this story, it also adds, as we shall see, to our understanding of women, writing, and the world of literature in antebellum America.

BORN CAROLINE MATILDA STANSBURY in 1801, Caroline Kirkland came from a background that encouraged her intellectual development, self-sufficiency, interest in writing and instincts for reform.[3] Her grandfather, the Tory poet Joseph Stansbury, was known for the appealing satire of his verse. Her father, Samuel Stansbury, though a most unsuccessful entrepreneur, was apparently a loving parent. Her mother, Eliza Alexander Stansbury, wrote poetry and fiction, and Caroline later paid tribute to her by publishing one of her mother's sketches in a collection of her own work.[4] The oldest child in the family, remarkably active and intelligent, Caroline was sent to the school of her father's sister, Lydia Mott, at the age of eight. Like Caroline's parents, her aunt appreciated and encouraged her abilities, writing enthusiastically to them in 1809 that "when compared to the general run of our scholars . . . [their treasure] has about twice as much in her as any we have got & needs about double the care, she is indeed . . . 'no common child'" (26 July, CHS). Eventually, Caroline read French as well as some German, Latin, and English literature—an unusual range for a young woman of her day.

"Aunt Mott's" school also provided Caroline with the foundation for moral development, for Lydia Mott taught Caroline Quaker religious practices and humanitarian theories. When she was in her fifties, Kirkland explained to a friend that "the instruction of the Quakers" "first turned my attention" to "a private, secret communication with a personal God, or supernatural intelligence" (to Henry Bellows, [1858?], MHS). Additionally, Aunt Mott gave Caroline professional training, for the niece taught at her aunt's schools into the 1820s. The economic independence that teaching gave her must have reinforced Caroline's status in her own family. When Samuel Stansbury died in 1822, she was teaching at a school her aunt owned in Clinton, New York, and she persuaded her mother to relocate the entire family there.

Commentators have suggested that Caroline wanted her family to move to Clinton because she had become engaged to a young tutor at Hamilton College, William Kirkland, and wished to remain near him. If this was the case, it was characteristic of Caroline's directness with regard to her feelings about William. The glimpses we have of their relationship suggests that it was extraordinarily open and reciprocal. The intellectual and emotional partnership they enjoyed was unusual at a time when the ideology of separate spheres and the actual confinement of middle-class women to the home tended to create marriages in which husbands dominated and spouses' activities were conceived as distinct. Like Caroline, William was well educated, intellectual, and enterprising. The grandson of a founder of Hamilton College, he was educated there and had just embarked on a career as a tutor of languages when a student prank, probably the explosion of a cannon outside his room, permanently impaired his hearing and ended his plan to make college teaching his profession. A period of separation followed, with Caroline continuing to teach in New York and William studying in Germany. When the two finally married on January 10, 1828, their marriage quickly took what was to be its enduring shape. In its first year they started a family—their first child, Elizabeth, was born in 1828—and founded a girl's school near Utica, New York. The picture of a companionate relationship emerges in one of Caroline's few extant letters to William: she reminds him to "give the baby some Castor oil—a large teaspoonful—with brown sugar & a little boiling water—." Her love is also explicit: she pictures him "[taking] a good deal of comfort reading in the parlor while I am gone nobody interrupting you" but hopes that he will not take "too much [comfort] for I cannot endure to think you can do so well without me when nothing can please me, without you—" (1 Nov. 1829, CHS).

In 1835 the Kirklands moved to Detroit to head jointly the Detroit Female Seminary. Two years later they embarked on a new kind of enterprise: William had taken advantage of the land boom in Michigan to acquire eight hundred acres of land sixty miles west of Detroit, and the couple decided to found a village there. In 1837 they moved to the frontier village of Pinckney, which Caroline would call Montacute in *A New Home*. Kirkland's letters from this period, like *A New Home* itself, show that though her family life continued to be deeply satisfying, she felt culturally and socially isolated on the frontier, where her neighbors were of a different educational and class background. Characteristically she was resourceful about such limitations, however, keeping herself amused, and keeping up eastern friendships, by writing letters filled with witty and detailed observations about life in a frontier village. The pleasure she and her friends took in these letters convinced her to try to expand her readership to the general public. Here is the way she later explained the genesis of *A New Home:* "I little thought of becoming an author before I lived in the wilderness—There, the strange things I saw and heard every day prompted me to description, for they always presented themselves to me under a humorous aspect—Finding my letters amusing to my friends, I thought of "more of the same sort" for a book—but always felt very serious doubts whether it would be possible to find a publisher for such stuff— A friend in N.Y. however was more hopeful—and in due time "A New Home" saw the light under the auspices of Mr Francis of this city" (to John S. Hart, 18 Jan. 1851, CUL).

This account illuminates the conditions that helped make *A New Home* the inventive, complicated book it is. That Kirkland found life in the wilderness "strange"—rather than, say, uncivilized, which is the way British traveler Francis Trollope's *Domestic Manners of the Americans* (1832) represented life in frontier Cincinnati—indicates a pleasure in observation which allowed her to go beyond debunking the West as crude; that Pinckney prompted her to "description" attests to the keen eye for the details of daily life which has given the book its reputation for realism; that her friends found her letters "amusing" suggests that the satiric approach of the book is a continuation—"more of the same sort"—of the tone of the letters. The continuity between Kirkland as a correspondant and Kirkland as author of *A New Home* shows, moreover, that at the beginning of her writing career she did not distinguish between her personal and public voices. *A New Home* is an exuberant book. Like Kirkland's letters to friends, it has a strongly personal tone; indeed, one of its most engaging features is the author's self-projection in the person of the narrator, Mrs. Mary Clavers, a name she also adopts as her *nom de plume.* Connected to the frank and direct voice is Kirkland's assumption of the right to comment on and satirize a range of habits, conventions, and states of mind of both the West to which she had come and the East she thought of as the locus of her readers, from standards of cleanliness to taste in literature and dress.

Its comprehensiveness and outspoken satire make *A New Home* virtually unique among published works by antebellum American women: the popular newspaper columns and novels of Fanny Fern (Sarah Willis Parton) are among the few other satiric works women writers published during the era. One reason for the scarcity of satire or large-scale sociocultural critique by women is that the scope and irreverence of satire were incompatible with prevailing ideas about white middle-class femininity.

The characteristics of such femininity—among them religiosity, an ethic of service, dedication to the domestic circle—inscribe an acceptance of social norms. Taken as a whole, femininity, like the nuclear family which it supported, was seen as the cornerstone of the social order. This ideology did not, to be sure, inexorably consign all writing by antebellum women to conventionality. Much of the output of Kirkland's female contemporaries called attention to limitations in prevailing constructions of gender and adapted aspects of femininity to grant women certain strengths.[5] However, whereas such African-American women as Harriet E. Wilson and Harriet Jacobs openly indicted the intertwinings of racism, slavery, and white femininity, white women writers seldom criticized fundamental social norms directly. When they did, it was usually on behalf of specific, delimited social changes, notably (as in *Uncle Tom's Cabin*) the abolition of slavery. Certainly the assumptions on which comprehensive social critique rested—the writer's ability to analyze the foundations of social and cultural practice and authority to pronounce skeptically on the ways of the world—was quintessentially at odds with prevailing constructions of femininity.

Though *A New Home* was the self-confident utterance of a woman who did not align her pronouncements with this ideology, Kirkland had not set out to defy true womanhood. The evidence we have suggests that she had simply continued to write in the voice of her correspondence, giving her wit full play, and had not thought deeply about the consequences. Certainly she did not anticipate the vehemence of her Michigan neighbors' responses. A contemporary recounts that *A New Home* "raised against [Mrs. Kirkland] a whirlwind of indignation among her Pinckney neighbors . . ." for which she was totally unprepared: "She had supposed that it was all concealed by calling the town Montacute and altering the names of the actors, and that no copies of the work would find their way to that remote settlement. But in this she was mistaken, and . . . all the persons thus truthfully depicted, were exasperated almost to frenzy. One woman threatened to have her put under bonds, and the life of the Kirkland family in Pinckney thereafter was the reverse of agreeable" (quoted by Osborne 44). Resentment still ran high several years after *A New Home*'s appearance. A lawyer from New York State traveling in Michigan in 1843 reported to his family that he had been in "Mrs Kirkland's neighborhood" and found her in "bad odure with her neighbors." He was treated to some rather menacing statements, of the kind she herself may have heard: it was, he was told, "well known who she meant, and she had better attend to her own family and let other people's alone" (quoted by Osborne 44–45).

All indications are that these hostilities prompted a fall from innocence about writing and gender in Caroline Kirkland.[6] She appears to have thought of herself henceforth not just as a writer, but as a woman writer—a writer who needed to preserve her status as a respectable woman by observing certain proprieties when appearing before the public. In 1843, in one of the few direct statements we have about her sense of herself as a writer, she identified *A New Home* as uninhibited in a way nothing else she wrote would ever be, and acknowledged that thereafter she separated her public voice from her private one. To Rufus Griswold, editor of *Graham's Magazine,* who was soliciting her work, she explained that "I shall probably never write any thing as amusing as my first effort, because I accomplished that under the assured belief that the author would never be discovered . . ." (21 Jan. 1843, DPL). Kirkland specifically linked her later circumspection to the desire to protect her femininity: in the sentence preceding the one just quoted, she requested a lady's prerogative to publish anonymously: "a lady always feels under a certain degree of restraint when she feels that the world is looking her in the face all the time—many a thought 'funny, free and flashy' is checked through a feeling of diffidence or pride— . . ."

But Kirkland did not retreat into unreflecting conventionality. She was never a prude, and she disliked mere respectability, saying of Melville's *Omoo,* for example, that she liked it because it was *not* respectable. In her letters, the satire and delight in exposing the hypocrisy of certain cultural practices still emerges strongly. Consider this zestful description of a group of statues of cherubs "*au naturel*" created for a local Episcopal church: they "so shocked the women members" that the sculptor "envelope[d] the little fellows in leaves . . . so effectually that the hand holding the cross was entirely wrapped up while that with the cup still appeared—giving the whole the effect of Infant Bacchusses, just issuing from cornucopia—Sixty of these along the walls of a church must have been great aids to devotion" (to Henry and Eliza Bellows, 6 Aug. 1847, MHS). But as a writer for the public she became extremely selective about what she critiqued, and after *A New Home* her published writing is almost never again comprehensive. Her next book, a collection of sketches about western life, *Forest Life* (1842), contains some satire of Michigan traits, but the targets are generally acceptable ones—dishonest land sharks, meddling spinsters. Most tellingly, her persona, Mary Clavers, no longer has a sharply defined sensibility and exhibits a new reticence about her neighbors which she links to her standing with her readership. Once one is known by one's neighbors, she explains, "it is impossible to describe minutely our own personal experiences without giving in some degree the experience of others; and this is a matter requiring careful handling, to say the least. We may say of ourselves what we must not say of others . . ." (*Forest Life* 2:48).

Kirkland had too much integrity not to be aware than she was muting her voice, and throughout her life, in letters to her closest friends, she castigated herself for what she termed her lack of courage. An indirect indication of her uneasiness about her self-suppression may also be detected in the severity with which she came to censure women writers who ventured beyond the boundaries of propriety. In what was perhaps the harshest review she ever published, she took the French feminist novelist George Sand sharply to task for what she considered a cavalier attitude toward marriage and a pernicious support of divorce, claiming that Sand would do "far better work for her sex and her race" if she showed women, or indeed couples, enduring unsatisfactory marriages with good grace ("George Sand and the Journeyman Joiner" 222). Similarly, Kirkland's reaction to the notoriety the English writer Elizabeth Gaskell suffered after publishing her *Life of Charlotte Brontë* in 1857 holds that the woman writer herself should be responsible for working within the boundaries of decorum and avoiding public censure. Gaskell had revealed that Charlotte Brontë's brother Branwell had had an affair with the mother of the children whom he tutored. Though Kirkland did not question Gaskell's facts (which were accurate), she held Gaskell herself accountable for Mrs. Robinson's much-publicized threat to sue for slander. "What a horrid position Mrs Gaskell has placed herself in being obliged to retract all she had said in a such a solemn way about that unhappy experience of Patrick Brontë—," she proclaimed. She then extended her censure to all women who lacked the sense to navigate within the status quo and thus protect themselves from public scorn. "Oh these women!," she exclaimed, "how little prudence they have!" (to Henry Bellows, 31 July 1857, MHS).

ADAPTING TO STRICTURES of convention, Kirkland continued to write for the public. In addition to *Forest Life* she contributed to such magazines as *Graham's* and the *Knickerbocker* and to Cary and Hart's *Annual*, a gift book of the type publishers began to find highly profitable in the late 1820s. She doubtlessly also wrote to bolster family finances, for Pinckney did not prosper. In 1843 the Kirklands—who now had five children—left Michigan and settled in New York City. Toward the end of the Pinckney years William had begun to write too, and in New York the collaborative character of their marriage apparently took on a new dimension; he became an editor of the New York *Mirror* and Caroline wrote for the newspaper.

During these early years in New York, Caroline Kirkland balanced several roles with her characteristic energy. In addition to being a mother she launched her own school for girls. Her social life became very active, her circle consisting in part of the growing group of "New York Literati" who were among the era's most prominent literary figures: her friends and acquaintances included Poe, the editor-writer-literary entrepreneurs Nathaniel P. Willis and Evert Duyckinck, literary hostess Ann Lynch, authors Lydia Maria Child and Catharine Maria Sedgwick, and the poets Lydia Sigourney and William Cullen Bryant. Kirkland's correspondence shows that she was liked and respected by the literati and that she felt herself their intellectual equal. This reaffirmation of her status may have inspired her to engage again, very tentatively, in selective cultural criticism, for the scope of her writing expanded during the mid 1840s. She wrote for a range of publications and in a range of modes, including reviews that appeared in numerous publications, essays, stories for *Godey's Lady's Book,* and even a satiric piece entitled "Biography of a Distinguée" for Duyckinck's humorous magazine *Yankee Doodle.* She prepared a modernized version of Book I of Spenser's *Fairy Queen* for publication, wrote an introduction to the American edition of Marion Hugo's feminist *A Plea for Women,* and produced a third collection of western sketches, *Western Clearings* (1845), in which she occasionally edged toward the more incisive commentary of *A New Home.*

Her firsthand knowledge of writers and markets and her expanded literary range might have prompted Kirkland to engage once more in fuller cultural commentary, but events cut short any such development. In the fall of 1846 William Kirkland died unexpectedly. Returning from a visit to the one of the Kirklands' sons in Fishkill, New York, William lost his footing as he boarded a night steamer and drowned. The devastation Caroline felt was overwhelming. She wrote a friend that she was cast into an emotional void, for she had "depended, heart and soul, on my husband—I feel unfit to walk alone—," and that she was also economically stranded: "My children are to be educated and provided for—on my own and their earnings principally—" (to Theodore Woolsey, 2 Mar. 1847, BC). Kirkland would teach sporadically for the rest of her life, sometimes educating young women in her home, occasionally giving instruction at one of New York's many girls' schools, but her skill as a writer and her connections among the literati enabled her to make writing and publishing her major source of income. Just before he died, William had become editor of a new Unitarian newspaper, the *Christian Inquirer,* of which Caroline was to be literary editor. Friends persuaded her to assume full editorship immediately. Though she held this post for only few months, in 1847 she also became editor of the new literary and art magazine, the *Union Magazine.* (After 1848, when John Sartain bought the magazine, renamed it *Sartain's Union Magazine,* and moved its offices from New York to Philadelphia, she shared editorial duties with John S. Hart, a Philadelphia educator and man of letters.) She also wrote for the *Union* and *Sartain's* as well as for *Putnam's* and other magazines. One sign of her success as a writer and her acumen as a businesswoman is that between 1853 and 1856 Charles Scribner published her magazine pieces in three book-length collections and the letters she sent to the *Union* while traveling in Europe in a fourth.

In leaving Caroline Kirkland little choice but to become a professional writer, William's death helped solidify her identity as one of the many women writers who saw their work as a vocation, "a profession and not a calling" in Nina Baym's phrase (*Woman's Fiction* 32). As a writer of nonfiction who intended her work for readers of both sexes, however, she differs from the novelists Baym discusses. In becoming an editor, moreover, Kirkland occupied a position unusual, though not unheard of, for antebellum literary women.[7] The sheer pace of her life after William died, combined with her need to be assured of the market appeal of her writing and of the *Union,* probably tempered any resurgence of enthusiasm she may have felt for full-scale cultural commentary or satire—including satire of literary conventions, to which she had devoted some of her best energy in *A New Home.* But her professionalization, far from channeling her intellectual and political energies into the mere reduplication of conventions, focused her efforts on reforming the conventions of her era, nonliterary as well as literary.

Most important, her experience in the marketplace taught her to manipulate conditions generally unaccommodating to women—conditions over which she had no direct control—in order to preserve her own values and her sense of herself as a woman professional. Most likely, her hard-won sense of the connections between propriety and womanly status trained her for this effort; certainly it strengthened her sense that it was incumbent upon her to insist on maintaining her status as a respectable woman. She appears to have conducted herself with extraordinary skill, and without the kind of ambivalence which Mary Kelley finds to have characterized so many of the women of the time who moved beyond the domestic into the public sphere. On a purely personal level, Kirkland welcomed the activity her work provided, calling employment a "grand panacea." She also quickly learned to negotiate skillfully within the public, masculine workplace to create a makeshift woman's space: explaining that she shunned her "lonely" home, she described to friends her success in fashioning proper dining arrangements (and the relative lack of success of her efforts to avoid repugnant male colleagues): "I . . . often [take] my dinner at the office . . . where I eat it off the corner of Joseph's table, with a newspaper for a cloth [her son Joseph was apparently an apprentice of the journal's printer]. . . . That old troglodyte [*Union* owner] Israel Post . . . hops up out of his dark corner, with glassy eyes, as I go in, and extends a toad-like paw, which I shake shudderingly, knowing that he will be content with nothing less" (to Eliza and Henry Bellows, 6 Aug. 1847, MHS). Though she was not always paid punctually by the *Union,* she was able to make the position work to her advantage when she wished to travel to Europe in 1848 with her friends the Bellows. While arranging for poet and essayist Bayard Taylor, whom she greatly respected, to substitute for her at the *Union,* she convinced the owners to pay her "about $300 in arrears . . . which they wd not other wise have felt able to do—in consideration of the advantage to be derived" from the sketches she was to furnish the magazine about her travels (to Henry Bellows, before 31 Mar. 1848, MHS).

To be sure, Kirkland did not always get her way. When John Sartain bought the *Union* while she was in Europe, he appointed John Hart the magazine's coeditor without consulting her. Furthermore, the men with whom she worked were wont to violate the observation of decorum she equated with womanliness, as when *Sartain's* cover once erased her gender and marital status by listing its editors as "John S. Hart and C. M. Kirkland." But Kirkland's reaction shows how decidedly she could invoke class-based notions of gender—what is gentlemanly, what is ladylike—to insist that her own codes prevail. Requesting that her full name be restored, she wrote to "Sartain & Co.": "I have never authorized any person to address me [without "Mrs."], and should take it as an incivility if any but a Quaker did so. . . . I have no desire to appear before the public in any unusual form" (30 Dec. 1850, CUL). And though in soliciting contributions for the *Union* and *Sartain's,* as in questions of design and artwork, she was subject to her publisher's ideas about what would sell, she became quite skilled as a literary agent and procurer of literary work of merit. Probably hired partly because of her contacts, she ably solicited contributions from prominent writers of her acquaintance—William Cullen Bryant, Evert Duyckinck—and arranged for the appearance of good, though lesser-known writers, as when she secured for *Sartain's* Elizabeth Gaskell's sketch "The Last Generation of England," which would become the basis of Gaskell's narrative *Cranford.* Indeed, she helped produce a publication of fairly high quality, with work by Poe, Whitman, Sigourney, and Thoreau, among others. Frank Luther Mott notes that *Sartain's* paid quite decently (Mott 771), and it did so partly because Kirkland became so adroit at manipulating marketplace codes to obtain fair payment for the writers. Her letters give glimpses of the way she accomplished this. When James Russell Lowell sent her a poem she liked, she urged him to "learn to put a price upon yourself," and suggested the amount he could expect to command: "Shall I ask [Hart for] twenty or twenty-five dollars—or what—for your poem, which I think very charming . . ." (30 Mar. 1849, HL). Soon she was able to inform Hart that "I have a letter from Mr Lowell saying that he wants $30 for his poem and for future poems—He says he will abide by any thing I have done as to the past—but mentions this sum for the future," skillfully attaining her objective for payment for Lowell by appealing to the superior business position that Hart occupied as male editor. She adds cleverly, "Now I believe I *did* nothing—but only suggested—however you will know best about that and act accordingly" (to John S. Hart, 3 May 1849, CUL).

Kirkland evidently identified Sartain's and Hart's competitive, market-based conduct as specifically masculine, and she tried to maneuver her male colleagues into adapting to more communitarian values, which she saw as feminine. Writing on behalf of another woman writer as well as herself when Hart was angry that *Godey's Lady's Book* had published an unauthorized sketch by Swedish author Frederika Bremer, a *Sartain's* contributor, Kirkland declared herself "much troubled at the idea of being implicated in any unfriendly rivalry with the Lady's Book—Mrs Hale's [*Godey's* editor] being considered both by Mrs Howitt and myself as a friend would make it particularly painful to be arrayed against her— Indeed I can imagine no pecuniary interest that would make me willing to get into a quarrel with anybody" (27 Oct. 1849, CUL).

Even more than her editorial work, Kirkland's writing was an impor-

tant source of family income, and here too she expressed her own principles. To her close friend Henry Bellows she wrote, "I never get a dollar
without earning it fully, and really as a matter of choice I care little where I
work. I shall try to do some good with my pen . . ." (27 May 1849, MHS).
Much of her writing adapts popular forms—the essay, the sketch—to
promote liberal social reform. While adhering scrupulously to conventions
about tone, scope, and attitudes, her work advocates greater social responsibility and a more communal culture. In an essay called "The Mystery of
Visiting" (*Sartain's*, Aug. 1850), she plays anthropologist to show that contemporary urban customs about hospitality and entertainment are cultural
constructs, not absolute standards, and indicts them for merely facilitating
social circulation rather than expressing community. She supported the
abolition of slavery and opposed capital punishment, and she sometimes
wrote to support specific progressive causes, producing *The Helping Hand,
Comprising an Account of the Home for Discharged Female Convicts and Appeal in
Behalf of that Institution* (1853) to aid the movement for the rehabilitation of
female convicts. On family organization she tended to be a conservative
reformer—"The Household," which was, she told Bellows, a "shadowing
forth of some of my notions" about social organization, depicts the patriar-
chal family in which the father plays a central role as the proper foundation
of the social order at large. About women's position, on the other hand,
she was often quite progressive. She opposed tight lacing and noted the
practicality of the much-maligned bloomers, though she found them ugly.
The witty and incisive "Literary Women" (reprinted in this volume) shows
that she could still be scathingly satiric when she chose: the essay mocks
the belief held by some of her contemporaries that writing defeminizes
women, and contains a pointed reminder that women's lives and creativity
continue into middle age, and beyond.

Kirkland's last significant literary effort, *Personal Memoirs of Washington*
(1856), shows that as an established and knowledgeable writer, she returned to writing a fairly comprehensive sociocultural critique when two
issues she cared deeply about, gender reform and Abolition, converged. In
Memoirs she implicitly takes exception to conventional political biographies
of Washington—the standard life by historian Jared Sparks, Washington
Irving's *Life*—to present an audience whom the standard biographies ignored, "women and young persons," as she explained to Sparks (20 Dec.
1853, HL), with reformed versions of gender. She begins by contesting the
prevalent view of Washington as a man who lived in the public realm and
had "no private character" (6). Her critique is tantamount to a rejection of

the value system in which true manhood and the fully public life are one. Repeatedly, she impugns the accuracy of the image of Washington as self-sufficient and aloof while linking these traits with a misguided ideal (the standard Washington is, she insists, "cold," a "statue," a "stern, rigid business machine," a man on a "pedestal" (vi, 7, 95, 191). Her expressed intention is to present "Washington, the man" (8), and in her hands the domestic and the public are intertwined in genuine manhood, much as they were for the domestic father in "The Household." "Home was always a prominent object in [Washington's] mind," she proclaims (414), and her Washington's capacity for leadership is enhanced by an abiding commitment to domestic life.

Memoirs also reflects Kirkland's intention to extend some form of citizenship to women. Dedicated to "*all* my young friends . . . and particularly to my own sons and daughters" (author's emphasis), it corrects Victorian American ideas about restrictions on femininity, showing the importance of women in American history. It contains a very favorable portrait of Martha Washington, whom Kirkland at times elevates into a quasi-political figure, paying considerable attention to her activities on behalf of the Revolutionary Army, her exemplary conduct as First Lady, even mentioning that she was sometimes credited with the authorship of a political pamphlet, "The Sentiments of American Women." In several sections devoted to Mary Washington, mother of the president, it portrays Republican motherhood—the late eighteenth-century idea that as mothers and educators of sons, women had an important, if indirect, public role to play—as an implicit counterweight to the later ideology of true womanhood, and goes so far as to imply that if George Washington is the father of his country, Mary Washington deserves recognition as its true mother (see esp. 34–38).

Kirkland also wanted *Memoirs* to aid the Abolitionist cause. Feeling that Washington's opposition to slavery was not well known, she devoted parts of the book to his views. A measured exposition of his antislavery sentiments constitutes the bulk of the final chapter, while comparisons between his principles and those of her contemporaries, sprinkled throughout, have a bite and forcefulness close to the commentary of *A New Home*. For instance, portraying Washington as a man who exceeded the mentality of his day in being able to question slavery, she asserts that "he would have been slow to believe, probably, that the day would ever come when good people could be found who would condemn dancing, yet refuse to condemn slavery; who would consider card-playing a sin, yet utter no fulminations against what Washington himself, born and bred in the midst of it, calls 'a wicked, cruel and unnatural trade'" (205).

In her preface, Kirkland expresses an awareness that materials reflecting everyday life contain important social and personal information—an approach that, though it would have been unthinkable to such political historians as Sparks, has become fundamental to twentieth-century social history. She explains that she will omit "much that is usually interwoven with the Life of Washington, such as details of battles and of politics," drawing instead on "extracts from the diary of daily life at Mount Vernon and descriptions of Washington's doings, appearance, habits, and manners as reported by himself and his contemporaries" (9). While *Memoirs* does detail much of Washington's public life (often dutifully citing Sparks and Irving as if to legitimate its veracity in political and military matters), it also pointedly corrects the authoritative biographies by including vital information about "Washington, the man" obtained from mundane records. One example will suffice. In a chapter on Washington's married life before the Revolution, Kirkland reproduces one of the annual purchase orders he sent his agent in England, treating it as a precious mirror of the Washingtons' home life. She sees in it the reflection of Washington's ignorance about womanly attire and his devotion to the women of his family: "In writing for the finery of the ladies of the family Washington evidently took the names of the different articles from viva voce communication and wrote them down as he could best guess at the spelling. As '6 yds. Jackenot Muslin'—'1 pr. Corded Dimothy'—(a farmer being more familiar with Timothy than with Dimity)— . . . 'Pinns,'—'Jarr Raisons' . . ." (181). This chapter concludes with a pointed statement about her intent to revise standard historical method and subject matter: "It is because these seeming trifles do assist in forming an estimate of Washington's condition, character and tastes at that period that I have thought it worth while to cite these specimens of the annual invoice" (182).

Memoirs caused Kirkland more anxiety and effort than anything she ever attempted. She researched it painstakingly, writing to experts to gather information, conducting interviews, spending the summer of 1855 in Washington, DC, reading Washington's papers. Her letters about the project are full of uncharacteristic doubts and fears. Not only did she feel herself to be poaching on male territory in making the country's father, and a national icon, her subject, she was, for the first time since *A New Home,* engaging in far-reaching public commentary, and she was doing so by drawing overtly on her perspective as a woman to challenge male authorities' construct of Washington. In spite of her qualms, however, she insists that it is precisely her gender that enables her to see the importance of such matters as the way Washington conducted his domestic affairs, for "men have hitherto scorned all this class of materials—those would show the *man* so plainly" (to Henry Bellows, 19 July 1855, author's emphasis, MHS). The force of this latter conviction seems to have helped give her the courage to insist on retaining all the antislavery material when her publisher, George Appleton, threatened not to publish *Memoirs* if she did not excise her own commentary. The ability to hold her own in the publishing world, gained through long experience, also helped: she was prepared to withdraw the book if need be, explaining to Bellows that "I *may* be obliged yet, to go to Boston for a publisher" (26 July 1856, author's emphasis, MHS). Finally her prediction that "they will let me have my own way in the end" was borne out (to Henry Bellows, 2 Aug. 1856, MHS). Appleton agreed to publish the manuscript intact.

IN THE LAST YEARS of her life, although she published some magazine pieces and prepared a book of educational materials for publication, Kirkland devoted herself more fully to her family.[8] She built a new home in Eagleswood, Perth Amboy, New Jersey; she made several trips to Illinois to visit her son Joseph, who was working there, and other family members. But she was also deeply committed to Abolition and to the Union cause, and when the war began she moved back to New York City and began working for the United States Sanitary Commission, the forerunner of the Red Cross. She headed a woman's sewing circle that produced clothing for Union soldiers; she organized drives to secure soldiers medical supplies and books; she tried to interest others in joining the war effort. She was active up to her death. On April 4, 1864, she opened a Metropolitan Fair, which she had organized to raise funds for the Sanitary Commission. On the morning of April 6 she suffered a stroke and died in her sleep.

The pallbearers at Kirkland's funeral, among them William Cullen Bryant and Nathaniel P. Willis, were prominent men whose presence reflects her public stature. The funeral oration, preached by the Reverend S. K. Lothrop of Boston, suggests that despite her decorum, she was an unsettling figure to some contemporaries who had strong convictions about the limitations of women and their absolute differences from men. Lothrup's praise for her as a writer was distinctly uneasy—she had "a masculine grasp of theme [and] . . . a feminine delicacy in illustrating it"—and he hastened to emphasize the greater importance of her more traditional activity as an educator of the young.[9] Some male contemporaries paid her similar compliments. Bayard Taylor cast her as the exception that proves the rule, maintaining that she "is, to my mind, possessor of more genius than any woman in America."[10] Abolitionist businessman and writer James Gilmore went through some striking contortions to reaffirm prevailing gender categories yet do her justice: lamenting to a friend that "her death cut . . . short" his plan to found a Woman's League which would flood the south with Abolitionist publications, he added, "and now, I know of no woman (it should be done by the women) brave enough, and 'man' enough to head the movement."[11] For the Swedish writer and feminist Frederika Bremer, on the other hand, Kirkland presented no dilemmas about gender, because, for her, Kirkland simply refuted the dichotomies of masculine and feminine to which so much of Victorian American ideology subscribed. "Hers is a character of great depth," Bremer wrote after meeting her in the early 1850s. "She is one of those natures in which the feminine and the manly attributes are harmoniously blended."[12]

WE TURN NOW to a closer examination of A New Home. As cultural commentary, Kirkland's narrative operates on several levels. Much of its satire is directed at literary practices: it critiques several popular genres within which contemporary writers evoked the West. It pillories sentimental representations by including several love stories in which eastern emigrants enact formulaic romances and display a remarkable obliviousness to their new western environment. It mocks the rosy depictions of the West's natural environment in the many guides intended to lure easterners into emigrating to the West and in such travel literature as Charles Feno Hoffman's popular A Winter in the West (1835). It exposes the supposedly "realistic" celebration of the West as the site of untrammeled nature in the newly emerging western literature (particularly James Hall's Legends of the West [1832]) as the mere reproduction of conventions of continental, British, and American Romanticism. Kirkland's satire is explicitly grounded in women's perspective, for women's experiences were ignored or falsified by these representations of the West and women were in reality often faced with learning to live among people unlike the friends and family they had left behind and with building a domestic life in alien and difficult circumstances.[13]

In addition, A New Home attends to depicting what life in the West is really like—to the process of community formation which, for Kirkland, constitutes the real drama of western life. In exploring this process, Kirkland works within a newly emerging genre, the village sketch. The village sketch provided an alternative to both Romantic-based formulas and to dramatic plots. Developed primarily by women,[14] it focused on the details of daily life and on village inhabitants' personal histories to render the dynamics and practice of the village as a community and a culture. Village sketches such as Lydia Sigourney's *Sketch of Connecticut* (1824) and Eliza Buckminster Lee's *Sketch of a New-England Village in the Last Century* (1838) displayed considerable sophistication, indeed protoethnographic sensitivity, in portraying local cultures as dynamic systems that negotiated the needs and interests of diverse community members. Though there is no evidence that Kirkland knew these narratives, her stated model was a work pivotal in the development of the village sketch, the English writer Mary Russell Mitford's *Our Village* (1824–32)—a series of sketches about the rural village of Aberleigh, where Mitford lived.

Although by putting village life in the foreground, Kirkland is explicit in her adaptation of Mitford, she does not reproduce the village sketch in full any more than she does the genres she satirizes. Rather, she tailors it to a situation and objectives that are unique. In contrast to Mitford, Sigourney, and others, she is writing not about an established village and culture but about the *creation* of both. Moreover, while other writers tend to be celebratory, Kirkland's representation of village and culture is complicated by her sense that community is formed in the American West within the parameters of certain unique paradoxes. While circumstances and democratic ideology presume the equality of all community members, and the settlers' necessary interdependence mandates this equality, communal life also reveals to her that in fact all the members of the community are not equal—or, rather, equally worthy. For her, the vulgarity of one group of settlers and the pretense to gentility of another present serious impediments to the achievement of community.

A New Home is thus about a complex process, the process by which the settlement on the Clavers's land becomes a village community. The situation of Montacute, as Kirkland portrays it, is always in flux. As was the case for most Michigan villages in the 1830s—the time of a great land boom—the actual village, Pinckney, was being established on land where certain white settlers had already lived for some time: the highly individualistic farmers and woodsmen who, with little formal education but considerable determination, formed the backbone of Jacksonian democracy. These "indigenous" settlers, as Kirkland sometimes calls them, were followed in the 1830s by a wave of immigrants coming from the East, of whom the Clavers were exemplary. They tended to be middle class, better educated, and tenacious of their alliances with the more genteel culture of the Northeast. For Kirkland, the "West" is a site where a culture must be created from these heterogeneous and often conflicting groups, and *A New Home* traces the process of their slow and usually testy mutual accommodation. Dwelling on their frequent clashes and adjustments, Kirkland takes a humorous and generally analytic perspective, reflecting on the assumptions, biases, and practices of both groups. To the extent that Montacute does succeed in becoming a bona fide village—a community and not a mere demographic entity in which various types of people live in proximity—she shows that it does so because something new is born, a pluralistic, polyphonic culture that honors the original viewpoints and practices of each constituent group and may well represent the future of America itself.

The slow process of community and culture formation is *A New Home*'s central "action," and while Kirkland's persona, Mary Clavers, plays a key role in it, this role is more culturally representative than individual: she embodies an eastern sensibility that must adjust to western life. An "actual settler," as she is called on the title page, she takes full part in the community's development. Furthermore, and in contrast to the unobtrusive participant/observer stance of the narrators of most antebellum village sketch literature, her participation in the community and the consequent changes in attitude she undergoes are central features of the narrative. She begins western life with an easterner's ambivalence about the "indigenous" settlers which never fully abates, and she continues to reflect on her experiences with considerable wryness. She also gradually learns to adapt to the developing community. In effect, the formation of Montacute thus occurs within Clavers as well as around her: her developing capacity to accommodate westerners as well as easterners constitutes one dimension of the community's development.

In representing the changes in Clavers's expectations and assumptions—and reproducing, yet also satirizing, her persistent ambivalences—*A New Home* achieves its most original cultural commentary, for it adopts an approach that is, I believe, unique in the protoethnographic literature of the period. Mary Clavers's cultural biases and her gradual acculturation are conveyed through her own self-observation. In addition to reflecting on the beliefs and attitudes of her neighbors of both eastern and indigenous origins, Clavers perpetually queries her *own* responses and behavior. Like her approach to others, her approach to herself is satirical. Her self-mockery consistently places her attitudes in question, as in the following comment on her adjustment to life in a log cabin: "My ideas of comfort were by this time narrowed down to a well-swept room with a bed in one corner, and cooking-apparatus in another—and this in some fourteen days from the city!" (ch. xii). *A New Home* thus extends the ethnographic dimension of village sketch literature by highlighting the narrator's own participation in village culture. Though the narrative's satire distinguishes it from most ethnography—for ethnography not only strives for objectivity, it often purports to have reverent respect for its subjects— Clavers's self-scrutiny anticipates the self-awareness of late twentieth-century ethnographers such as Vincent Crapanzano in *Waiting: The Whites of South Africa*. Like them, she suggests that the pose of objectivity generally masks a host of unacknowledged assumptions that are as culturally marked as the assumptions and practices of those whom the ethnographer observes.

A combination of reflexivity with the satiric demolition of Romantic clichés and tropes and of sentimental fiction help make *A New Home* an agreeably complicated book. Filled with folksy anecdotes and sketches, consistently dramatizing a community's daily life rather than featuring an individualized central protagonist, *A New Home* can also be most confusing to late twentieth-century readers. We may initially be tempted to accept at face value Clavers's own description of her narrative technique as an "[unorthodox] way of telling a story" peppered with "rambling gossip" (ch. XXI) and fail to see that such formulations constitute yet another dimension of the book's satire—a means by which Kirkland destabilizes readers' expectations of a tightly unified plot. Still, *A New Home* is undergirded by a discernible narrative line, though not one that traces an individual life. Like that of most village sketches, the "story" is communal and delineates the gradual formation of the community of Montacute.

Because village sketch literature and communal narratives are unfamiliar to most twentieth-century readers, we should review briefly the way *A New Home* folds the story of Mary Clavers's gradual adjustment to material and cultural conditions in the West into that of Montacute's growth. By the time the Clavers family moves into a frame house (chapter XXVII), Montacute has some other settlers, a grain mill, a store. More settlers arrive; a neighboring town, Tinkerville, is begun; and finally local institutions take hold—a (wildcat) bank in Tinkerville, a school and a library, a Montacute's women's sewing circle, a system of justice. By the end, Montacute has become a lively, flourishing community and Mary Clavers a committed, if rueful and self-mocking participant in it.

Complicating this concentration on community development is Kirkland's sense that egalitarianism in the West is excessive, often allowing the settlers to follow their worst inclinations. Believing in order in all its forms—from manners and decorum through family life to social organization—Kirkland saw in many "indigenous" westerners a combination of ignorance, arrogance, lack of restraint, and irresponsible individualism that not only offended her sensibilities but also seemed to her to jeopardize the formation of a stable and functioning community. *A New Home* is unflinching in its representation of the shiftlessness and opportunism of several Montacute families, of the penchant in the West for mobbism, of drunkenness and wife abuse, of sexual license that results in one young woman's death because of a botched abortion and another's success in framing a hapless schoolmaster as the father of her illegitimate child. Mary Clavers dwells at particular length on practices whose vulgarity makes genuine community with some of her neighbors sometimes appear out of the question to a person of her refinement. These include the ignorant schoolmarm Cleory Jenkins's insistence on smoking a pipe—and spitting at Clavers's hearth—and the crassness of Simeon Jenkins, Montacute's "Justas of the Piece," who achieved his prosperity partly by having provided for his neighbors the entertainment of stoning a large turkey "at twenty-five cents a throw" and his status partly by changing political parties when expedience mandated. Further impeding the achievement of community, in Kirkland's eyes, is the insistence of a number of the more "genteel" settlers on retaining class-based attitudes inappropriate to life on the frontier, in particular a conviction that any sort of work would lower their status and a refusal to acknowledge any bond with their more "vulgar" neighbors. Such an outlook, she shows, does more than maintain class barriers and foster the resentment of the "indigenous" settlers: it undergirds out-and-out exploitation. Thus Mr. Harley Rivers, whose laziness and pretentions to gentility do not preclude a penchant for dishonest activity, is so determined to live "like a gentleman" (ch. XXXII) that he takes part in a dishonest banking scheme that ruins many of the region's poor farmers. Still, irreducible physical and economic circumstances do ultimately force the development of a communal bond among people who, in the more class-stratified world of the East, would have remained irremediably divided. Taken as a whole the narrative registers the gradual emergence of what to Clavers seems a more civilized state—made possible, to be sure, partly by the move further west of the most lawless families (ch. XXVIII), the gradual refinement of a character like Simeon Jenkins, the departure of dishonest Harley Rivers.

We should keep in mind both the narrative line and the complex attitudes outlined above as we examine *A New Home*'s depiction of the fascinating process by which a community is created. Three stages in the village's growth will be discussed. The first (chs. I–III) satirizes an eastern-based vision of the West as unspoiled "nature" and establishes the existence of an indigenous western culture. Stage two (as epitomized in chapter XX) exemplifies the central drama of *A New Home,* the vexed coexistence of western- and eastern-based cultures, and highlights Mary Clavers's own snobbery. In the third and final stage (chs. XLVI–XLVII), Clavers has developed an empathic approach to each group in the West, an approach that exemplifies the mutual acceptance on which a new and genuinely hybrid culture of the West must be founded; though she remains critical of the crudeness of many of her neighbors, the main target of the text's satire is East-Coast elitism, which emerges as the major source of continuing cultural polarization in the United States.

A NEW HOME initially locates itself within the eastern-based culture of the book's readers, which is also Mary Clavers's culture of origin. It begins with her first experience of the wilderness of Michigan, her trip to the site of what will become the village of Montacute. Reflecting Clavers's cultural insularity and resistance to the West, the first chapter moves through a series of contrasts in which she first articulates her expectations about the region, then depicts the "real" West as it departs from or contradicts these expectations. A mixture of styles reflects different currents in the popular literature that has shaped Clavers's expectations. These are expressed in the flowery language of Romantic-based literature about the West: the actual frontier, seldom sublime and often filled with physical discomfort, is rendered in a literal language that ironizes her European and East-Coast American mentality. For instance, Clavers embarks on her trip feeling "a little sentimental" and is consumed by "floral enthusiasm" shaped by popular poets in the British Romantic vein: Shelley, Lamb, Bulwer-Lytton. The overvoice of the retrospective narrator suggests dryly that these modes of description are inappropriate—"[Michigan] must have a poet of [its] own" (ch. I)—and the narrative proceeds to an aspect of nature these poets did not celebrate: the mudhole.

Introduction

As Clavers gains more experience of Michigan's wilds, a new voice, the demotic one, disrupts the Romantic poetic diction and by the end of the first chapter, she is setting these voices in counterpoint by satirizing her own attitudes. On the third day of the Clavers' journey, she relates,

> I began to complain of the sameness of the oak-openings and to wish we were fairly at our journey's end. We were crossing a broad expanse of what seemed at a little distance a smooth shaven lawn of the most brilliant green, but which proved on trial little better than a quaking bog—embracing within its ridgy circumference all possible varieties of
> "Muirs, and mosses, slaps and styles"—
> I had just indulged in something like a yawn and wish that I could see our hotel. At the word, my companion's face assumed a rather comical expression, and I was preparing to inquire somewhat testily what there was so laughable . . . when down came our good horse to the very chin in a bog-hole, green as Erin on top, but giving way on a touch . . . Down came the horse . . . down came the driver; and I could do no less than follow . . . our good steed kicking and floundering—covering us with hieroglyphics, which would be readily decyphered by any Wolverine we should meet, though perchance strange to the eyes of our friends at home (ch. I).

Mocking Charles Feno Hoffman's description of Michigan's "oak clearings," which she herself earlier appropriated when waxing rapturous about the landscape's beauty, Clavers now emphasizes her rueful recognition that her initial way of perceiving the West was through the filters of a "foreign" culture. She also shows herself continuing to embrace that culture. She tries to familiarize the strange landscape by describing it through genteel poetry; she expects a genuine "hotel"; and as she continues to adapt the landscape to an alien terrain (perceiving the bog's surface to be "green as Erin"), she obscures its true character and perils. Growing textual emphasis on a "native" way of seeing—in which the indigenous inhabitants, experienced in bogs and mudholes, employ a different vocabulary and grammar—also indicates that she is projecting a set of poetic conventions inappropriately, not actually seeing the Michigan landscape. If to eastern friends the Clavers would appear merely dirty and strange, "Wolverines" (long-term Michigan inhabitants) would easily "decypher" the story the mud "hieroglyphs" tell.

The narrative line quickly expands to portray the "Wolverines" as a bona fide group that must play a full part in the establishment of Montacute. To sophisticated easterners who scorn a "particular class" she says, "'those creatures' are partakers with [yourselves] of a common nature" (ch. I), and she delineates that nature in depth. Western language, initially reproduced only in short phrases, is now linked to individualized speakers who share a discrete body of values, attitudes and customs, as well as a way of speaking. Mary Clavers encounters her "Hotel" (the phrase is capitalized, satirizing her eastern expectations), "a log-house of diminutive size" (ch. II) and the proprietor, Mrs. Danforth, immediately "decyphers" the Clavers' experience: "Well! Is this Miss Clavers? . . . why do tell if you've been upset in the mash? why, I want to know!—and didn't ye hurt ye none?" This scene represents a striking departure from contemporaneous depictions of the West. In James Hall's popular, romanticized *Legends of the West,* for instance, only secondary backwoods characters speak "non-standard" English. Their language is in the tradition of dialect, marked off by italics and spelling as inferior, and their behavior is similarly relegated to stock activities, notably tracking down Indians and hunting. In *A New Home* the indigenous language not only has the status of a vernacular—a full-bodied popular language—, the prominence given Mrs. Danforth and others quickly establishes it as one aspect of a legitimate culture.[15]

Once indigenous life is established as a culture, *A New Home* subjects western ways to the same satiric scrutiny to which it subjects the East, representing the continual tension and renegotiation between the two cultures as a drama centering in both discourse and practice. The mutual dependence of new and older settlers forces them to live together, but each tries to prevail over the ways of the other. Mary Clavers quickly learns that her dependence on neighbors for household help makes her home a cultural battlefield. Hiring Mrs. Jennings to "chore round," she is also subjected to Mrs. Jennings's western ways. These "required a strong green tea at least three times a day; and between these three times she drank the remains of the tea from the spout of the tea-pot, saying 'it tasted better so.' 'If she hadn't it,' she said, 'she had the 'sterics so that she wasn't able to do a chore.' And her habits were equally imperious in the matter of dipping with her own spoon or knife into every dish on the table. . . . It was in vain one offered her any thing, she replied invariably with a dignified nod: 'I'll help myself, I thank ye. I never want no waitin on'" (ch. XIV). Mrs. Jennings's language and behavior are bracketed off from the rest of the narrative in a discrete paragraph (much as Mary Clavers would like to contain Mrs. Jennings), but they nevertheless insist on the woman's individualistic Jacksonian pride and her adroitness in getting around Mary Clavers's efforts to keep her in her place. Mary Clavers is equally insistent that *her* culture prevail. Not only does she try to contain Mrs. Jennings, but—in an appropriation of the latter's expression of "choring round"— she reports that *she* learned to "wear round": to maintain her own sense of propriety by manipulating the women who work for her into dining separately.

A New Home's cultural commentary continues to deepen. By the time Mary Clavers has been in Montacute a year, she excels at what sociolinguist Basil Bernstein has called code-switching, and her counterpointing of eastern and western language constitutes a major mode of cultural critique. Chapter XX, which centers on gardening, exemplifies the intricacy with which Kirkland presents Montacute's oscillation between cultural recalcitrance and cultural negotiation. In describing Clavers's efforts at gardening and her indigenous neighbors' skepticism about it, *A New Home* explores the easterners' penchant for envisioning themselves as cultivated and the westerners boorish by interrogating Clavers's attitudes along with those of her neighbors. Now a village resident, Clavers identifies herself as one of "us," a Montacutian, yet she also remains an easterner whose cultural values are those of "my reader" (ch. XX). At points, she plays linguistic registers against each other to satirize what she sees as the indigenous westerners' pig-headed practicality:

> The ordinary name with us for a rose is "a rosy-flower"; our vase of flowers usually a broken-nosed pitcher, is a "posy-pot"; and "yaller lilies" are among the most dearly-prized of all the gifts of Flora. . . . A neighbor . . . coolly broke off a spike of my finest hyacinths, and after putting it to his undiscriminating nose, threw it on the ground with a "pah!" as contemptuous as Hamlet's. But I revenged myself when I set him sniffing at a crown imperial—so we are at quits now. [*ch. XX*]

Clavers's own insularity is mocked here as much as is the older Michigan residents' anti-aestheticism, for her neighbors' versatility comes into focus immediately after she debunks them for their narrowness. Local floral interest is not, it appears, limited to "yaller lilies," for Clavers soon concedes that both gardener and florist are to be found within three miles of Montacute. More important, Clavers is momentarily able to abandon her rigid categorizing and take note of the impressive diversity of the local culture, including the fact that it is often expressed in multiple talents and practical expertise rather than in the gardening to which she herself is so attached. In a catalogue of occupations which anticipates those of Whitman, she celebrates the local blacksmith, cooper, milliner, and the "'hen-tailor' for your little boy's pantaloons" and she envisons one neighbor's versatility as a magnificent form of pan-culturalism: "Is one of your guests dependent upon a barber? Mr. Jenkins can shave. Does your husband [. . .] demolish his boot upon a *grub?* Mr. Jenkins is great at a *rifacciamento.* Does Billy lose his cap in the pond? Mr. Jenkins makes caps *comme il y en a peu.* Does your bellows get the asthma? Mr. Jenkins is a famous Francis Flute" (ch. XX).

Such an appreciation of difference is only temporary at this point, as we see by the way the brief harmony of this passage is disrupted. Clavers tartly labels her rhapsody a mere digression ("wandering"), and the chapter ends by reasserting Montacute's persisting and factionalizing cultural differences. Its final sentences take the form of snide commentary on the part of Mary Clavers: "I hope my reader will not be disposed to reply in that terse and forceful style which is cultivated at Montacute, and which has more than once been employed in answer to my enthusiastic lectures on [gardening]. 'Taters grows in the field, and 'taters is good enough for me.'" She has abandoned her appreciation of her neighbors' diversity to re-ally herself with her eastern readers and gloat over browbeating Montacutians for their taste in flora. And she again reproduces the vernacular merely to mock Michigan practicality. Kirkland exposes Clavers's bias, however, for though Clavers cannot see the implications of the "taters" remark, its placement—it ends the chapter—gives her neighbors the last word, and it stands as their resentful parody of her condescending image of them.

IN THE COURSE of the three years that *A New Home* covers, Montacute begins to become a community and Mary Clavers's participation in local life intensifies, however ambivalently. Appropriately, her capacity to understand and portray the perspective of members of both groups grows: increasingly, she places western farm families' cultural attitudes in the context of their material circumstances. In consequence *A New Home* becomes more emotionally colored, as it evokes the "indigenous" settlers' lives with greater sympathy, and its deconstruction of easterners' elitism expands. By the penultimate chapter, though Clavers still identifies herself primarily as an eastern emigrant, *A New Home* makes it clear that easterners must undergo profound questioning of *many* of their cultural assumptions, not just those held about the West. In an extended reflection on the material and cultural discomfort easterners experience in living side by side and interdependently with the West's poor but aggressive indigenous settlers, Kirkland suggests that the experience of settlement contributes importantly to dismantling class, regional, and cultural polarities that permeate American life. "It would require volumes to enumerate all the cases in which the fastidiousness, the taste, the pride, the self-esteem of the refined child of civilization, must be wounded by a familiar intercourse with the persons among whom he will find himself thrown, in the ordinary course of rural life," she observes. "He is continually reminded in how great a variety of particulars his necessities, his materials for comfort, his courses of pain, are precisely those of the humblest of his neighbors." (Her ambivalence does resurface at the end of this meditation, which reads wryly: "The humblest, did I say? He will find that he has no humble neighbors" [ch. XLVI]). The chapter opens by qualifying the elitism of easterners; it shows that life in the woods has the salutary effect of revealing their general sense of entitlement to material luxury as an unexamined privilege. At the same time, Clavers acknowledges the rawness of western manners. Putting herself in the new emigrant's place, she notes how "unreasonable and absurd" a neighbor's brusque claims to the newcomer's possessions appear, but she also maintains that once "the barriers of pride and prejudice are [. . .] broken, we discover a certain satisfaction in the homely fellowship with our kind, which goes far towards repaying whatever sacrifices or concessions we may have been induced to make" (ch. XLVI). As the chapter moves to the situation of indigenous westerners, Clavers's capacity for empathy increases. The lingering condescension apparent here gives way to the greater tolerance of a genuinely bicultural stance—a stance that forecasts what a plural western culture may look like. As usual, Clavers satirizes western outlooks by incorporating the vernacular within her account: westerners are represented by a string of defensive statements made to new migrants, such as speaking of the latters' carpets as "*one* way to hide dirt." But the sting of her satire lessens as Clavers turns to the material circumstances that lie behind such truculence. As she had earlier assumed the easterner's point of view, she now assumes that of the westerner. In a leap of imagination, she tries to see the new settler from the perspective of the indigenous one, dwelling at length on what appears, from the latter's standpoint, a privileged standard of living: "To the tenant of a log-cabin whose family, whatever be its numbers, must burrow in a single room, while a bed or two, a chest, a table, and a wretched handful of cooking utensils, form the chief materials of comfort, an ordinary house, small and plain it may be, yet amply supplied, looks the very house of luxury."

Assuming the perspectives of each group, contextualizing those perspectives within material circumstances, and moving fluidly between the two, Mary Clavers's voice and mentality thus become a model of what, to Caroline Kirkland, the new and communitarian culture of the West might become. Significantly, this chapter concludes by directing the satiric voice outward from the West toward the East, which is now located as the primary source of divisive elitism. Clavers notes that her acceptance of community with western farmers jeopardizes her standing among eastern readers, for "I have not so far forgotten the rules of the sublime *clique* as not to realize, that in acknowledging even a leaning toward the 'vulgar' side, I place myself forever beyond its pale." Then, circling back to the "wild woods" of Michigan (the phrase echoes the romantic diction about the West which the opening of *A New Home* satirized and explicitly mocks the equation of the "West" with "nature" as an East-Coast invention), she parodies eastern elitism by playing out a scenario in which she is in the mock-elevated position of being able to institutionalize a hierarchical social structure by founding a local aristocracy: "Several of us have as many as three cows; some few, carpets and shanty kitchens; and one or two, pianofortes and silver tea-sets. I myself, as *dame de la seigneurie,* have had secret thoughts of an astral lamp! but even if I should go so far, I am resolved not to be either vain-glorious or over-bearing, although this kind of superiority forms the usual ground for exclusiveness. I shall visit my neighbours just as usual, and take care not to say a single word about dipped candles, if I can possibly help it" (ch. XLVI).

Clavers's satiric tone is directed here at both the pretension of social ambition and her own ambition's laughable modesty, and though her humor may convey her special bond with her readers in the East, it is nevertheless as an appreciative participant in Montacute that she ends the narrative. *A New Home*'s closing chapter dramatizes her newly inclusive, if self-consciously ironic, mentality, embracing a comprehensive vision of Montacute which attests to its final status as a discrete and vital community, "our secluded little village" (ch. XLVII). In an echo of the closing chapter of Mitford's *Our Village,* Clavers surveys the present status and prospects of various residents, recounts the building of a meeting house, and discusses the village's place in county and state affairs. Clavers's status as exemplar of this new community's culture is reaffirmed. All her interest now lies in Montacute, and she interweaves the lives of commonplace settlers—nosey Mrs. Nippers, feisty "Squire" Jenkins—with those of more cultivated eastern-based citizens. Now the blending of linguistic registers exemplifies the cultural mix appropriate to Montacute's newly developed community. Clavers, who now refers to herself zestfully as a midge fancier, delights in melding sentimental jargon with pithy localese to describe the villagers' lives, as in her reference to a "nascent *tendresse* between Mrs. Nippers and Mr. Phlatt, a young lawyer, whose resplendent 'tin' [sign] . . . graces . . . the side-post of Squire Jenkins' door." And she positions this plural language against the hackneyed, misleading language of the advertisements designed to lure new settlers by hawking developing western villages as paragons of material progress: They cannot be described, she reports, by such phrases as "brilliant success!" "splendid fortune!" "march of improvement!" The note of mockery on which she closes is again directed outward at the snobbish eastern reader. Parodying this reader's judgments, she compares herself to an awkward "rustic damsel" imposing too long on a city acquaintance, and her narrative to a country dance, a "Scotch [reel] . . . which [has] no natural ending, save the fatigue of those engaged." Though she ends with "an unceremonious adieu to the kind and courteous reader," her identification of her narrative as a "simple and sauntering story" that has no natural ending once more locates the narrow eastern reader outside a life that is ongoing, a life, *A New Home* suggests, that will continue to take shape through the vital, often difficult, always absorbing process of cultural interchange and re-formation.

CLAVERS'S RENDERING of the development of culture and community in Montacute is distinctly female. Her own domestic activities, particularly housekeeping, provide a major arena for the emergence of Montacute; her participation in the village's daily life—visiting, listening to her neighbors gossip and tell their personal histories, taking part in local events—is another. A conviction that certain principles are generally connected to each gender also permeates *A New Home,* informing Kirkland's depiction of the West as a battleground in which incompatible modes of socioeconomic conduct vie for ascendancy. One, the ethic of interdependence, is specifically associated with women and constitutes the heartbeat of community. The women consistently (though not always graciously) assist the ague stricken and the destitute, and even institutionalize their cooperative ways in a much satirized Ladies' Beneficent Society. However lackadasically, many of Montacute's men also carry out this ethic, contributing to the development of the community by being neighborly and particularly by hiring out their labor: they build the grain mill, the general store, the Clavers's frame house. *A New Home* makes it clear that scarcity makes interdependence an absolute necessity in the West: survival can occur only in groups, and is possible only through the practice of reciprocity—the sharing of goods and possessions which most typically takes the form of constant borrowing. One dimension of Mary Clavers's adjustment to the new culture is that she learns to embrace interdependence. Though the borrowing irritates her, she comes to understand the material necessity of the communitarian ethic—"If I treat Mrs. Timson with neglect to-day, can I with any face borrow her broom tomorrow?" she declares (ch. XVII)—and we have seen that she learns to entertain this ethic as an ideal by the end of the three years the narrative covers.

Though *A New Home* charts the rise of communal interdependence, it also shows community to be constantly endangered by a wanton and individualistic pursuit of profit. This is an attitude which Mary Clavers identifies as peculiarly masculine, and its holders view the West as no more than an arena for profit. Whereas women have a sense of responsibility toward new settlers, Clavers maintains, men see each new arrival to the West "merely as an additional business-automaton—a somebody more with whom to try the race of enterprize, i.e. money-making" (ch. XVII). The growth of community occurs when goods and cultures are shared; for the profit economy, with its dedication to quick and easy gain, material production is a waste of time. Its devotees, all men, are interested only in making money, which they achieve through the continual sale and resale of land. Clavers likens this process to "Robin's alive," a game similar to hot potato in which many "thousand acres were transferred from hand to hand with a rapidity . . . [in which] all gained save him in whose hand Robin died" (ch. IX). Appropriately, whereas the communal economy is based on literal and life-sustaining production, particularly of wheat, the profit economy generates only images: false representations designed to promote the sale of inferior land.

A New Home exposes the language of the profit economy as the opposite of the vernacular of the indigenous settlers and of the genteel lingo of the newer ones, both of which reflect specific cultures appropriate to the specific contexts within which they have developed. The commercial language is shown to entail the production only of an elaborate system of

Sounds Marxist

ever-shifting and fraudulent signifiers which advance the interests of a few individuals at the expense of the community as a whole. The drive to keep reselling the same land, Kirkland shows, leads to the creation of an elaborate, deceitful discourse: misleading visual images (flyers depicting "with bewitching minuteness" the docks, harbors, mills, factories, railroads, and bridges of a thriving metropolis to lure settlers to sites where not even a village yet exists), the printed word in a new mode (the text accompanying the pictures on the flyers is "choicely worded and carefully vague," and an artful oral style in which auctioneers become "[men] of genius, or ready invention, of fluent speech" whose collateral for the land they hawk is empty words—their self-proclaimed respectability (ch. IX). The naming of Montacute itself involves this sort of image production, for though the "tricksy" land agent, Mr. Mazard, suggests that Mary Clavers name the village, his objections to her choices reflect his dedication to words that do *not* correspond in any way to the realities of the land parcels he advertises. All her choices of Indian names prove unacceptable: "One was too long, another signified *Slippery Eel,* another *Big Bubble;* and these would be so inappropriate!" she comments sarcastically. Clavers eventually chooses randomly from slips of paper on which she has written "ten of the most sounding names I could muster from my novel reading stores" (ch. III). Her method is fully commensurate with the fictitious but "sounding" language produced by Mazard and his ilk.

A New Home critiques the profit economy by balancing Montacute's slowly developing community and language against the story of the village's monitory double, the neighboring village of Tinkerville. Tinkerville seems inhabited solely by men and comes into being for the sake of profit alone. Its first purchaser is so discouraged when he lays eyes on the swampy land he has bought sight unseen that he sells it below cost to Mr. Mazard. Mazard then uses an "emblazoned chart" of the land, much like the dazzling flyers, to seduce Mr. Tinker, a Maine resident with no knowledge of the West, into buying the land. The village's subsequent history delineates the way an economy devoted to profit making without material productivity necessitates the proliferation of misrepresentations. Eventually a group of land speculators ("enterprising men") purchases the languishing village and founds the "Merchants' and Manufacturers' Bank of Tinkerville" (the name is a typical misrepresentation: there are no manufacturers in or around Tinkerville, and, as there is little to sell, few merchants). The land the speculators cannot sell becomes the basis for the production of a new set of images, again analogous to the advertising flyers:

paper currency. The aptly titled "General Naming Law" allows "any dozen of men who could pledge real estate to a nominal amount, to assume the power of making money." The paper money the Tinkerville bankers generate—"lighter in the pocket" than "gold or silver," based on valueless land, made of "rags," but "beautifully engraved"—is a gilded eye-catcher. A "new species of gramarye" (ch. XXXI)—the word means both a language and a book of sorcery—it constitutes a new level of fraudulent signification as the game of poor Robin continues. Bank inspectors discover that the specie currency (currency backed by gold and silver) with which the bank supposedly supports its paper currency is "locomotive"—moved from one bank to another to convince inspectors that the notes of each bank are adequately backed—and that the metal boxes supposed to contain gold and silver are filled with broken glass and nails and covered with what looks like actual specie but is in fact mainly "*bogus*" (ch. XXXII, author's emphasis).

Kirkland insists that the discourse and economy of runaway profits are not abstract "gramarye" but have powerful material consequences. Unravelling the connections between riches and rags, she dramatizes the literal consequences of the individualistic economy by showing that the bankers' gains are reaped from the settlers' losses. The deep-woods settlers who have exchanged their produce for the Tinkerville notes go to town "with their splendid-looking bank-notes, their hard-earned all, for the flour which was to be the sole food of wife and babes through the long winter, [and are told] that these hoarded treasures were as valueless as the ragged paper which wrapped them" (ch. XXXII). Produced from rags like those in which these settlers wrap them, the flashy notes are shown to signify nothing less than the calculated theft that lies at the heart of the profit economy. In the western settlers' impoverishment, Kirkland insists, lies the enrichment of the bank's officers. For the latter, the paper currency does indeed become riches: it "transmute[s] . . . acres of wood and meadow into splendid metropolitan residences" (ch. XXXI) as Harley Rivers, president of the Tinkerville Bank, removes his wife and newly purchased elegant furniture to "one of the Eastern cities," and lives "like a gentleman . . . on the spoils of the Tinkerville Wild-Cat" (ch. XXXII).

THE DYNAMISM AND INVENTIVENESS of Caroline Kirkland's regionalism represent one of the most important ways in which she complicates conventions. Both before *A New Home* and after it, much regional literature in the United States has portrayed the region as a discrete unit, culturally and sometimes economically isolated from the country's centers. Sometimes it is cast as grim backwater (as is the Midwest in Edgar W. Howe's *Story of a Country Town* and Hamlin Garland's *Main-Travelled Roads*). Often women writers develop the region as physically, psychically, and culturally female; or—and the second and third modes often overlap—it is represented as a self-contained locale whose coherence and purity contrast with the fragmentation of modern life, as in Harriet Beecher Stowe's New England tales and novels and Sarah Orne Jewett's *Country of the Pointed Firs*. Still, we have had other writers for whom regionalism entailed the representation of a complex and ongoing relationship between a region and the country's center. Not surprisingly, the work of the best of these has, like Kirkland's, developed that relationship as it is enacted in daily life—in language, domestic activities, local affairs—rather than using the region to illustrate a political or historical analysis. It should also come as no surprise that many of these writers have been women. Willa Cather's novels frequently depict frontier values and ways of life yielding to capitalism and its ethics. In *The Goodness of St. Roque* (1896), the African-American writer Alice Dunbar Nelson evokes the ethnically diverse culture of New Orleans, at the same time showing it to be threatened by the commercialism and homogenization of modernization. In our own time, Jayne Anne Phillips in *Machine Dreams* and Bobbie Ann Mason in *In Country* explore the interplay between a national economy and politics, with its mass culture, and the more communal and family-centered traditions of Appalachia. That their works seem ambivalent about disclosing their understanding of the dynamics of regional life to an outside readership, as if wishing to protect the life they portray, may well be because the tensions within regions and between regions and the national center have been resolved in favor of the cultural-economic hegemony of the latter. Though Kirkland did not predict this outcome, she did foreshadow it; and in focusing on the dynamics of economic communitarianism and the emergence of a unique culture within Montacute as her most compelling subject, she showed herself almost uncannily atuned to a key struggle in American history. In the kind of regionalism she practices, in her later writing, and in the patterns of her own life, she challenges our understanding of our culture and its history. *A New Home*—in offering modern readers brought up on personal narratives the pleasures of a text that features cultural interchange and creation—also reminds us that in retrieving neglected writers we expand the way we read and bestow upon ourselves new and unanticipated enjoyment.

NOTES TO INTRODUCTION

1. A synopsis of the book's critical reception from its initial appearance to the 1920s can be found in Langley Carlton Keyes, "Caroline Matilda Kirkland," 330–36. Since the early 1970s, several critics who have sought to reestablish Kirkland's reputation have agreed with Keyes in according Kirkland the status of a pioneer realist: among them are William Osborne, *Caroline M. Kirkland;* Audrey Roberts, introduction to "The Letters of Caroline M. Kirkland"; Annette Kolodny, *The Land before Her;* and Judith Fetterley, *Provisions.*

2. See Susan M. Coultrap-McQuin, "Why Their Success? Some Observations on Publishing by Popular Nineteenth-Century Women Writers," for an excellent analysis of the reasons writers and publishers relied on such conventions. See also Joanne Dobson's introduction to *The Hidden Hand or, Capitola the Madcap* by E.D.E.N. Southworth for a sensitive discussion of the way in which the mutually profitable relationship between Robert Bonner, editor and owner of the *New York Ledger,* and E.D.E.N. Southworth preserved the familial contours of conventional masculinity and femininity. Little has been written as yet about women as editors. For a discussion of the fundamental concessions the era's most successful woman editor, Sarah Hale, made to Louis Godey when he bought her *Ladies Magazine* and made her editor of *Godey's Lady's Book,* see Nancy Woloch, *Women and the American Experience* 97–112.

3. Although there is no full-scale biography of Caroline Kirkland, I have relied on several indispensible synopses of her life and work by Langley Keyes, William Osborne, Audrey Roberts. I have also drawn on Roberts's edition of the letters, which contains all of Kirkland's extant letters and is the immediate source

for the letters I quote. For additional information about Kirkland's children I have consulted Clyde E. Henson, *Joseph Kirkland*.

4. "An Incident in Dreamland" appears in *Autumn Hours and Fireside Readings* (1854).

5. See Jane Tompkins, *Sensational Designs*, and Joanne Dobson, "The Hidden Hand," for fine discussions of the way in which several antebellum women novelists maneuvered within conventions of gender and genre. Some women writers, taking the explicit position of reformers, sought to expand women's province beyond domesticity as narrowly conceived; Catherine Beecher and Harriet Beecher Stowe, for instance, appropriated the view that women were the repositories of moral and religious principles to strengthen women's claims as the source of improvement of the social order.

6. Though she does not analyze Kirkland's response in terms of gender or investigate her later career as a writer, Kolodny suggests that Kirkland's neighbors' outrage caused her to subdue her satire, and she sees signs of a new self-restraint in Kirkland's next book, *Forest Life* (see esp. 148–49).

7. Sarah Hale, editor of *Godey's Lady's Book*, and Margaret Fuller, editor of the Transcendentalist journal the *Dial*, are the most famous women to have held such positions. Lydia Maria Child founded and edited the first children's magazine in the United States, the *Juvenile Miscellany*, and edited the weekly *National Anti-Slavery Standard* for two years; Ann Stephens, originator of the dime novel and enterprising editor of several annuals, edited the *Portland Magazine* and *Peterson's Magazine*.

8. Writing about Washington was a family affair. Kirkland's oldest daughter, Elizabeth, was part of the project from the beginning, assisting in the composition of a two-part essay on Washington's early life which appeared in *Putnam's* in January and February of 1854, and "Lizzy" and her brother Joseph both accompanied their mother to Washington to comb through Washington's papers. Such activity was characteristic of the Kirklands, for after William's death it was imperative that the family function as a collaborative unit even more fully than it had before, and this encouraged the children's resourcefulness. Elizabeth taught for a time, then opened a school in Chicago in the 1860s with her sister Cordelia. The oldest son, Joseph, began to work shortly after his father's death. He became a successful businessman and lawyer, and a regional writer of note. His *Zury: The Meanest Man in Spring County* (1887), a fairly realistic rendering of western life, has long been considered a landmark work (though it lacks his mother's scope and pioneering satire), and he was an important influence on other western regionalists, particularly Hamlin Garland.

9. Keyes, 315, quotes the funeral oration as it was reported by the New York *Evening Post* 11 Apr. 1864.

10. Bayard Taylor to John Phillips, 8 Sept. 1847, quoted in *Life and Letters of Bayard Taylor,* ed. Marie Hansen (Boston: Houghton Mifflin, 1885) 1 : 100–01.

11. To E. P. Whipple, 9 May 1864, MHS.

12. *Homes of the New World* (New York: Harper and Brother, 1853) 1 : 245.

13. Such commentators as Keyes and Osborne were instrumental in delineating Kirkland's knowledge of Romantic literature; it has taken feminist scholars, particularly Kolodny and Fetterley, with their understanding of *A New Home* as a woman's text, to show that Kirkland draws on a woman's perspective to take popular representations of western life to task and to reveal the consequences for women settlers of life in the West. David Leverenz, on the other hand, reads *A New Home* as a personal narrative, the story of Clavers's adherence to genteel ladyhood. He sees this adherence to be crucial in granting the book its status as "one of the most flagrant and insouciant instances of the patrician paradigm, surviving and at least temporarily prospering in the American wilderness" (p. 152).

14. See Josephine Donovan, *New England Local Color Literature* ch. 2, for a brief discussion of village sketch literature as a women's tradition; Percy Westbrook, *The New England Town in Fact and Fiction,* and Lawrence Buell, *New England Literary Culture* ch. 13, for general discussions of New England village sketch literature. Elizabeth Ammons, in her introduction to *How Celia Changed Her Mind and Selected Stories,* Fetterley, introduction to *Provisions,* and my "Expanding 'America'" discuss formal and cultural aspects of the sketch as a literary genre.

15. According to Richard Bridgeman, the vernacular was still primarily a source of broad humor in American literature in the 1830s and 1840s, though if we follow the thinking of Mikhail Bakhtin, we can recognize that the vernacular generally also disrupts the genteel and literate language within which writers tried to contain it (see Richard Bridgeman, *The Colloquial Style in America* [New York, 1966], and Mikhail Bakhtin, *Rabelais and His World,* trans. Helene Iswolsky [Cambridge, MA, 1968]). Theory aside, *A New Home*'s explicit focus on cultural tension and negotiation results partly from the unusual complexity with which it renders the vernacular, though there are other instances of village sketch literature in which the vernacular is also reproduced with some nuance.

SELECTED BIBLIOGRAPHY

ARCHIVAL MATERIAL

The following abbreviations are used in the introduction to designate archival sources:

BC   Beinecke Rare Book and Manuscript Collection, Yale University
CHS   Chicago Historical Society
CUL   Cornell University Library
DPL   Detroit Public Library
HL   Houghton Library, Harvard University
MHS   Massachusetts Historical Society

SELECTED WORKS BY CAROLINE M. KIRKLAND

Works are listed in chronological order. Many of Kirkland's magazine pieces are reprinted in the book-length collections of her work published by Scribners in the 1850s, and only those to which I have specifically referred are listed separately as well.

A New Home, Who'll Follow? or, Glimpses of Western Life. By Mrs. Mary Clavers, an actual settler. New York: C. S. Francis, 1839.

Selected Bibliography

Forest Life. 2 vols. By the Author of "A New Home." New York: C. S. Francis, 1842.

Western Clearings. 2 vols. New York: Wiley and Putnam, 1845.

Introduction. *A Plea for Women.* By Mrs. Hugo Reid. New York: Farmer and Daggers, 1845.

Spenser and the Fairy Queen. New York: Wiley and Putnam, 1847.

"George Sand and the Journeyman Joiner." *Union Magazine* 1 (Nov. 1847): 222–23.

Preface. *Dahcotah, or, Life and Legends of the Sioux around Fort Snelling.* By Mrs. Mary Eastman. New York: John Wiley, 1849.

Holidays Abroad, or Europe from the West. 2 vols. New York: Baker and Scribner, 1849.

"Literary Women." *Sartain's* 6 (Feb. 1850): 150–54.

"The Mystery of Visiting." *Sartain's* 6 (May 1850): 317–21.

"The Household." *Sartain's* 7 (Aug. 1850): 42–46.

The Evening Book, or, Fireside Talk on Morals and Manners, with Sketches of Western Life. New York: Charles Scribner, 1852.

A Book for the Home Circle, or, Familiar Thoughts on Various Topics, Literary, Moral, and Social. A Companion for the Evening Book. New York: Charles Scribner, 1853.

The Helping Hand, Comprising an Account of the Home for Discharged Female Convicts and an Appeal in Behalf of that Institution. New York: Charles Scribner, 1853.

Autumn Hours and Fireside Reading. New York: Charles Scribner, 1854.

Personal Memoirs of Washington. New York: D. Appleton, 1857.

The School-Girl's Garland. New York: Charles Scribner, 1864.

Patriotic Eloquence: Being Selections from 100 Years of National Literature. New York: Charles Scribner; Cleveland: Ingham and Bragg, 1866.

WORKS CITED AND FURTHER READING

Ammons, Elizabeth. Introduction. *How Celia Changed Her Mind and Selected Stories.* By Rose Terry Cooke. American Women Writers Series. New Brunswick: Rutgers UP, 1986.

Baym, Nina. *Women's Fiction: A Guide to Novels by and about Women in America, 1820–1870.* Ithaca: Cornell UP, 1978.

Selected Bibliography

Buell, Lawrence. *New England Literary Culture.* Cambridge: Cambridge UP, 1986.

Coultrap-McQuin, Susan M. "Why Their Success? Some Observations on Publishing by Popular Nineteenth-Century Women Writers." *Legacy* 1984 (Fall) 1 (2): 1, 8–9.

Dobson, Joanne. Introduction. *The Hidden Hand or, Capitola the Madcap* by E.D.E.N. Southworth. American Women Writers Series. New Brunswick and London: Rutgers UP, 1988.

——— "The Hidden Hand: Subversion of Cultural Ideology in Three Mid-Nineteenth Century American Women's Novels." *American Quarterly* 1986 (Summer) 38 (2): 223–42.

Donovan, Josephine. *New England Local Color Literature: A Women's Tradition.* New York: Frederick Ungar, 1983.

Fetterley, Judith. *Provisions: A Reader from 19th-Century American Women.* Bloomington: Indiana UP, 1985.

Griswold, Rufus W. *The Prose Writers of America.* 3rd ed. Philadelphia: Carey and Hart, 1849.

Hart, John S. *Female Prose Writers of America.* 1851. Philadelphia: E. H. Butler, 1855.

Henson, Clyde E. *Joseph Kirkland.* New York: Twayne, 1962.

Kelley, Mary. *Private Woman, Public Stage: Literary Domesticity in Nineteenth-Century America.* New York: Oxford UP, 1984.

Keyes, Langley Carlton. "Caroline Matilda Kirkland: A Pioneer in American Realism." Diss. Harvard U, 1935.

Kolodny, Annette. *The Land before Her.* Chapel Hill and London: U of North Carolina P, 1984.

Leverenz, David. *Manhood and the American Renaissance.* Ithaca and London: Cornell UP, 1989.

Mott, Frank Luther. *A History of American Magazines, 1741–1850.* New York: Appleton, 1930.

Osborne, William S. *Caroline M. Kirkland.* New York: Twayne, 1972.

Pattee, F. W. *The Feminine Fifties.* New York: Appleton, 1940.

Poe, Edgar Allan. "The Literati of New York." In *Essays and Reviews.* New York: Library of America, 1984.

Roberts, Audrey. "The Letters of Caroline M. Kirkland." Diss. U of Wisconsin, 1976.

Tompkins, Jane. *Sensational Designs: The Cultural Work of American Fiction, 1790–1829.* New York: Oxford UP, 1985.

Selected Bibliography

Westbrook, Perry. *The New England Town in Fact and Fiction.* Rutherford: Farleigh Dickinson UP, 1982.

Woloch, Nancy. *Women and the American Experience.* New York: Knopf, 1984.

Zagarell, Sandra A. "Expanding 'America': Lydia Sigourney's *Sketch of Connecticut,* Catharine Sedgwick's *Hope Leslie.*" *Tulsa Studies in Women's Literature* 1987 (Fall) 6(2): 225–45.

1

This edition of *A New Home* is set from the first edition (1839). Obvious typographical and a few spelling errors have been silently changed, but period spelling has been retained. The text of "Literary Women," which originally appeared in *Sartain's* in 1850, is taken from Kirkland's second collection of essays, *A Book for the Home Circle*.

An unusually well educated woman who was proficient in several languages, Caroline Kirkland quoted freely from a wide range of sources, from Renaissance English through continental Romantic to contemporary American works. In many cases, she appears to have quoted from memory; I suspect she sometimes also made use of collections of quotations, of the sort she may have used in teaching. While many of the sources of quoted materials and allusions have been identified, many remain untraced. Except with regard to the epigraphs at the chapter heads, the latter have not been specially noted.

A NEW HOME, WHO'LL FOLLOW?

Ladies—or fair ladies—I would wish you—or I would request you, or
I would entreat you, not to fear—not to tremble; my life for yours.
—*A Midsummer Night's Dream* [1]

A shew, as it were, of an accompaniable solitariness, and of a civil wildness.
—Sidney's *Arcadia* [2]

PREFACE

I AM GLAD to be told by those who live in the world, that it has lately become fashionable to read prefaces. I wished to say a few words, by way of introduction, to a work which may be deemed too slight to need a preface, but which will doubtless be acknowledged to require some recommendation.

I claim for these straggling and cloudy crayon-sketches of life and manners in the remoter parts of Michigan, the merit of general truth of outline. Beyond this I venture not to aspire. I felt somewhat tempted to set forth my little book as being entirely, what it is very nearly—a veritable history; an unimpeachable transcript of reality; a rough picture, in detached parts, but pentagraphed from the life; a sort of "Emigrant's Guide:"—considering with myself that these my adventurous journeyings and tarryings beyond the confines of civilization, might fairly be held to confer the traveller's privilege. But conscience prevailed, and I must honestly confess, that there be glosses, and colourings, and lights, if not shadows, for which the author is alone accountable. Journals published entire and unaltered, should be Parthian darts,[1] sent abroad only when one's back is turned. To throw them in the teeth of one's every-day associates might diminish one's popularity rather inconveniently. I would desire the courteous reader to bear in mind, however, that whatever is quite unnatural, or absolutely incredible, in the few incidents which diversify the following pages, is to be received as literally true. It is only in the most commonplace parts (if there be comparisons) that I have any leasing-making to answer for.

A New Home, Who'll Follow?

It will of course be observed that Miss Mitford's charming sketches of village life[2] must have suggested the form of my rude attempt. I dare not flatter myself that any one will be led to accuse me of further imitation of a deservedly popular writer. And with such brief salvo, I make my humble curtsey.

M. C.

CHAPTER I

Here are seen
No traces of man's pomp and pride; no silks
Rustle, nor jewels shine, nor envious eyes
Encounter ***
    Oh, there is not lost
One of earth's charms; upon her bosom yet
After the flight of untold centuries
The freshness of her far beginning lies.
        —Bryant [1]

OUR FRIENDS in the "settlements" have expressed so much interest in such of our letters to them, as happened to convey any account of the peculiar features of western life, and have asked so many questions, touching particulars which we had not thought worthy of mention, that I have been for some time past contemplating the possibility of something like a detailed account of our experiences. And I have determined to give them to the world, in a form not very different from that in which they were originally recorded for our private delectation; nothing doubting, that a veracious history of actual occurrences, an unvarnished transcript of real characters, and an impartial record of every-day forms of speech (taken down in many cases from the lips of the speaker) will be pronounced "graphic," by at least a fair proportion of the journalists of the day.

'Tis true there are but meagre materials for anything which might be called a story. I have never seen a cougar—nor been bitten by a rattlesnake. The reader who has patience to go with me to the close of my desultory sketches, must expect nothing beyond a meandering recital of common-place occurrences—mere gossip about every-day people, little enhanced in value by any fancy or ingenuity of the writer; in short, a very ordinary pen-drawing; which, deriving no interest from colouring, can be valuable only for its truth.

What makes a good story? a good autobios?

3

A home on the outskirts of civilization—habits of society which allow the maid and her mistress to do the honours in complete equality, and to make the social tea visit in loving conjunction—such a distribution of the duties of life as compels all, without distinction, to rise with the sun or before him—to breakfast with the chickens—then,

"Count the slow clock and dine exact at noon"—[2]

to be ready for tea at four, and for bed at eight—may certainly be expected to furnish some curious particulars for the consideration of those whose daily course almost reverses this primitive arrangement—who "call night day and day night," and who are apt occasionally to forget, when speaking of a particular class, that "those creatures" are partakers with themselves of a common nature.

I can only wish, like other modest chroniclers, my respected prototypes, that so fertile a theme had fallen into worthier hands. If Miss Mitford, who has given us such charming glimpses of Aberleigh, Hilton Cross and the Loddon,[3] had by some happy chance been translated to Michigan, what would she not have made of such materials as Tinkerville, Montacute, and the Turnip?

When my husband purchased two hundred acres of wild land on the banks of this to-be-celebrated stream, and drew with a piece of chalk on the bar-room table at Danforth's the plan of a village, I little thought I was destined to make myself famous by handing down to posterity a faithful record of the advancing fortunes of that favoured spot.

"The madness of the people" in those days of golden dreams took more commonly the form of city-building; but there were a few who contented themselves with planning villages, on the banks of streams which certainly never could be expected to bear navies, but which might yet be turned to account in the more homely way of grinding or sawing— operations which must necessarily be performed somewhere for the well-being of those very cities. It is of one of these humble attempts that it is my lot to speak, and I make my confession at the outset, warning any fashionable reader who may have taken up my book, that I intend to be "decidedly low."

Whether the purchaser of *our* village would have been moderate under all possible circumstances, I am not prepared to say, since, never having enjoyed a situation under government, his resources have not been unlimited;—and for this reason any remark which may be hazarded in the course of these my lucubrations touching the more magnificent plans of wealthier aspirants, must be received with some grains of allowance. "Il est plus aisé d'être sage pour les autres, que de l'être pour soi-même."[4]

When I made my first visit to these remote and lonely regions, the scattered woods through which we rode for many miles were gay in their first gosling-green suit of half-opened leaves, and the forest odours which exhaled with the dews of morning and evening, were beyond measure delicious to one "long in populous cities pent."[5] I desired much to be a little sentimental at the time, and feel tempted to indulge to some small extent even here—but I forbear; and shall adhere closely to matters more in keeping with my subject.

I think, to be precise, the time was the last, the very last of April, and I recollect well that even at that early season, by availing myself with sedulous application, of those times when I was fain to quit the vehicle through fear of the perilous mud-holes, or still more perilous half-bridged marshes, I picked upwards of twenty varieties of wild-flowers—some of them of rare and delicate beauty;—and sure I am, that if I had succeeded in inspiring my companion with one spark of my own floral enthusiasm, one hundred miles of travel would have occupied a week's time.

The wild flowers of Michigan deserve a poet of their own. Shelley, who sang so quaintly of "the pied wind-flowers and the tulip tall,"[6] would have found many a fanciful comparison and deep-drawn meaning for the thousand gems of the road-side. Charles Lamb[7] could have written charming volumes about the humblest among them. Bulwer[8] would find means to associate the common three-leaved white lily so closely with the Past, the Present, and the Future—the Wind, the stars, and the tripod of Delphos, that all future botanists, and eke all future philosophers, might fail to unravel the "linked sweetness."[9] We must have a poet of our own.

Since I have casually alluded to a Michigan mud-hole, I may as well enter into a detailed memoir on the subject, for the benefit of future travellers, who, flying over the soil on rail-roads, may look slightingly back upon the achievements of their predecessors. In the "settlements," a mud-hole is considered as apt to occasion an unpleasant jolt—a breaking of the thread of one's reverie—or in extreme cases, a temporary stand-still or even an overturn of the rash or the unwary. Here, on approaching one of these characteristic features of the "West"—(How much does that expression mean to include? I never have been able to discover its limits)—the driver stops—alights—walks up to the dark gulf—and around it if he can get round it. He then seeks a long pole and sounds it, measures it across to ascertain how its width compares with the length of his wagon—

tries whether its sides are perpendicular, as is usually the case if the road is much used. If he find it not more than three feet deep, he remounts cheerily, encourages his team, and in they go, with a plunge and a shock rather apt to damp the courage of the inexperienced. If the hole be narrow the hinder wheels will be quite lifted off the ground by the depression of their precedents, and so remain until by unwearied chirruping and some judicious touches of "the string" the horses are induced to struggle as for their lives; and if the fates are propitious they generally emerge on the opposite side, dragging the vehicle, or at least the fore wheels after them. When I first "penetrated the interior" (to use an indigenous phrase) all I knew of the wilds was from Hoffman's tour[10] or Captain Hall's "graphic" delineations[11]: I had some floating idea of "driving a barouche-and-four anywhere through the oak-openings"[12]—and seeing "the murdered Banquos of the forest" haunting the scenes of their departed strength and beauty. But I confess, these pictures, touched by the glowing pencil of fancy, gave me but incorrect notions of a real journey through Michigan.

Our vehicle was not perhaps very judiciously chosen;—at least we have since thought so. It was a light high-hung carriage—of the description commonly known as a buggy or shandrydan—names of which I would be glad to learn the etymology. I seriously advise any of my friends who are about flitting to Wisconsin or Oregon, to prefer a heavy lumber-waggon, even for the use of the ladies of the family; very little aid or consolation being derived from making a "genteel" appearance in such cases.

At the first encounter of such a mud-hole as I have attempted to describe, we stopped in utter despair. My companion indeed would fain have persuaded me that the many wheel tracks which passed through the formidable gulf were proof positive that it might be forded. I insisted with all a woman's obstinacy that I could not and would not make the attempt, and alighted accordingly, and tried to find a path on one side or the other. But in vain, even putting out of the question my paper-soled shoes— sensible things for the woods. The ditch on each side was filled with water and quite too wide to jump over; and we were actually contemplating a return, when a man in an immense bear-skin cap and a suit of deer's hide, sprang from behind a stump just within the edge of the forest. He "poled" himself over the ditch in a moment, and stood beside us, rifle in hand, as wild and rough a specimen of humanity as one would wish to encounter in a strange and lonely road, just at the shadowy dusk of the evening. I did *not* scream, though I own I was prodigiously frightened. But our stranger said

immediately, in a gentle tone and with a French accent, "Me watch deer—
you want to cross?" On receiving an answer in the affirmative, he ran in
search of a rail which he threw over the terrific mud-hole—aided me to
walk across by the help of his pole—showed my husband where to
plunge—waited till he had gone safely through and "slow circles dimpled
o'er the quaking mud"[13]—then took himself off by the way he came,
declining any compensation with a most polite "rien, rien!" This instance
of true and genuine and generous politeness I record for the benefit of all
bearskin caps, leathern jerkins and cowhide boots, which ladies from the
eastward world may hereafter encounter in Michigan.

Our journey was marked by no incident more alarming than the one
I have related, though one night passed in a wretched inn, deep in the
"timbered land"—as all woods are called in Michigan—was not without
its terrors, owing to the horrible drunkenness of the master of the house,
whose wife and children were in constant fear of their lives, from his
insane fury. I can never forget the countenance of that desolate woman,
sitting trembling and with white, compressed lips in the midst of her
children. The father raving all night, and coming through our sleeping
apartment with the earliest ray of morning, in search of more of the poison
already boiling in his veins. The poor wife could not forbear telling me her
story—her change of lot—from a well-stored and comfortable home in
Connecticut to this wretched den in the wilderness—herself and children
worn almost to shadows with the ague, and her husband such as I have
described him. I may mention here that not very long after I heard of this
man in prison in Detroit, for stabbing a neighbour in a drunken brawl, and
ere the year was out he died of delirium tremens, leaving his family destitute. So much for turning our fields of golden grain into "fire water"—a
branch of business in which Michigan is fast improving.

Our ride being a deliberate one, I felt, after the third day, a little
wearied, and began to complain of the sameness of the oak-openings and
to wish we were fairly at our journey's end. We were crossing a broad
expanse of what seemed at a little distance a smooth shaven lawn of the
most brilliant green, but which proved on trial little better than a quaking
bog—embracing within its ridgy circumference all possible varieties of

"Muirs, and mosses, slaps and styles"—

I had just indulged in something like a yawn, and wished that I could see
our hotel. At the word, my companion's face assumed rather a comical
expression, and I was so preparing to inquire somewhat testily what there

7

was so laughable—I was getting tired and cross, reader—when down came our good horse to the very chin in a bog-hole, green as Erin on the top, but giving way on a touch, and seeming deep enough to have engulfed us entirely if its width had been proportionate. Down came the horse— and this was not all—down came the driver; and I could not do less than follow, though at a little distance—our good steed kicking and floundering—covering us with hieroglyphics, which would be readily decyphered by any Wolverine we should meet, though perchance strange to the eyes of our friends at home. This mishap was soon amended. Tufts of long marsh grass served to assoilize[14] our habiliments a little, and a clear stream which rippled through the marsh aided in removing the eclipse from our faces. We journeyed on cheerily, watching the splendid changes in the west, but keeping a bright look-out for bog-holes.

CHAPTER II

Think us no churls, nor measure our good minds
By this rude place we live in.
　　　—Shakespeare, *Cymbeline*[1]

THE SUN had just set when we stopped at the tavern, and I then read the cause of my companion's quizzical look. My Hotel was a log-house of diminutive size, with corresponding appurtenances; and from the moment we entered its door I was in a fidget to know where we could possibly sleep. I was then new in Michigan. Our good hostess rose at once with a nod of welcome.

"Well! is this Miss Clavers?" (my husband had been there before.) "well! I want to know! why do tell if you've been upsot in the mash? why, I want to know!—and didn't ye hurt ye none? Come, gals! fly round, and let's git some supper."

"But you'll not be able to lodge us, Mrs. Danforth," said I, glancing at three young men and some boys, who appeared to have come in from their work, and who were lounging on one side of the immense open chimney.

"Why, bless your heart! yes I shall; don't you fret yourself: I'll give you as good a bed as any-body need want."

I cast an exploring look, and now discovered a door opposite the fire.

A New Home, Who'll Follow?

"Jist step in here," said Mrs. Danforth, opening this door, "jist come in, and take off your things, and lop down, if you're a mind to, while we're a getting supper."

I followed her into the room, if room it might be called, a strip partitioned off, just six feet wide, so that a bed was accurately fitted in at each end, and a square space remained vacant between the two.

"We've been getting this room made lately, and I tell you it's real nice, so private, like!" said our hostess, with a complacent air. "Here," she continued, "in this bed the gals sleeps, and that's my bed and the old man's; and then here's a trundle-bed for Sally and Jane," and suiting the action to the word, she drew out the trundle-bed as far as our standing-place would allow, to show me how convenient it was.

Here was my grand problem still unsolved! If "me and the old man," and the girls, and Sally and Jane, slept in this strip, there certainly could be no room for more, and I thought with dismay of the low-browed roof, which had seemed to me to rest on the tops of the window-frames. And, to make a long story short, though manifold were the runnings up and down, and close the whisperings before all was ready, I was at length ushered up a steep and narrow stick-ladder, into the sleeping apartment. Here, sur-rounded by beds of all sizes spread on the floor, was a bedstead, placed under the peak of the roof, in order to gain space for its height, and round this state-bed, for such it evidently was, although not supplied with pillows at each end, all the men and boys I had seen below stairs, were to repose. Sundry old quilts were fastened by forks to the rafters in such a way as to serve as a partial screen, and with this I was obliged to be content. Exces-sive fatigue is not fastidious. I called to mind some canal-boat experiences, and resigned myself to the "honey-heavy dew of slumber."[2]

I awoke with a sense of suffocation—started up—all was dark as the Hall of Eblis.[3] I called—no answer came; I shrieked! and up ran one of the "gals."

"What on airth's the matter?"

"Where am I? What ails me?" said I, beginning to feel a little awk-ward when I heard the damsel's voice.

"Why, I guess you was scairt, wa' n't ye?"

"Why am I in the dark? Is it morning?"

"Morning? why, the boys has been gone away this hour, and, you see, there ain't no winder up here, but I'll take down this here quilt, and then I guess you'll be able to see some."

She did so, and I began to discern

"A faint shadow of uncertain light,"[4]

which, after my eyes had become somewhat accustomed to it, served very well to dress by.

Upon descending the ladder, I found our breakfast prepared on a very neat-looking table, and Mrs. Danforth with her clean apron on, ready to do the honours.

Seeing me looking round with inquiring eye, she said, "Oh! you 'm lookin' for a wash-dish, a' n't ye!" and forthwith put some water into a little iron skillet, and carried it out to a bench which stood under the eaves, where I performed my very limited ablutions *al fresco,* not at all pleased with this part of country habits.

I bethought me of a story I had heard before we crossed the line, of a gentleman travelling in Michigan, who instead of a "wash-dish" was directed to the spring, and when he requested a towel received for answer: "Why, I should think you had a hankercher!"

After breakfast, I expressed a wish to accompany Mr. Clavers to the village tract; but he thought a very bad marsh would make the ride unpleasant.

"Lord bless ye!" said Mr. Danforth, "that *mash* has got a real handsome bridge over it since you was here last."

So we set out in the buggy and rode several miles through an alternation of open glades with fine walnut trees scattered over them, and "bosky dells" fragrant as "Araby the blest"[5] at that delicious hour, when the dews filled the air with the scent of the bursting leaves.

By and bye, we came to the "beautiful bridge," a newly-laid causeway of large round logs, with a slough of despond to be crossed in order to reach it. I would not consent to turn back, however, and in we went, the buggy standing it most commendably. When we reached the first log our poor Rozinante[6] stopped in utter despair, and some persuasion was necessary to induce him to rear high enough to place his fore feet upon the bridge, and when he accomplished this feat, and after a rest essayed to make the buggy rear too, it was neck or nothing. Yet up we went, and then came the severe part of the achievement, a "beautiful bridge" half a mile long!

Half a rod was enough for me, I cried for quarter, and was permitted to pick my way over its slippery eminences to the utter annihilation of a pair of Lane's shoes.

CHAPTER III

The greatness of an estate, in bulk and territory doth fall under measure; and the greatness of finances and revenue doth fall under computation. *** By all means it is to be procured, that the trunk of Nebuchadnezzar's tree of monarchy be great enough to bear the branches and the boughs.
    —Bacon [1]

THE MORNING passed in viewing and reviewing the village site and the "Mill privilege," under the condescending guidance of a regular land spec-ulator, into whose clutches—but I anticipate.

The public square, the water lots, the value *per foot* of this undulating surface, clothed as it then was with burr-oaks, and haunted by the red deer; these were almost too much for my gravity. I gave my views, how-ever, as to the location of the grand esplanade, and particularly requested that the fine oaks which now graced it might be spared when the clearing process commenced.

"Oh, certainly, mem!" said our Dousterswivel,[2] "a place that's de-signed for a public promenade must not be divested of shade trees!" Yet I believe these very trees were the first "Banquos" at Montacute. The water lots, which were too valuable to sell save by the foot, are still in the market, and will probably remain there for the present.

This factotum, this Mr. Mazard, was an odd-looking creature, with "diverse ocular foci,"[3] and a form gaunt enough to personify Grahamism.[4] His words sometimes flowed in measured softness, and sometimes tumbled over each other, in his anxiety to convince, to persuade, to inspire. His air of earnest conviction, of sincere anxiety for your interest, and, above all, of entire forgetfulness of his own, was irresistible. People who did not know him always believed every word he said; at least so I have since been informed.

This gentleman had kindly undertaken to lay out our village, to build a mill, a tavern, a store, a blacksmith's shop; houses for cooper, miller, &c. &c., to purchase the large tracts which would be required for the mill-pond, a part of which land was already improved; and all this, although sure to cost Mr. Clavers an immense sum, *he,* from his experi-ence of the country, his large dealings with saw-mills, &c., would be able to accomplish at a very moderate cost. The mill, for instance, was to be a story and a half high, and to cost perhaps twenty-five hundred dollars at the utmost. The tavern, a cheap building of moderate size, built on the most popular plan, and connected with a store, just large enough for the infant needs of the village, reserving our strength for a splendid one, (I quote Mr. Mazard) to be built out of the profits in about three years. All these points being thus satisfactorily arranged, Mr. Mazard received *carte blanche* for the purchase of the lands which were to be flowed, which he had ascertained might be had for a mere trifle.

The principal care now was to find a name—a title at once simple and dignified—striking and euphonious—recherché and yet unpretending. Mr. Mazard was for naming it after the proprietor. It was a proper opportunity, he thought, of immortalizing one's-self. But he failed in convincing the proprietor, who relished not this form of fame, and who referred the matter entirely to me. Here was a responsibility! I begged for time, but the matter must be decided at once. The village plot was to be drawn instanter—lithographed and circulated through the United States, and, to cap the climax, printed in gold, splendidly framed, and hung up in Detroit, in the place "where merchants most do congregate."

I tried for an aboriginal designation, as most characteristic and unworn. I recollected a young lady speaking with enthusiastic admiration of our Indian names, and quoting *Ypsilanti* as a specimen. But I was not fortunate in my choice; for to each of the few which I could recollect, Mr. Mazard found some insuperable objection. One was too long, another signified *Slippery Eel,* another *Big Bubble;* and these would be so inappropriate! I began to be very tired. I tried romantic names; but these again did not suit any of us. At length I decided by lot, writing ten of the most sounding names I could muster from my novel reading stores, on slips of paper, which were mingled in a *shako,* and out came—Montacute.[5] How many matters of greater importance are thus decided.

CHAPTER IV

As I am recording the sacred events of History, I'll not bate one nail's breadth of the honest truth.—W. Irving, *Knickerbocker* [1]

Hope, thou bold taster of delight,
Who, while thou should'st but taste, devours't it quite.
—Cowley [2]

MUCH was yet to be done this morning, and I was too much fatigued to wander about the hills any longer; so I sought shelter in a log-house at no great distance, to await the conclusion of the survey. I was received with a civil nod by the tall mistress of the mansion, and with a curiously grave and somewhat sweeping curtsey by her auburn-tressed daughter, whose hair was in curl papers, and her hands covered with dough. The room was occupied at one end by two large beds not partitioned off "private like," but curtained in with cotton sheets pinned to the unhewn rafters. Between them stood a chest, and over the chest hung the Sunday wardrobe of the family; the go-to-meeting hats and bonnets, frocks and pantaloons of a goodly number of all sizes.

The great open hearth was at the opposite end of the house, flanked on one side by an open cupboard, and on the other by a stick ladder.

Large broadside sheets, caravan show bills were pasted on the logs in different places, garnished with mammoth elephants, and hippopotamuses, over which "predominated" Mr. Van Amburgh, with his head in the lion's mouth. [3] A strip of dingy listing was nailed in such a way as to afford support for a few iron spoons, a small comb, and sundry other articles grouped with the like good taste; but I must return to my fair hostesses.

They seemed to be on the point of concluding their morning duties. The hearth was newly swept, a tin reflector was before the fire, apparently full of bread, or something equally important. The young lady was placing some cups and plates in a pyramidal pile on the cupboard shelf, when the mother, after taking my bonnet with grave courtesy, said something, of which I could only distinguish the words "slick up."

She soon after disappeared behind one of the white screens I have mentioned, and in an incredibly short time emerged in a different dress.

Then taking down the comb I have hinted at, as exalted to a juxtaposition with the spoons, she seated herself opposite to me, unbound her very abundant brown tresses, and proceeded to comb them with great deliberateness; occasionally speering a question at me, or bidding Miss Irene (pronounced Irenee) "mind the bread." When she had finished, Miss Irene took the comb and went through the same exercise, and both scattered the loose hairs on the floor with a coolness that made me shudder when I thought of my dinner, which had become, by means of the morning's ramble, a subject of peculiar interest. A little iron "wash-dish," such as I had seen in the morning, was now produced; the young lady vanished— reappeared in a scarlet circassian dress, and more combs in her hair than would dress a belle for the court of St. James; and forthwith both mother and daughter proceeded to set the table for dinner.

The hot bread was cut into huge slices, several bowls of milk were disposed about the board, a pint bowl of yellow pickles, another of apple sauce, and a third containing mashed potatoes took their appropriate stations, and a dish of cold fried pork was brought out from some recess, heated and re-dished, when Miss Irene proceeded to blow the horn.

The sound seemed almost as magical in its effects as the whistle of Roderick Dhu;[4] for, solitary as the whole neighbourhood had appeared to me in the morning, not many moments elapsed before in came men and boys enough to fill the table completely. I had made sundry resolutions not to touch a mouthful; but I confess I felt somewhat mortified when I found there was no opportunity to refuse.

After the "wash dish" had been used in turn, and various handkerchiefs had performed, not for that occasion only, the part of towels, the lords of creation seated themselves at the table, and fairly demolished in grave silence every eatable thing on it. Then, as each one finished, he arose and walked off, till no one remained of all this goodly company but the red-faced heavy-eyed master of the house. This personage used his privilege by asking me five hundred questions, as to my birth, parentage, and education; my opinion of Michigan, my husband's plans and prospects, business and resources; and then said, "he guessed he must be off."

Meanwhile his lady and daughter had been clearing the table, and were now preparing to wash the dishes in an iron pot of very equivocal-looking soapsuds, which stood in a corner of the chimney place, rinsing each piece in a pan of clean water, and then setting it to "*dreen*" on a chair. I watched the process with no increasing admiration of Michigan economics—thought wofully of dinner, and found that Mrs. Danforth's breakfast table, which had appeared in the morning frugal and homely enough, was filling my mind's eye as the very acme of comfort. Every thing is relative.

But now, prospects began to brighten; the tea-kettle was put on; the table was laid again with the tea equipage and a goodly pile of still warm bread, redolent of milk yeast—the unfailing bowls of apple-sauce and pickles, a plate of small cakes, and a saucer of something green cut up in vinegar. I found we had only been waiting for a more lady-like meal, and having learned wisdom by former disappointment, I looked forward with no small satisfaction to something like refreshment.

The tea was made and the first cup poured, when in came my husband and Mr. Mazard. What was my dismay when I heard that I must mount and away on the instant! The buggy at the door—the sun setting, and the log causeway and the black slough yet to be encountered. I could not obtain a moment's respite, and I will not pretend to describe my vexation, when I saw on looking back our projector already seated at my predestined cup of tea, and busily engaged with my slice of bread and butter!

I walked over the logs in no very pleasant mood and when we reached the slough it looked blacker than ever. I could not possibly screw up my fainting courage to pass it in the carriage, and after some difficulty, a slender pole was found, by means of which I managed to get across, thinking all the while of the bridge by which good Mussulmans skate into Paradise, and wishing for no houri[5] but good Mrs. Danforth.

We reached the inn after a ride which would have been delicious under other circumstances. The softest and stillest of spring atmospheres, the crimson rays yet prevailing, and giving an opal changefulness of hue to the half-opened leaves;—

"The grass beneath them dimly green"—

could scarcely pass quite unfelt by one whose delight is in their beauty: but, alas! who can be sentimental and hungry?

I alighted with gloomy forebodings. The house was dark—could it be that the family had already stowed themselves away in their crowded nests? The fire was buried in ashes, the tea-kettle was cold—I sat down in the corner and cried. ***

I was awakened from a sort of doleful trance by the voice of our cheery hostess.

"Why, do tell if you've had no supper! Well, I want to know! I went off to meetin' over to Joe Bunner's and never left nothing ready."

But in a space of time which did not seem long even to me, my cup of tea was on the table, and the plate of snow-white rolls had no reason to complain of our neglect or indifference.

CHAPTER V

Such soon-speeding geer
As will dispense itself through all the veins.
—Shakespeare[1]

By her help I also now
Make this churlish place allow
Some things that may sweeten gladness
In the very heart of sadness.
—Withers[2]

THE NEXT DAY I was to spend in the society of my hostess; and I felt in no haste to quit my eyrie, although it was terribly close, but waited a call from one of the little maidens before I attempted my twilight toilet. When I descended the ladder, nobody was visible but the womankind.

After breakfast Mrs. Danforth mentioned that she was going about a mile into the woods to visit a neighbour whose son had been bitten by a Massisanga (I spell the word by ear) and was not expected to live.

I inquired of course—"Why, law! it's a rattlesnake; the Indians call them Massisangas and so *folks* calls 'em so too."

"Are they often seen here?"

"Why, no, not very; as far from the *mash* as this. I han't seen but two this spring, and them was here in the garden, and I killed 'em both."

"*You* killed them!"

"Why, law, yes!—Betsey come in one night after tea and told me on 'em, and we went out, and she held the candle while I killed them. But I tell you we had a real chase after them!"

My desire for a long walk through the woods, was somewhat cooled by this conversation; nevertheless upon the good dame's reiterated assurance that there was no danger, and that she would "as lief meet forty on 'em as not," I consented to accompany her, and our path through the dim forest was as enchanting as one of poor Shelley's gemmed and leafy dreams. The distance seemed nothing and I scarcely remembered the rattle-snakes.

We found the poor boy in not quite so sad a case as had been expected. A physician had arrived from ———, about fourteen miles off, and had brought with him a quantity of spirits of Hartshorn,[3] with which the poisoned limb had now been constantly bathed for some hours, while frequent small doses of the same specific had been administered. This course had produced a change, and the pale and weary mother had begun to hope.

The boy had been fishing in the stream which was to make the fortune of Montacute, and in kneeling to search for bait, had roused the snake which bit him just above the knee. The entire limb was frightfully swollen and covered with large livid spots "exactly like the snake," as the woman stated with an air of mysterious meaning.

When I saw the body of the snake, which the father had found without difficulty, and killed very near the scene of the accident, so slow are these creatures generally—I found it difficult to trace the resemblance between its brilliant colours, and the purplish brown blotches on the poor boy's leg. But the superstition once received, imagination supplies all deficiencies. A firm belief in some inscrutable connexion between the spots on the snake and the spots on the wounded person is universal in this region, as I have since frequently heard.

During our walk homeward, sauntering as we did to prolong the enjoyment, my hostess gave me a little sketch of her own early history, and she had interested me so strongly by her unaffected kindliness, and withal a certain dash of espièglerie,[4] that I listened to the homely recital with a good deal of pleasure.

"I was always pretty lucky" she began—and as I looked at her benevolent countenance with its broad expansive brow and gentle eyes, I thought such people are apt to be "lucky" even in this world of disappointments.

"My mother did'n't live to bring me up," she continued, "but a man by the name of Spangler that had no children took me and did for me as if I had been his own; sent me to school and all. His wife was a real mother to me. She was a weakly woman, hardly ever able to sit up all day. I don't believe she ever spun a hank of yarn in her life; but she was a proper nice woman, and Spangler loved her just as well as if she had been ever so smart."

Mrs. Danforth seemed to dwell on this point in her friend's character with peculiar respect,—that he should love a wife who could not do her own work. I could not help telling her she reminded me of a man weeping for the loss of his partner—his neighbours trying to comfort him, by urging the usual topics; he cut them short, looking up at the same time with an inconsolable air—"Ah! but she was such a dreadful good creature to work!"

Mrs. Danforth said gravely, "Well, I suppose the poor feller had a family of children to do for;" and after a reflective pause continued— "Well, *Miss* Spangler had a little one after all, when I was quite a big girl, and you never see folks so pleased as they! Mr. Spangler seemed as if he could not find folks enough to be good to, that winter. He had the prayers of the poor, I tell ye. There was'nt a baby born anywheres in our neighbourhood, that whole blessed winter, but what he found out whether the mother had what would make her comfortable, and sent whatever was wanted.

"He little thought that baby that he thought so much on was going to cost him so dear. His wife was never well again! She only lived through the summer and died when the frost came, just like the flowers; and he never held up his head afterwards. He had been a professor[5] for a good many years, but he did'nt seem then to have neither faith nor hope. He would'nt hear reason from nobody. I always thought that was the reason the baby died. It only lived about a year. Well, I had the baby to bring up by hand, and so I was living there yet when Mr. Spangler took sick. He seemed always like a broken-hearted man, but still he took comfort with the baby, and by and bye the little dear took the croup and died all in a minute like. It began to be bad after tea and it was dead before sunrise. Then I saw plain enough nothing could be done for the father. He wasted away just like an April snow. I took as good care on him as I could, and when it came towards the last he would'nt have any body else give him even so much as a cup of tea. He set his house in order if ever any man did. He settled up his business and gave receipts to many poor folks that owed him small debts, besides giving away a great many things, and paying all those that had helped take care of him. I think he knew what kind of a feller his nephew was, that was to have all when he was gone.

"Well, all this is neither here nor there. George Danforth and I had been keeping company then a good while, and Mr. Spangler knew we'd been only waiting till I could be spared, so he sent for George one day and told him that he had long intended to give me a small house and lot jist back of where he lived, but, seein things stood jist as they did, he advised

George to buy a farm of his that was for sale on the edge of the village, and he would credit him for as much as the house and lot would have been worth, and he could pay the rest by his labour in the course of two or three years. Sure enough, he gave him a deed and took a mortgage, and it was so worded, that he could not be hurried to pay, and every body said it was the greatest bargain that ever was. And Mr. Spangler gave me a nice settin out besides.—But if there is n't the boys comin in to dinner, and I bet there's nothin ready for 'em!" So saying, the good woman quickened her pace, and for the next hour her whole attention was absorbed by the "savoury cates," fried pork and parsnips.

CHAPTER VI

A trickling stream from high rock tumbling down,
And ever drizzling rain upon the loft,
Mixt with a murmuring wind, much like the sound
Of swarming bees.
      —Spenser, *House of Sleep*[1]

While pensive memory traces back the round
Which fills the varied interval between;
Much pleasure, more of sorrow, marks the scene.
      —Warton[2]

WHEN we were quietly seated after dinner, I requested some further insight into Mrs. Danforth's early history, the prosy flow of which was just in keeping with the long dreamy course of the afternoon, unbroken as it was by any sound more awakening than the ceaseless click of knitting-needles, or an occasional yawn from the town lady who found the *farniente*[3] rather burdensome.

She smiled complacently and took up the broken thread at the right place, evidently quite pleased to find she had excited so much interest.

"When Mr. Spangler's nephew came after he was dead and gone, he was very close in asking all about the business, and seein' after the mortgages and such like. Now, George had never got his deed recorded. He felt as if it was'nt worth while to lose a day's work, as he could send it any time by one of his neighbours. But when we found what sort of a man Mr.

A New Home, Who'll Follow?

Wilkins was, we tho't it was high time to set about it. He had talked a good
deal about the place and said the old man must have been crazy to let us
have it so cheap, and once went so far as to offer my husband a hundred
dollars for his bargain. So John Green, a good neighbour of ours, sent us
word one morning that he was going, and would call and get the deed, as
he knew we wanted to send it up, and I got it out and laid it ready on the
stand and put the big bible on it to keep it safe. But he did not come,
something happened that he could not go that day: and I had jist took up
the deed to put it back in the chest, when in came Wilkins. He had an eye
like a hawk; and I was afraid he would see that it was a deed, and ask to
look at it, and then I could n't refuse to hand it to him, you know, so I jist
slipped it back under the bible before I turned to ask him what was his will.

"'Did n't John Saunderson leave my bridle here?' says he. So I stepped
into the other room and got it, and he took it and walked off without
speaking a word; and when I went to put away the deed, it was gone!

"My husband came in while I sat crying fit to break my heart; but
all I could do I could not make him believe that Wilkins had got it. He
said I had put it somewhere else without thinking, that people often felt
just as sure as I did, and found themselves mistaken after all. But I knew
better, and though I hunted high and low to please him, I knew well
enough where it was. When he found we must give it up he never gave
me a word of blame, but charged me not to say anything about the loss,
for, wherever the deed was, Wilkins was just the man to take advantage
if he knew we had lost it.

"Well, things went on in this way for a while, and I had many a
good cryin' spell, I tell ye! and one evening when George was away, in
comes Wilkins, I was sittin' alone at my knittin', heavy hearted enough,
and the schoolmaster was in the little room; for that was his week to
board with us.

"'Is your man at home?' says he; I said—No; but I expected him
soon, so he sat down and began the old story about the place, and at last
he says,

"'I'd like to look at that deed if you've no objection, Mrs. Danforth.' I was so mad, I forgot what George had told me, and spoke right
out.

"I should think, says I, you'd had it long enough to know it all by
heart.

"'What does the woman mean?' says he.

"You know well enough what I mean, says I, you know you took it

20

from off this table, and from under this blessed book, the very last time you was in this house.

"If I had not known it before, I should have been certain then, for his face was as white as the wall and he trembled when he spoke in spite of his impudence. But I could have bit off my own tongue when I tho't how imprudent I had been, and what my husband would say. He talked very angry as you may think.

" 'Only say that where anybody else can hear you,' says he, 'and I'll make it cost your husband all he is worth in the world.'

"He spoke so loud that Mr. Peeler, the master, came out of the room to see what was the matter, and Wilkins bullied away and told Peeler what I had said, and dared me to say it over again. The master looked as if he knew something about it but did not speak. Just then the door opened, and in came George Danforth led between two men as pale as death, and dripping wet from head to foot. You may think how I felt! Well, they would n't give no answer about what was the matter till they got George into bed—only one of 'em said he had been in the canal. Wilkins pretended to be too angry to notice my husband, but kept talking away to himself—and was jist a beginning at me again, when one of the men said, 'Squire, I guess Henry 'll want some looking after; for Mr. Danforth has just got him out of the water.'

"If I live to be an hundred years old I shall never forget how Wilkins looked. There was every thing in his face at once. He seemed as if he would pitch head-foremost out of the door when he started to go home—for Henry was his only child.

"When he was gone, and my husband had got warm and recovered himself a little, he told us, that he had seen Henry fall into the lock, and soused right in after him, and they had come very near drowning together, and so stayed in so long that they were about senseless when they got into the air again. Then I told him all that had happened—and then Peeler, he up, and told that he saw Wilkins take a paper off the stand the time I opened the bed-room door, to get the bridle, for he was at our house then.

"I was very glad to hear it to be sure; but the very next morning came a new deed and the mortgage with a few lines from Mr. Wilkins, saying how thankful he was, and that he hoped George would oblige him by accepting some compensation. George sent back the mortgage, saying he would rather not take it, but thanked him kindly for the deed. So then I was glad Peeler had n't spoke, 'cause it would have set Wilkins against him. After that we thought it was best to sell out and come away, for such feelings, you know, a' n't pleasant among neighbours, and we had talked some of coming to Michigan afore.

"We had most awful hard times at first. Many 's the day I've worked from sunrise till dark in the fields gathering brush heaps and burning stumps. But that's all over now; and we 've got four times as much land as we ever should have owned in York-State."

I have since had occasion to observe that this forms a prominent and frequent theme of self-gratulation among the settlers in Michigan. The possession of a large number of acres is esteemed a great good, though it makes but little difference in the owner's mode of living. Comforts do not seem to abound in proportion to landed increase, but often on the contrary, are really diminished for the sake of it: and the habit of selling out so frequently makes that *home*-feeling, which is so large an ingredient in happiness elsewhere, almost a nonentity in Michigan. The man who holds himself ready to accept the first advantageous offer, will not be very solicitous to provide those minor accommodations, which, though essential to domestic comfort, will not add to the moneyed value of his farm, which he considers merely an article of trade, and which he knows his successor will look upon in the same light. I have sometimes thought that our neighbours forget that "the days of man's life are three score and ten," since they spend all their lives in getting ready to begin.

CHAPTER VII

🦋🦋🦋🦋🦋🦋

Offer me no money, I pray you; that kills my heart. ***

> Will you buy any tape
> Or lace for your cape,
> My dainty duck, my dear-a?
> Any silk, any thread,
> Any toys for your head,
> Of the newest and finest wear-a?
> —Shakespeare, *The Winter's Tale* [1]

OUR RETURN to Detroit was accomplished without any serious accident, although we were once overturned in consequence of my enthusiastic admiration of a tuft of splendid flowers in a marsh which we were crossing by the usual bridge of poles, or *corduroy* as it is here termed.

While our eyes were fixed upon it, and I was secretly determining not to go on without it, our sober steed, seeing a small stream at a little distance on one side, quietly walked towards it, and our attention was withdrawn from the contemplation of the object of my wishes by finding ourselves *spilt* into the marsh, and the buggy reposing on its side, while the innocent cause of the mischief was fairly planted, fetlock deep, in the tenacious black-mud: I say the innocent cause, for who ever expected any proofs of education from a livery-stable beast?—and such was our brown friend.

'T were vain to tell how I sat on the high bog, (the large tufted masses in a marsh are so called in Michigan,) which had fortunately received me in falling, and laughed till I cried to see my companion hunting for his spectacles, and D'Orsay (whom I ought sooner to have introduced to my reader) looking on with a face of most evident wonder. D'Orsay, my beautiful greyhound, was our *compagnon de voyage,* and had caused us much annoyance by her erratic propensities, so that we were obliged to tie him in the back part of the buggy, and then watch very closely that he did not free himself of his bonds.

Just at this moment a pedestrian traveller, a hard-featured, yellow-haired son of New England, came up, with a tin trunk in his hand, and a small pack or knapsack strapped on his shoulders.

"Well! I swan!" said he with a grim smile, "I never see any thing slicker than that! Why, you went over jist as *easy!* You was goin' to try if the mash wouldn't be softer ridin', I s'pose."

Mr. Clavers disclaimed any intention of quitting the causeway, and pointed to my unfortunate pyramid of pale pink blossoms as the cause of our disaster.

"What! them posies? Why, now, to my thinking, a good big double marygold is as far before them pink lilies as can be: but I'll see if I can't get 'em for you if you want 'em."

By this time, the carriage was again in travelling trim, and D'Orsay tolerably resigned to his imprisoned state. The flowers were procured, and most delicately beautiful and fragrant they were.

Mr. Clavers offered guerdon-remuneration, but our oriental friend seemed shy of accepting any thing of the sort.

"If you've a mind to trade, I've got a lot o' notions I'd like to sell you," said he.

So my travelling basket was crammed with essences, pins, brass thimbles, and balls of cotton; while Mr. Clavers possessed himself of a valuable outfit of pocket-combs, suspenders, and cotton handkerchiefs— an assortment which made us very popular on that road for some time after.

We reached the city in due time, and found our hotel crowded to suffocation. The western fever was then at its height, and each day brought its thousands to Detroit. Every tavern of every calibre was as well filled as ours, and happy he who could find a bed any where. Fifty cents was the price of six feet by two of the bar-room floor, and these choice lodgings were sometimes disposed of by the first served at "thirty per cent. advance." The country inns were thronged in proportion; and your horse's hay cost you nowhere less than a dollar *per diem;* while, throughout the whole territory west of Detroit, the only masticable articles set before the thousands of hungry travellers were salt ham and bread, for which you had the satisfaction of paying like a prince.

CHAPTER VIII

Notre sagesse n'est pas moins à la merci de la fortune que nos biens.—Rochefoucault[1]

> Your horse's hoof-tread sounds too rude,
> So stilly is the solitude.
> —Scott[2]

OUR BREAKFAST-TABLE at ———— House was surrounded by as motley a crew as Mirth ever owned. The standing ornament of the upper end was a very large light-blue crape turban, which turban surmounted the prolonged face of a lady, somewhere (it is not polite to be exact in these matters) between forty and fifty, and also partly concealed a pair of ears from which depended ear-rings whose pendants rested not far from the Apalachian collar-bones of the dignified wearer. This lady, turban and ear-rings, were always in their places before the eggs came, and remained long after the last one had disappeared—at least, I judge so; for I, who always take my chance (rash enough in this case) for a breakfast, never saw her seat vacant. Indeed, as I never met her anywhere else, I might have supposed her a fixture, the production of some American Maelzel,[3] but that the rolling of her very light grey eyes was quite different from that of the dark Persian orbs of the chess-player; while an occasional word came to my ear with a sharp sound, even more startling than the "Echec" of that celebrated personage.

Another very conspicuous member of our usual party was a lady in mourning, whom I afterwards discovered to be a great beauty. I had indeed observed that she wore a great many curls, and that these curls were carefully arranged and bound with a ribbon, so as to make the most of a pair of dark eyes; that nothing that could be called throat was ever enviously shaded, even at breakfast; and that a pair of delicately white hands, loaded with rings of all hues, despite the mourning garments, were never out of sight. But I did not learn that she was a beauty till I met her long after at a brilliant evening party in rouge and blonde, and with difficulty recognized my neighbour of the breakfast-table.

But if I should attempt to set down half my recollections of that *piquant* and changeful scene, I should never get on with my story: so, begging pardon, I will pass over the young ladies, who never were hungry, and their papas, who could never be satisfied, and their brothers, who could not get any thing fit to eat; the crimson-faced *célibataire*,[4] who always ate exactly three eggs, and three slices of bread and butter, and drank three cups of tea, and then left the table, performing the whole in perfect silence; the lady, who played good mamma, and would ever have her two babies at the table with her, and feed them on sausage and strong coffee, without a mouthful of bread; and the shoals of speculators, fat and lean, rich and poor, young and old, dashing and shabby, who always looked very hungry, but could not take time to eat. I saw them only at breakfast, for the rest of the day we usually spent elsewhere.

While we were awaiting the arrival of our chattels from the east, Mr. Clavers accepted an invitation to accompany a party of these breakfast-table companions last mentioned, men of substance literally and figuratively, who were going to make a tour with a view to the purchase of one or two cities. Ponies, knapsacks, brandy-bottles, pocket-compasses, blankets, lucifers, great India rubber boots, coats of the same, and caps with immense umbrella capes to them: these things are but a beginning of the outfit necessary for such an expedition. It was intended to "camp out" as often as might be desirable, to think nothing of fasting for a day or so, and to defy the ague and all its works by the aid of the potent exorcisor contained in the bottles above mentioned. One of the company, an idler from ————, was almost as keen in his pursuit of game as of money, and he carried a double-barrelled fowling-piece, with all things thereunto appertaining, in addition to his other equipments, giving a finishing touch to the grotesque cortége. My only parting charge to my quota of the expedition was to keep out of the water, and to take care of his spectacles. I should have cautioned him against buying a city, but that he was never very ambitious, and already owned Montacute. He went merely *pour se désennuyer;*[5] and I remained at the very focus of this strange excitement as unconcerned spectator, weary enough of the unvarying theme which appeared to fill the whole soul of the community.

The party were absent just four days; and a more dismal sight than they presented on their return cannot well be imagined. Tired and dirty, cross and hungry, were they all. No word of adventures, no boasting of achievements, not even a breath of the talismanic word "land," more interesting to the speculator of 1835–6 than it ever was to the shipwrecked mariner. They seemed as if they would, Esau-like,[6] have sold their city lots for a good supper, though I doubt whether the offer of a "trade" would not have aroused all their energies, and so prevented the bargain.

After tea, however, things brightened a little: I speak for one of the party only. The bath, the razor, the much needed change of those "lendings" on which so much of the comfort of life depends, produced their usual humanizing effect; and by questions skilfully timed and cautiously worded, I drew from my toil-worn spouse a tolerably circumstantial account of the journey.

The first day had been entirely consumed in reaching Shark River, or rather its junction with another considerable stream. Twilight had already shaded the woody path, when the surveyor, who was acquainted with the whole region, informed them that they had yet some miles of travel before they could hope to reach any kind of shelter. They had been for some hours following an Indian trail, and some of the city gentlemen recollecting, as the day declined, that they were a little rheumatic, began to give vent to their opinion that the evening was going to be particularly damp. One went so far as to hint that it would have been as well if Mr. ———— (the sportsman) had not taken quite so long to ascertain whether that white moving thing he had seen in the woods was a deer's tail or not.

To this the city Nimrod had replied, that as to its being a deer's tail, there was no possibility of question; that if the other gentlemen had been a little more patient, they might have had venison for supper; and this little discussion, growing more and more animated as it proceeded, at length occupied the attention of the whole party so completely, that they lost the trail and found themselves at the end of what had seemed to them an open path. There was nothing for it, but to turn the horses' heads right about, and retrace the last mile or more, while the faint gleam of daylight was fast disappearing.

The good humour of the party was, to say the least, not increased by this little *contretemps,*[7] and the following of a trail by star-light is an exercise of skill and patience not likely to be long agreeable to gentlemen who have been for many years accustomed to pavements and gas-lamps. Not a word was said of "camping out," so manfully planned in the morning. The loads of preparations for a bivouac seemed entirely forgotten by every body—at least, no one thought proper to mention them; and after some few attempts of the younger members to be funny, the whole caravan yielded to fate, and plodded on in gloomy and determined silence.

The glimmer of a distant light had an electrical effect. The unlucky sportsman was fortunately in the van, and so had an opportunity of covering up his offences by being the announcer of joyous tidings.

He sang out cheerily, "So shines a good deed in this naughty world!" and pricked on his tired Canadian into something akin to a trot, while the soberer part of the cavalcade followed as fast as they could, or as they dared. Ere long they reached the much desired shelter, and found that their provident care in regard to the various items requisite for food and lodging had not been in vain.

The log cabin which received the weary way-farers was like many others which have served for the first homes of settlers in Michigan. It was logs and nothing else, the fire made on the ground, or on a few loose stones, and a hole in the roof for the escape of the smoke. A family of tolerably decent appearance inhabited this forlorn dwelling, a man and his wife and two young children. They seemed little moved at the arrival of so large a company, but rendered what assistance they could in providing for the ponies and preparing the meal from such materials as were afforded by the well-stored hampers of the baggage pony.

After the conclusion of the meal, the blankets were spread on the ground, and happy he who could get a bag for a pillow. But the night's rest was well earned, and Nature is no niggard paymaster.

CHAPTER IX

Night came; and in their lighted bower, full late
The joy of converse had endured; when, hark!
Abrupt and loud, a summons shook their gate—
Upris'n each wondering brow is knit and arch'd.
        —Campbell[1]

If thou wert the lion, the fox would beguile thee: if thou wert
the lamb, the fox would eat thee.—Shakespeare, *Timon of Athens*[2]

THE MORNING SUN showed the river and its adjunct bright and beautiful, though a *leetle* marshy at the sides. The dead silence, the utter loneliness, the impenetrable shade, which covered the site of the future city, might well call to mind the desolation which has settled on Tadmor and Palmyra;[3] the anticipation of future life and splendour contrasting no less forcibly with the actual scene than would the retrospect of departed grandeur. The guide, who had been much employed in these matters, showed in the course of the day six different points, each of which, the owners were fully satisfied, would one day echo the busy tread of thousands, and see reflected in the now glassy wave the towers and masts of a great commercial town. If already this infatuation seems incredible, how shall we make our children believe its reality!

The day was to be spent in exploring, and as it was desirable to see as much as could be seen of the river so important to the future fortunes of the company, it was concluded to follow the bank as closely as the marshes would allow, and pass the night at the house of a French trader near the outlet of the stream.

The spirits of the party were not very high during the ride. There was something a little cooling in the aspect of the marshes, and, although nobody liked to say so, the ground seemed *rather* wet for city building. However, the trader's dwelling looked very comfortable after the accommodations of the preceding night, and a few Indian huts at no great distance gave some relief to the extreme solitariness of the scene, which had contributed not a little to the temporary depression of the party.

The Frenchman was luckily at home, and with his Indian wife treated the travellers with much civility: the lady, however, declining conversation, or indeed notice of any sort unless when called on to perform the part of interpreter between the gentlemen and some wretched looking Indians who were hanging about the house. Several children with bright, gazelle-like eyes, were visible at intervals, but exhibited nothing of the staring curiosity which is seen peeping from among the sun-bleached locks of the whiter broods of the same class of settlers.

The Indians to whom I have alluded, had come to procure whiskey of the trader, and after they had received the baleful luxury which performs among their fated race the work of fire, famine and pestilence, they departed with rapid steps. They had scarcely quitted the house when another was seen approaching the door with that long easy *trot* which is habitual with the savage when on a journey. He was well dressed, in his way; his hat boasted a broad band of silver lace; his tunic, leggins and moccasins were whole and somewhat ornamented; his blanket glorying in a bright red border; and on his shoulders, slung by a broad thong, was a pack of furs of considerable value. He seemed an old acquaintance of the family, and was received with some animation even by the grave and dignified mistress of the mansion. The trader examined and counted the skins, spoke to the Indian in his own tongue, and invited him to eat, which however he declined, with a significant gesture towards the huts before alluded to.

This evening's supper was made quite luxurious by the preserved cranberries and maple syrup furnished by the settlers; and our friends retired to rest in much more comfortable style than on the preceding night.

The first nap was in all its sweetness, when the whole party were aroused by a hideous yelling, which to city ears could be no less than an Indian war-whoop. Every one was on foot in an instant; and the confusion which ensued in the attempt to dress in the dark was most perplexing and would have been amusing enough but for certain unpleasant doubts. The noise continued to increase as it approached the house, and terror had reached its acmé,—every one catching at something which could be used as a weapon; when a violent knocking at the door aroused the trader, who slept in an inner room or closet, and who had not been disturbed by the bustle within doors or the yelling without. He seemed much surprised at the confusion which reigned among his guests—assured them it was "noting at all" but the Indians coming for more whiskey; and then admitting one of them, and coolly shutting the door in the face of the rest, spoke to the desperate looking savage very sharply, evidently reprobating in no gentle terms the uproar which had disturbed the sleepers.

The Indian made scarce any reply, but pointed with an impatient ire to the keg, repeating "Whiskey! whiskey!" till the trader re-filled it; he then departed leaving our party once more to repose.

The next morning, much was said of the disturbance of the night. The Frenchman seemed to look upon it as a thing of course, and un-blushingly vindicated his own agency in the matter. He said that they would get whiskey from some one—that an Indian could not live without it, and that they would pay honestly for what they got, although they would steal anything they could lay their hands on, from the farmers who lived within reach of their settlements. Bitter complaints he said were often made of corn, potatoes, or cucumbers being spirited away in the night, and the Indians got the blame at least, but from him they took nothing. His lady listened with no pleased aspect to this discussion of the foibles of her countrymen, and seemed quite willing to expedite the depar-ture of the guests.

The way to the "Grand Junction" seemed shortened as they went. The day was fine and the ponies in excellent spirits. The sportsman came very near shooting a fat buck, and this miss kept him in talk for all day. The old gentlemen were much pleased with certain statistical accounts fur-nished them by the trader, whom they decided on the whole to be a very sensible fellow: and when they reached once more the chosen spot, they saw at a glance how easily the marshes could be drained, the channel of the Shark deepened, and the whole converted into one broad area on which to found a second New-York.

They passed another night at the log hut which had first received them, and leaving with the poor couple who inhabited it, what cheered their lonely dwelling for many a day, they returned to Detroit.

Our friends considered the offers which had been made them so very advantageous that the bargain for the site at the "Grand Junction" was concluded the very next day. "Only one hundred shares at three hundred dollars each!" the money might be quadrupled in a month. And some of the knowing ones, who took shares "merely to oblige," did realize the golden vision, while the more careful, who held on to get the top of the market—but why should I tell secrets?

Nobody happened to mention to these eastern buyers that the whole had been purchased for four hundred dollars, just a week before they reached Detroit.

These things certainly cost a good deal of trouble after all. They ought to have paid well, unquestionably. When lots were to be sold, the whole fair dream was splendidly emblazoned on a sheet of super-royal size;

things which only floated before the mind's eye of the most sanguine, were portrayed with bewitching minuteness for the delectation of the ordinary observer. Majestic steamers plied their paddles to and fro upon the river; ladies crowding their decks and streamers floating on the wind. Sloops dotted the harbours, while noble ships were seen in the offing. Mills, factories, and light-houses—canals, rail-roads and bridges, all took their appropriate positions. Then came the advertisements, choicely worded and carefully vague, never setting forth any thing which might not come true at some time or other; yet leaving the buyer without excuse if he chose to be taken in.

An auctioneer was now to be procured (for lots usually went rather heavily at private sale,) and this auctioneer must not be such a one as any Executive can make, but a man of genius, or ready invention, of fluent speech; one who had seen something of the world, and above all, one who must be so thoroughly acquainted with the property, and so entirely convinced of its value, that he could vouch on his own personal *respectability,* for the truth of every statement. He must be able to exhibit certificates from—no matter whom—Tom-a-Nokes[4] perhaps—but "residing on the spot"—and he must find men of straw to lead the first bids. And when all this had been attended to, it must have required some nerve to carry the matter through; to stand by, while the poor artizan, the journeyman mechanic, the stranger who had brought his little all to buy government land to bring up his young family upon, staked their poor means on strips of land which were at that moment a foot under water. I think many of these gentlemen earned their money.

It is not to be supposed that the preliminaries I have enumerated, preceded every successful land-sale. Many thousand acres were transferred from hand to hand with a rapidity which reminded one irresistably of the old French game of "le petit bon homme" (anglicised into 'Robin's alive')[5]—while all gained save him in whose hand Robin died.

I have known a piece of property bought at five hundred dollars, sold at once for twenty thousand; five thousand counted down, and the remainder secured by bond and mortgage. Whether these after payments were ever made, is another question, and one which I am unable to answer. I mention the transaction as one which was performed in all truth and fairness savouring nothing of the "tricksy spirit" on which I have been somewhat diffuse.

I must not omit to record the friendly offer of one of the gentlemen whose adventures I have recapitulated, to take "two Montacute lots at five hundred dollars each." As this was rather beyond the price which the owner had thought fit to affix to his ordinary lots, he felt exceedingly obliged, and somewhat at a loss to account for the proposition, till his friend whispered, "and you shall have in payment a lot at New-New-York at a thousand; and we have not sold one at that I can assure you."

The obliged party chanced to meet the agent for New-New-York about a year after and inquired the fortunes of the future emporium—the number of inhabitants, &c.

"There's nobody there," said he "but those we hire to come."

CHAPTER X

Mrs. Hardcastle. I wish we were at home again. I never met so many accidents in so short a journey. Drenched in the mud, over-turned in the ditch, jolted to a jelly, and at last to lose our way.
—Goldsmith, *She Stoops to Conquer* [1]

AT LENGTH came the joyful news that our moveables had arrived in port; and provision was at once made for their transportation to the banks of the Turnip. But many and dire were the vexatious delays, thrust by the cruel Fates between us and the accomplishment of our plan; and it was not till after the lapse of several days that the most needful articles were selected and bestowed in a large waggon which was to pioneer the grand body. In this waggon had been reserved a seat for myself, since I had far too great an affection for my chairs and tables, to omit being present at their debarcation at Montacute, in order to ensure their undisturbed possession of the usual complement of legs. And there were the children to be packed this time,—little roley-poley things, whom it would have been in vain to have marked—"this side up," like the rest of the baggage.

A convenient space must be contrived for my plants among which were two or three tall geraniums and an enormous Calla Ethiopica. Then D'Orsay must be accommodated, of course; and, to crown all, a large basket of live fowls; for we had been told that there were none to be purchased in the vicinity of Montacute. Besides these, there were all our travelling trunks; and an enormous square box crammed with articles which we then in our greenness considered indispensable. We have since learned better.

After this enumeration, which yet is only partial, it will not seem strange that the guide and director of our omnibus was to ride

"On horseback after we."[2]

He acted as a sort of adjutant—galloping forward to spy out the way, or provide accommodations for the troop—pacing close to the wheels to modify our arrangements, to console one of the imps who had bumped its pate, or to give D'Orsay a gentle hint with the riding-whip when he made demonstrations of mutiny—and occasionally falling behind to pick up a stray handkerchief or parasol.

The roads near Detroit were inexpressibly bad. Many were the chances against our toppling load's preserving its equilibrium. To our inexperience the risks seemed nothing less than tremendous—but the driver so often reiterated, "that a'n't nothin'," in reply to our despairing exclamations, and, what was better, so constantly proved his words by passing the most frightful inequalities (Michiganicé "sidlings") in safety, that we soon became more confident, and ventured to think of something else besides the ruts and mud-holes.

Our stopping-places after the first day were of the ordinary new country class—the very coarsest accommodations by night and by day, and all at the dearest rate. When every body is buying land and scarce any body cultivating it, one must not expect to find living either good or cheap: but, I confess, I was surprised at the dearth of comforts which we obeserved every where. Neither milk, eggs, nor vegetables were to be had, and those who could not live on hard salt ham, stewed dried apples, and bread raised with "salt risin'," would necessarily run some risk of starvation.

One word as to this and similar modes of making bread, so much practised throughout this country. It is my opinion that the sin of bewitching snow-white flour by means of either of those abominations, "salt risin'," "milk emptin's," "bran 'east," or any of their odious compounds, ought to be classed with the turning of grain into whiskey, and both made indictable offences. To those who know of no other means of producing the requisite sponginess in bread than the wholesome hop-yeast of the brewer, I may be allowed to explain the mode to which I have alluded with such hearty reprobation. Here follows the recipe:

To make milk emptin's. Take quantum suf. of good sweet milk—add a teaspoon full of salt, and some water, and set the mixture in a warm place till it ferments, then mix your bread with it; and if you are lucky enough to catch it just in the right moment before the fermentation reaches the putrescent stage, you may make tolerably good rolls, but if you are five minutes too late, you will have to open your doors and windows while your bread is baking.—Verbum sap.

"Salt risin'" is made with water slightly salted and fermented like the other; and becomes putrid rather sooner; and "bran 'east" is on the same plan. The consequences of letting these mixtures stand too long will become known to those whom it may concern, when they shall travel through the remoter parts of Michigan; so I shall not dwell upon them here—but I offer my counsel to such of my friends as may be removing westward, to bring with them some form of portable yeast (the old-fashioned dried cakes which mothers and aunts can furnish, are as good as any)—and also full instructions for perpetuating the same; and to plant hops as soon as they get a corner to plant them in.

> "And may they better rock the rede,
> Than ever did th' adviser." [3]

The last two days of our slow journey were agreeably diversified with sudden and heavy showers, and intervals of overpowering sunshine. The weather had all the changefulness of April, with the torrid heat of July. Scarcely would we find shelter from the rain which had drenched us completely—when the sunshine would tempt us forth; and by the time all the outward gear was dried, and matters in readiness for a continuation of our progress, another threatening cloud would drive us back, though it never really rained till we started.

We had taken a newly opened and somewhat lonely route this time, in deference to the opinion of those who ought to have known better, that this road from having been less travelled would not be quite so *deep* as the other. As we went farther into the wilderness the difficulties incnreased. The road had been but little "worked," (the expression in such cases) and in some parts was almost in a state of nature. Where it wound round the edge of a marsh, where in future times there will be a bridge or drain, the wheels on one side would be on the dry ground while the others were sinking in the long wet grass of the marsh—and in such places it was impossible to discern inequalities which yet might overturn us in an instant. In one case of this sort we were obliged to dismount the "live lumber"—as the man who helped us through phrased it, and let the loaded waggon pass on, while we followed in an empty one which was fortunately at hand—and it was, in my eyes, little short of a miracle that our skillful friend succeeded in piloting safely the top-heavy thing which seemed thrown completely off its centre half a dozen times.

At length we came to a dead stand. Our driver had received special cautions as to a certain *mash* that "lay between us and our home"—to "keep to the right"—to "follow the travel" to a particular point, and then "turn up stream:" but whether the very minuteness and reiteration of the directions had puzzled him, as is often the case, or whether his good genius had for once forsaken him, I know not. We had passed the deep centre of the miry slough, when by some unlucky hair's-breadth swerving, in went our best horse—our sorrel—our "Prince,"—the "off haus," whose value had been speered three several times since we left Detroit, with magnificent offers of a "swop!" The noble fellow, unlike the tame beasties that are used to such occurrences, shewed his good blood by kicking and plunging, which only made his case more desperate. A few moments more would have left us with a "single team," when his master succeeded in cutting the traces with his penknife. Once freed, Prince soon made his way out of the bog-hole and pranced off, far up the green swelling hill which lay before us—out of sight in an instant—and there we sat in the marsh.

There is but one resource in such cases. You must mount your remaining horse if you have one, and ride on till you find a farmer and one, two, or three pairs of oxen—and all this accomplished, you may generally hope for a release in time.

The interval seemed a *leetle* tedious, I confess. To sit for three mortal hours in an open waggon, under a hot sun, in the midst of a swamp, is not pleasant. The expanse of inky mud which spread around us, was hopeless, as to any attempt at getting ashore. I crept cautiously down the tongue, and tried one or two of the tempting green tufts, which looked as if they *might* afford foothold; but alas! they sank under the slightest pressure. So I was fain to re-gain my low chair, with its abundant cushions, and lose myself in a book. The children thought it fine fun for a little while, but then they began to want a drink. I never knew children who did not, when there was no water to be had.

There ran through the very midst of all this black pudding, as clear a stream as ever rippled, and the waggon stood almost in it!—but how to get at it? The basket which had contained, when we left the city, a store of cakes and oranges, which the children thought inexhaustible, held now, nothing but the napkins, which had enveloped those departed joys, and those napkins, suspended corner-wise, and soaked long and often in the crystal water, served for business and pleasure, till papa came back.

"They're coming! They're coming!" was the cry, and with the word, over went Miss Alice, who had been reaching as far as she could, trying how large a proportion of her napkin she could let float on the water.

Oh, the shrieks and the exclamations! how hard papa rode, and how hard mamma scolded! but the little witch got no harm beyond a thorough wetting, and a few streaks of black mud, and felt herself a heroine for the rest of the day.

CHAPTER XI

Rous'd at his name, up rose the boozy sire,
. . . .
In vain, in vain,—the all-composing hour
Resistless falls: the Muse obeys the power."
　—Pope[1]

THE NIGHT DEWS were falling chill and heavy when we crossed the last log-causeway, and saw a dim glimmering in the distance. The children were getting horribly cross and sleepy. The unfortunate anchoring in the black swamp had deranged our plans by about three hours, and when we reached our destined resting-place, which was the log-house where I had been so happy as to make the acquaintance of Miss Irene Ketchum, and her dignified mamma, the family had retired to rest, except Mr. Ketchum, who rested without retiring.

The candle, a long twelve I should judge, was standing on the table, and wasting rapidly under the influence of a very long snuff, which re-clined upon its side. Upon the same table, and almost touching the tall iron candlestick, was a great moppy head; and this head rested in heavy slumber on the brawny arms of the master of the house.

"Ketchum! Ketchum!" echoed a shrill voice from within the pinned-up sheets in one corner, and I might have thought the woman was setting the dog at us, if I had not recognized the dulcet-treble of the fair Irene from the other bed—"Pa, pa, get up, can't you?"

Thus conjured, the master of the mansion tried to overcome the still potent effects of his evening potations, enough to understand what was the matter, but in vain. He could only exclaim, "What the devil's got into the women?" and down went the head again.

Mrs. Ketchum had, by this time, exchanged the night for the day cap, and made herself, otherwise, tolerably presentable. She said she had supposed we were not coming, it was so late; (it was just half-past eight,) and then, like many other poor souls I have known, tried hard to hide her husband's real difficulty.

"He was *so* tired!" she said.

How long the next hour seemed! A summer day in some company I wot of, would not seem half as tedious. It took all papa's ingenuity, and more than all mamma's patience to amuse the poor children, till matters were arranged; but at length the important matter of supper being in some sort concluded, preparations were made for "*retiracy.*"

Up the stick-ladder we all paced "slowly and sadly," Miss Irene preceding us with the remnant of the long twelve, leaving all below in darkness. The aspect of our lodging-place was rather portentous. Two bedsteads, which looked as if they might, by no very violent freak of nature, have grown into their present form, a good deal of bark being yet upon them, occupied the end opposite the stairs; and between them was a window, without either glass or shutter—that is to say, politeness aside, a square hole in the house. Three beds spread upon the floor, two chests, and a spinning-wheel, with reel and swifts, completed the plenishing of the room. Two of the beds were already tenanted, as the vibrations of the floor might have told us without the aid of ears, (people snore incredibly after ploughing all day,) and the remainder were at our service. The night air pouring in at the aperture seemed to me likely to bring death on its dewy wings, and when I looked up and saw the stars shining through the crevices in the roof, I thought I might venture to have the wider rent closed, although I had been sensible of some ill resulting from the close quarters at Danforth's. So a quilt, that invaluable resource in the woods, was stuck up before the window, and the unhinged cover of one of the chests was used as a lid for the stair-way, for fear the children might fall down. Sheets served to partition off a "tyring room" round my bed—an expedient frequently resorted to—and so dangerous that it is wonderful that so few houses are burnt down in this country. And thus passed my first night in Montacute.

I do not remember experiencing, at any time in my life, a sense of more complete uncomfortableness than was my lot, on awaking the next morning. It seemed to arise entirely from my anticipations of the awkward and tedious inconveniences of our temporary sojourn at this place, where every thing was so different from our ideas of comfort, or even decency.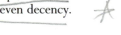

But I have since been convinced, that sleeping in an exhausted atmosphere, of which those who slept on the bedsteads felt the effect more sensibly than those who lay on the floor, had no small agency in producing this depression of spirits, so unusual with me.

Be this as it may, my troubles, when the children were to be washed and dressed, became real and tangible enough; for, however philosophical grown people may sometimes be under disagreeables consequent upon a change of habits, children are very epicures, and will put up with nothing that is unpleasant to them, without at least making a noise, which I do detest and dread; though I know mothers ought to "get used to such things." I have heard that eels get accustomed to being skinned, but I doubt the fact.

That morning was the first and the last time I ever attempted to carry through the ordinary nursery routine, in a log-hut, without a servant, and with a skillet for a wash-basin.

The little things did get dressed after a while, however, and were safely escorted down the stick-ladder, and it was really a pleasure to see them careering round the house, rioting in their freedom, and to hear now and then a merry laugh, awakening the echoes. Children are the true *bijouterie*[2] of the woods and wilds. How weary would my last three years have been, without the cares and troubles they have brought me?

Our breakfast, of undistinguishable green tea, milk-rising bread, and salt ham, did not consume much time, and most fortunately we here found milk for the children, who of course made out sumptuously. It was the first time since we left Detroit, that we had been able to procure more than a small allowance for the tea.

My first care was to inquire where I might be able to procure a domestic, for I saw plainly I must not expect any aid from Miss Irene or her younger sister, who were just such "captive-princess" looking damsels as Miss Martineau mentions having seen at a country inn somewhere on her tour.[3]

"Well, I don't know," said Mrs. Ketchum in reply to my questions; "there was a young lady here yesterday that was saying she did n't know but she 'd live out a spell till she 'd bought her a new dress."

"Oh! but I wish to get a girl who will remain with me; I should not like to change often."

Mrs. Ketchum smiled rather scornfully at this, and said there were not many girls about here that cared to live out long at a time.

My spirits fell at this view of the matter. Some of my dear theorizing friends in the civilized world had dissuaded me most earnestly from bringing a maid with me.

"She would always be discontented and anxious to return; and you'll find plenty of good farmer's daughters ready to live with you for the sake of earning a little money."

Good souls! how little did they know of Michigan! I have since that day seen the interior of many a wretched dwelling, with almost literally nothing in it but a bed, a chest, and a table; children ragged to the last degree, and potatoes the only fare; but never yet saw I one where the daughter was willing to own herself obliged to live out at service. She would "hire out" long enough to buy some article of dress perhaps, or "because our folks have been sick, and want a little money to pay the doctor," or for some such special reason; but never as a regular calling, or with an acknowledgment of inferior station.

This state of things appalled me at first; but I have learned a better philosophy since. I find no difficulty now in getting such aid as I require, and but little in retaining it as long as I wish, though there is always a desire of making an occasional display of independence. Since living with one for wages is considered by common consent a favour, I take it as a favour; and, this point once conceded, all goes well. Perhaps I have been peculiarly fortunate; but certainly with one or two exceptions, I have little or nothing to complain of on this essential point of domestic comfort.

To be sure, I had one damsel who crammed herself almost to suffocation with sweatmeats and other things which she esteemed very nice; and ate up her own pies and cake, to the exclusion of those for whom they were intended; who would put her head in at a door, with—"*Miss* Clavers, did you holler? I thought I *heered* a yell."

And another who was highly offended, because room was not made for her at table with guests from the city, and that her company was not requested for tea-visits. And this latter high-born damsel sent in from the kitchen a circumstantial account *in writing,* of the instances wherein she considered herself aggrieved; well written it was too, and expressed with much *naiveté,* and abundant respect. I answered it in the way which "turneth away wrath." Yet it was not long before this fiery spirit was aroused again, and I was forced to part with my country belle. But these instances are not very tremendous even to the city habits I brought with me; and I cannot say I regret having been obliged to relinquish what was, after all,

rather a silly sort of pride. But bless me! how I get before my story! I
viewed the matter very differently when I was at Ketchum's. My philosophy was of slow growth.

On reflection, it was thought best not to add another sleeper to the
loft, and I concluded to wait on myself and the children while we remained
at Ketchum's, which we hoped would be but for a day or two. I can only
say, I contrived to *simplify* the matter very much, when I had no one to
depend on but myself. The children had dirty faces, and aprons which
would have effected their total exclusion from genteel society more than
half the time; and I was happy to encourage the closest intimacy between
them and the calves and chickens, in order to gain some peace within
doors. Mrs. Ketchum certainly had her own troubles during our sojourn
under her leaky roof; for the two races commingled not without loud and
long effervescence, threatening at times nothing short of a Kilkenny cat
battle,⁴ ending in mutual extermination.

My office, on these occasions, was an humble imitation of the plan of
the celestials in ancient times; to snatch away the combatant in whom I was
most interested, and then to secrete him for a while, using as a desert island
one of the beds in the loft, where the unfortunate had to dree a weary
penance, and generally came down quite tame.

CHAPTER XII

The ripeness or unripeness of the occasion must ever be well
weighed; and generally, it is good to commit the beginnings of all
great actions to Argus with his hundred eyes, and the ends to
Briareus with his hundred hands.—Bacon¹

Trust not yourself; but your defects to know
Make use of every friend.
—Pope²

THE LOG-HOUSE, which was to be our temporary home, was tenanted at
this time; and we were obliged to wait while the incumbent could build a
framed one; the materials for which had been growing in the woods not
long before; I was told it would take but a short time, as it was already
framed.

What was my surprise, on walking that way to ascertain the progress of things, to find the materials still scattered on the ground, and the place quite solitary.

"Did not Mr. Ketchum say Green's house was framed?" said I to the *dame du palais,* on my return; "the timbers are all lying on the ground, and nobody at work."

"Why, la! so they be all framed, and Green's gone to ———— for the sash. They'll be ready to raise tomorrow."

It took me some time to understand that *framing* was nothing more than cutting the tenons and mortices ready for putting the timbers together, and that these must be *raised* before there could be a frame. And that "sash," which I in my ignorance supposed could be but for one window, was a *generic* term.

The "raising" took place the following afternoon, and was quite an amusing scene to us cockneys, until one man's thumb was frightfully mashed, and another had a severe blow upon the head. A jug of whiskey was pointed out by those who understood the matter, as the true cause of these disasters, although the Fates got the blame.

"Jem White always has such bad luck!" said Mr. Ketchum, on his return from the raising, "and word spake never more," for that night at least; for he disappeared behind the mysterious curtain, and soon snored most sonorously.

The many raisings which have been accomplished at Montacute, without that ruinous ally, strong drink, since the days of which I speak, have been free from accidents of any sort; Jem White having carried his "bad luck" to a distant county, and left his wife and children to be taken care of by the public.

Our cottage bore about the same proportion to the articles we had expected to put into it, that the "lytell hole" did to the fiend whom Virgilius[3] cajoled into its narrow compass; and the more we reflected, the more certain we became that without the magic powers of necromancy, one half of our moveables at least must remain in the open air. To avoid such necessity, Mr. Clavers was obliged to return to Detroit and provide storage for sundry unwieldy boxes which could by no art of ours be conjured into our cot.

While he was absent, Green had enclosed his new house; that is to say put on the roof and the siding, and laid one floor, and forthwith he removed thither without door, window or chimney, a course by no means unusual in Michigan.

As I was by this time, truth to speak, very nearly starved, I was anxious to go as soon as possible to a place where I could feel a little more at home; and so completely had my nine days at Ketchum's brought down my ideas, that I anticipated real satisfaction in a removal to this hut in the wilderness. I would not wait for Mr. Clavers's return; but insisted on setting up for myself at once.

But I should in vain attempt to convey to those who know nothing of the woods, any idea of the difficulties in my way. If one's courage did not increase, and one's invention brighten under the stimulus of such occasions, I should have given up at the outset, as I have often done with far less cause.

It was no easy matter to get a "lady" to clean the place, and ne'er had place more need of the tutelary aid of the goddess of scrubbing brushes. Then this lady must be provided with the necessary utensils, and here arose dilemma upon dilemma. Mrs. Ketchum rendered what aid she could, but there was little superfluous in her house.

And then, such racing and chasing, such messages and requisitions! Mrs. Jennings "could n't do nothin' without a mop, and I had not thought of such a thing and was obliged to sacrifice on the spot sundry nice towels, a necessity which made all the housekeeping blood in my veins tingle.

After one day's experience of this sort, I decided to go myself to the scene of action, so as to be at hand for these trying occasions; and I induced Mr. Ketchum to procure a waggon and carry to our new home the various articles which we had piled in a hovel on his premises.

Behold me then seated on a box, in the midst of as anomalous a congregation of household goods as ever met under one roof in the backwoods, engaged in the seemingly hopeless task of calling order out of chaos, attempting occasionally to throw out a hint for the instruction of Mrs. Jennings, who uniformly replied by requesting me not to fret, as she knew what she was about.

Mr. Jennings, with the aid of his sons, undertook the release of the pent up myriads of articles which crammed the boxes, many of which though ranked when they were put in as absolutely essential, seemed ridiculously superfluous when they came out. The many observations made by the spectators as each new wonder made its appearance, though at first rather amusing, became after a while quite vexatious; for the truth began to dawn upon me that the common sense was all on their side.

"What on airth's them gimcracks for?" said my lady, as a nest of delicate japanned tables were set out upon the uneven floor.

I tried to explain to her the various convenient uses to which they were applicable; but she looked very scornfully after all and said "I guess they'll do better for kindlin's than any thing else, here." And I began to cast a disrespectful glance upon them myself, and forthwith ordered them up stairs, wondering in my own mind how I could have thought a log house would afford space for such superfluities.

All this time there was a blazing fire in the chimney to accommodate Mrs. Jennings in her operations, and while the doors and windows were open we were not sensible of much discomfort from it. Supper was prepared and eaten—beds spread on the floor, and the children stowed away. Mrs. Jennings and our other "helps" had departed, and I prepared to rest from my unutterable weariness, when I began to be sensible of the suffocating heat of the place. I tried to think it would grow cooler in a little while, but it was absolutely insufferable to the children as well as myself, and I was fain to set both doors open, and in this exposed situation passed the first night in my western home, alone with my children and far from any neighbour.

If I could live a century, I think, that night will never fade from my memory. Excessive fatigue made it impossible to avoid falling asleep, yet the fear of being devoured by wild beasts, or poisoned by rattlesnakes, caused me to start up after every nap with sensations of horror and alarm, which could hardly have been increased by the actual occurrence of all I dreaded. Many wretched hours passed in this manner. At length sleep fairly overcame fear, and we were awakened only by a wild storm of wind and rain which drove in upon us and completely wetted every thing within reach.

A doleful morning was this—no fire on the hearth—streams of water on the floor, and three hungry children to get breakfast for. I tried to kindle a blaze with matches, but alas! even the straw from the packing-boxes was soaked with the cruel rain; and I was distributing bread to the hungry, hopeless of anything more, when Mr. Jennings made his appearance.

"I was thinking you'd begin to be sick o' your bargain by this time," said the good man, "and so I thought I'd come and help you a spell. I reckon you'd ha' done better to have waited till the old man got back."

"What old man?" asked I, in perfect astonishment.

"Why, *your* old man to be sure," said he laughing. I had yet to learn that in Michigan, as soon as a man marries he becomes "th' old man," though he may be yet in his minority. Not long since I gave a young bride the how d' ye do in passing, and the reply was, "I'm pretty well, but my old man 's sick a-bed."

But to return, Mr. Jennings kindled a fire which I took care should be a very moderate one; and I managed to make a cup of tea to dip our bread in, and then proceeded to find places for the various articles which strewed the floor. Some auger-holes bored in the logs received large and long pegs, and these served to support boards which were to answer the purpose of shelves. It was soon found that the multiplicity of articles which were to be accommodated on these shelves would fill them a dozen times.

"Now to my thinkin'," said my good genius, Mr. Jennings, "that 'ere soup-t'reen, as you call it, and them little ones, and these here great glass-dishes, and all *sich,* might jist as well go up chamber for all the good they'll ever do you here."

This could not be gainsaid; and the good man proceeded to exalt them to another set of extempore shelves in the upper story; and so many articles were included in the same category, that I began to congratulate myself on the increase of clear space below, and to fancy we should soon begin to look very comfortable.

My ideas of comfort were by this time narrowed down to a well-swept room with a bed in one corner, and cooking-apparatus in another— and this in some fourteen days from the city! I can scarcely, myself, credit the reality of the change.

It was not till I had occasion to mount the ladder that I realized that all I had gained on the confusion below was most hopelessly added to the confusion above, and I came down with such a sad and thoughtful brow, that my good aid-de-camp perceived my perplexity.

"Had n't I better go and try to get one of the neighbour's *gals* to come and help you for a few days?" said he.

I was delighted with the offer, and gave him carte-blanche as to terms, which I afterwards found was a mistake, for, where sharp bargains are the grand aim of every body, those who express anything like in-difference on the subject, are set down at once as having more money than they know what to do with; and as this was far from being my case, I found reason to regret having given room for the conclusion.

The damsel made her appearance before a great while—a neat look-ing girl with "scarlet hair and belt to match;" and she immediately set about "reconciling" as she called it, with a good degree of energy and ingenuity. I was forced to confess that she knew much better than I how to make a log-house comfortable.

She began by turning out of doors the tall cup-board, which had puzzled me all the morning, observing very justly, "Where there ain't no room for a thing, why, there ain't;" and this decision cut the Gordian knot of all my plans and failures in the disposal of the ungainly convenience. It did yeoman's service long afterwards as a corn-crib.

When the bedsteads were to be put up, the key was among the missing; and after we had sent far and wide and borrowed a key, or the substitute for one, no screws could be found, and we were reduced to the dire necessity of trying to keep the refractory posts in their places by means of ropes. Then there were candles, but no candle-sticks. This seemed at first rather inconvenient, but when Mr. Jennings had furnished blocks of wood with auger-holes bored in them for sockets, we could do nothing but praise the ingenuity of the substitute.

My rosy-haired Phillida [4] who rejoiced in the euphonius appellation of Angeline, made herself entirely at home, looking into my trunks, &c., and asking the price of various parts of my dress. She wondered why I had not my hair cut off, and said she reckoned I would before long, as it was all the fashion about here.

"When d' ye expect *Him?*" said the damsel, with an air of sisterly sympathy, and ere I could reply becomingly, a shout of "tiny joy" told me that Papa had come.

I did not cry for sorrow this time.

CHAPTER XIII

✹ ✹ ✹ ✹ ✹

Dans toutes les professions et dans tous les arts, chacun se fait une mine et un extérieur qu' il met en la place de la chose dont il veut avoir la merite; de sorte que tout le monde n'est composé que de mines; et c'est inutilement que nous travaillons à y trouver rien de réel.
—Rochefoucault [1]

We see the reign or tyranny of custom, what it is. The Indians lay themselves quietly upon a stack of wood, and so sacrifice themselves by fire. ***

Since custom is the principal magistrate of man's life, let men by all means endeavour to obtain good customs.—Bacon [2]

custom

45

DIFFICULTIES began to melt away like frosty rime after this. Some were removed, but to many we became habituated in a far shorter time than I could have imagined possible. A carpenter constructed a narrow flight of board-steps which really seemed magnificent after the stick-ladder. The screws came before the bed-steads were quite spoiled, and the arrival of my bureau—the unpacking of the box among whose multifarious contents appeared the coffee-mill, the smoothing-irons, the snuffers, gave more real delight than that of any case of splendid Parisian millinery that ever drew together a bevy of belles at Mrs. ———'s show-rooms. I never before knew the value of a portable desk, or realized that a bottle of ink might be reckoned among one's treasures.

Our preparations for residence were on a very limited scale, for we had no idea of inhabiting the loggery more than six weeks or two months at farthest. Our new dwelling was to be put up immediately, and our arrangements were to be only temporary. So easily are people deluded!

The Montacute mill was now in progress, and had grown (on paper,) in a short time from a story and a half to four stories; its capabilities of all sorts being proportionately increased. The tavern was equally fortunate, for Mr. Mazard had undertaken its erection entirely on his own account, as a matter of speculation, feeling, he said, quite certain of selling it for double its cost whenever he should wish. The plan of the public-house was the production of his teeming brain, and exhibited congenial intricacies; while the windows resembled his own eyes in being placed too near together, and looking all manner of ways. Several smaller buildings were also in progress, and for all these workmen at a high rate of wages were to be collected and provided for.

I could not but marvel how so many carpenters had happened to "locate" within a few miles of each other in this favoured spot; but I have since learned that a plane, a chisel, and two dollars a day make a carpenter in Michigan.

Mill-wrights too are remarkably abundant; but I have never been able to discover any essential difference between them and the carpenters, except that they receive three dollars per diem, which, no doubt, creates a distinction in time.

Our mill-wright was a little round-headed fellow with a button nose, a very Adonis, in his own eyes, and most aptly named Puffer, since never did a more consequential dignitary condescend to follow a base mechanical calling. His statements, when he condescended to make any, were always given with a most magisterial air; and no suggestion, however skilfully insinuated or gently offered, was ever received without an air of insulted dignity, and a reiteration of his own conviction that it was probable he understood his business.

It is to be ascribed to this gentleman's care and accuracy that Mr. Clavers has since had the satisfaction of appearing as defendant in several suits at law, brought by those of his neighbours whose property had been doubled in value by the erection of the mill, and who therefore thought they might as well see what else they could get, to recover the value of sundry acres of wet marsh made wetter by the flowing back of the pond, while Mr. Puffer's calculations and levels prove most satisfactorily (on paper) that the pond had no business to flow back so far, and that therefore malice itself could ascribe no fault to his management.

But to return. Our own dwelling was to be built at the same time with all those I have mentioned; and materials for the whole were to be brought by land carriage from two to thirty miles. To my inexperienced brain, these undertakings seemed nothing less than gigantic. I used to dream of the pyramids of Egypt, and the great wall of China, and often thought, during my waking hours, of the "tower on Shinar's plain," [3] and employed myself in conjectural comparisons between the confusion which punished the projectors of that edifice, and the difficulties which beset the builders of Montacute.

"No brick come yet, sir! Dibble couldn't get no white wood lumber at I————, (thirty miles off,) so he stopt and got what lime there was at Jones's; but they hadn't only four bushels, and they wouldn't burn again till week after next; and that 'ere sash that came from ———— is all of three inches too large for the window frames; and them doors was made of such green stuff, that they won't go together no how."

"Well, you can go on with the roof surely!"

"Why, so we could; but you know, sir, oak-shingle wouldn't answer for the mill, and there's no pine shingle short of Detroit."

"Can't the dwelling-house be raised to-day then?"

"Why, we calc'lated to raise to-day, sir; but that fellow never came to dig the cellar."

"Go on with the blacksmith's shop, then, since nothing else can be done."

"Yes, sir, certainly. Shall we take that best white wood siding? for you know the oak siding never came from Tacker's mill."

"Send Thomson for it, then."

"Well, Thomson's best horse is so lame that he can't use him to-day, and the other is a-drawin' timber for the dam."

"Let John go with my horses."

"John's wife 's sick, and he's got your horses and gone for the doctor."

But if I should fill pages with these delays and disappointments, I should still fail to give any idea of the real vexations of an attempt to build on any but the smallest scale in a new country. You discover a thousand requisites that you had never thought of, and it is well if you do not come to the angry conclusion that every body is in league against you and your plans. Perhaps the very next day after you have by extra personal exertion, an offer of extra price, or a bonus in some other form, surmounted some prodigious obstacle, you walk down to survey operations with a comfortable feeling of self-gratulation, and find yourself in complete solitude, every soul having gone off to election or town meeting. No matter at what distance these important affairs are transacted, so fair an excuse for a *ploy* can never pass unimproved; and the virtuous indignation which is called forth by any attempt at dissuading one of the sovereigns from exercising "the noblest privilege of a freeman," to forward your business and his own, is most amusingly provoking.

I once ventured to say, in my feminine capacity merely, and by way of experiment, to a man whose family I knew to be suffering for want of the ordinary comforts:

"I should suppose it must be a great sacrifice for you, Mr. Fenwick, to spend two days in going to election."

The reply was given with the air of Forrest's William Tell,[4] and in a tone which would have rejoiced Miss Martineau's heart—"Yes, to be sure; but ought not a man to do his duty to his country?"

This was unanswerable, of course. I hope it consoled poor Mrs. Fenwick, whose tattered gown would have been handsomely renewed by those two days' wages.

As may be conjectured from the foregoing slight sketch of our various thwartings and hinderances, the neat framed house which had been pictured on my mind's eye so minutely, and which I coveted with such enthusiasm, was not built in a month, nor in two, nor yet in three;—but I anticipate again.

The circumstance of living all summer, in the same apartment with a cooking fire, I had never happened to see alluded to in any of the elegant sketches of western life which had fallen under my notice. It was not until I actually became the inmate of a log dwelling in the wilds, that I realized fully what "living all in one room" meant. The sleeping apparatus for the children and the sociable Angeline, were in the loft; but my own bed, with its cunning fence of curtains; my bureau, with its "Alps on Alps" of boxes and books; my entire cooking array; my centre-table, which bore, sad change! the remains of to-day's dinner, and the preparations for to-morrow, all covered mysteriously under a large cloth, the only refuge from the mice: these and ten thousand other things, which a summer's day would not suffice me to enumerate, cumbered this one single apartment; and to crown the whole was the inextinguishable fire, which I had entirely forgotten when I magnanimously preferred living in a log-house, to re-maining in Detroit till a house could be erected. I had, besides the works to which I have alluded, dwelt with delight on Chateaubriand's Atala,[5] where no such vulgar inconvenience is once hinted at; and my floating visions of a home in the woods were full of important omissions, and always in a Floridian clime, where fruits serve for *vivers*.

The inexorable dinner hour, which is passed *sub silentio* in imaginary forests, always recurs, in real woods, with distressing iteration, once in twenty-four hours, as I found to my cost. And the provoking people for whom I had undertaken to provide, seemed to me to get hungry oftener than ever before. There was no end to the bread that the children ate from morning till night—at least it seemed so; while a tin reflector was my only oven, and the fire required for baking drove us all out of doors.

Washing days, proverbial elsewhere for indescribable horrors, were our times of jubilee. Mrs. Jennings, who long acted as my factotum on these occasions, always performed the entire operation, *al fresco*, by the side of the creek, with

> "A kettle slung
> Between two poles, upon a stick transverse."[6]

I feel much indebted to Cowper for having given a poetical grace to the arrangement. "The shady shadow of an umbrageous tree" (I quote from an anonymous author) served for a canopy, and there the bony dame generally made a pic-nic meal, which I took care to render as agreeable as possible, by sending as many different articles as the basket could be per-suaded to receive, each contained in that characteristic of the country, a pint bowl.

But, oh! the ironing days! Memory shrinks from the review. Some of the ordinary household affairs could be managed by the aid of a fire made on some large stones at a little distance from the house; and this did very well when the wind sat in the right quarter; which it did not always, as witness the remains of the pretty pink gingham which fell a sacrifice to my desire for an afternoon cup of coffee. But the ironing and the baking were imperious; and my forest Hecate, who seemed at times to belong to the salamander tribe, always made as much fire as the stick-chimney, with its crumbling clay-lining, would possibly bear. She often succeeded in bringing to a white heat the immense stone which served as a chimney-back, while the deep gaps in the stone hearth, which Alice called the Rocky Mountains, were filled with burning coals out to the very floor. I have sometimes suspected that the woman loved to torment me, but perhaps I wrong her. She was used to it, I dare say, for she looked like one exsiccated in consequence of ceaseless perspiration.

When the day declined, and its business was laid aside, it was our practice to walk to and fro before the door, till the house had been thoroughly cooled by the night-air; and these promenades, usually made pleasant by long talks about home, and laughing conjectures as to what ———— and ———— would say if they could see our new way of life, were frequently prolonged to a late hour. And to this most imprudent indulgence we could not but trace the agues which soon prostrated most of us.

We had, to be sure, been warned by our eastern friends that we should certainly have the ague, do what we might, but we had seen so many persons who had been settled for years in the open country, and who were yet in perfect health, that we had learned to imagine ourselves secure. I am still of the opinion that care and rational diet will enable most persons to avoid this terrible disease; and I record this grave medical view of things for the encouragement and instruction of such of my city friends as may hereafter find themselves borne westward by the irresistible current of affairs; trusting that the sad fate of their predecessors will deter them from walking in the open air till ten o'clock at night without hat or shawl.

CHAPTER XIV

Down with the topmast; yare; lower, lower; bring her to try with main-course.—*The Tempest*[1]

WHEN ANGELINE left me, which she did after a few days, I was obliged to employ Mrs. Jennings to "chore round," to borrow her own expression; and as Mr. Clavers was absent much of the time, I had the full enjoyment of her delectable society with that of her husband and two children, who often came to meals very sociably, and made themselves at home with small urgency on my part. The good lady's habits required strong green tea at least three times a day; and between these three times she drank the remains of the tea from the spout of the tea-pot, saying "it tasted better so." "If she had n't it," she said, "she had the 'sterics so that she was n't able to do a chore." And her habits were equally imperious in the matter of dipping with her own spoon or knife into every dish on the table. She would have made out nobly on kibaubs, for even that unwieldly morsel a boiled ham, she grasped by the hock and cut off in mouthfuls with her knife, declining all aid from the carver, and saying cooly that she made out very well. It was in vain one offered her any thing, she replied invariably with a dignified nod, "I'll help myself, I thank ye. I never want no waitin' on." And this reply is the universal one on such occasions, as I have since had vexatious occasion to observe.

Let no one read with an incredulous shake of the head, but rather let my sketch of these peculiar habits of my neighbours be considered as a mere beginning, a shadow of what might be told. I might

"Amaze indeed
The very faculty of eyes and ears,"[2]

but I forbear.

If "grandeur hear with a disdainful smile"[3]—thinking it would be far better to starve than to eat under such circumstances, I can only say such was not my hungry view of the case; and that I often found rather amusing exercise for my ingenuity in contriving excuses and plans to get the old lady to enjoy her meals alone. To have offered her outright a separate table, though the board should groan with all the delicacies of the

51

city, would have been to secure myself the unenviable privilege of doing my own "chores," at least till I could procure a "help" from some distance beyond the reach of my friend Mrs. Jennings' tongue.

It did not require a very long residence in Michigan, to convince me that it is unwise to attempt to stem directly the current of society, even in the wilderness, but I have since learned many ways of *wearing round* which give me the opportunity of living very much after my own fashion, without offending, very seriously, any body's prejudices.

No settlers are so uncomfortable as those who, coming with abundant means as they suppose, to be comfortable, set out with a determination to live as they have been accustomed to live. They soon find that there are places where the "almighty dollar" is almost powerless; or rather, that powerful as it is, it meets with its conqueror in the jealous pride of those whose services must be had in order to live at all.

"Luff when it blows," is a wise and necessary caution. Those who forget it and attempt to carry all sail set and to keep an unvarying course, blow which way it will, always abuse Michigan, and are abused in their turn. Several whom we have known to set out with this capital mistake have absolutely turned about again in despair, revenging themselves by telling very hard stories about us nor'westers.

Touchstone's philosophy is your only wear for this meridian.

"*Corin.* And how like you this shepherd's life, Master Touchstone?

"*Touch.* Truly, shepherd, in respect of itself it is a good life; but in respect it is a shepherd's life, it is naught. In respect that it is solitary, I like it very well; but in respect that it is private, it is a very vile life. Now, in respect that it is in the fields, it pleaseth me well; but in respect it is not in the court, it is tedious. As it is a spare life, look you, it fits my humour well; but as there is no plenty in it, it goes much against my stomach. Hast any philosophy in thee, shepherd?[4]

Nobody will quarrel with this view of things. You may say any thing you like of the country or its inhabitants: but beware how you raise a suspicion that you despise the homely habits of those around you. This is never forgiven.

It would be in vain to pretend that this state of society can ever be agreeable to those who have been accustomed to the more rational arrangements of the older world. The social character of the meals, in particular, is quite destroyed, by the constant presence of strangers, whose manners, habits of thinking, and social connexions are quite different from your own, and often exceedingly repugnant to your taste. Granting the correctness of the opinion which may be read in their countenances that they are "as good as you are," I must insist, that a greasy cook-maid, or a redolent stable-boy, can never be, to my thinking, an agreeable table companion—putting pride, that most terrific bug-bear of the woods, out of the question.

If the best man now living should honour my humble roof with his presence—if he should happen to have an unfortunate *penchant* for eating out of the dishes, picking his teeth with his fork, or using the fire-place for a pocket handkerchief, I would prefer he should take his dinner *solus* or with those who did as he did.

But, I repeat it; those who find these inconveniences most annoying while all is new and strange to them, will by the exertion of a little patience and ingenuity, discover ways and means of getting aside of what is most unpleasant, in the habits of their neighbours: and the silent influence of example is daily effecting much towards reformation in many particulars. Neatness, propriety, and that delicate forebearance of the least encroachment upon the rights or the enjoyments of others, which is the essence of true elegance of manner, have only to be seen and understood to be admired and imitated; and I would fain persuade those who are groaning under certain inflictions to which I have but alluded, that the true way of overcoming all the evils of which *they* complain is to set forth in their own manners and habits, all that is kind, forbearing, true, lovely, and of good report. They will find ere long that their neighbours have taste enough to love what is so charming, even though they see it exemplified by one who sits *all day* in a carpeted parlor, teaches her own children instead of sending them to the district school, hates "the breath of garlic eaters," and—oh fell climax!—knows nothing at all of soap-making.

CHAPTER XV

Honester men have stretch'd a rope, or the law has been sadly cheated. But this unhappy business of yours? Can nothing be done? Let me see the charge.

He took the papers, and as he read them, his countenance grew hopelessly dark and disconsolate.—*The Antiquary* [1]

A strange fish! Were I in England now, and had but this fish painted, not a holiday fool there but would give me a piece of silver.—Shakespeare, *The Tempest* [2]

Sorrow chang'd to solace, and solace mixed with sorrow.
   —*The Passionate Pilgrim* [3]

SEVERAL LOTS had already been purchased in Montacute and some improvement marked each succeeding day. The mill had grown to its full stature, the dam was nearly completed; the tavern began to exhibit promise of its present ugliness, and all seemed prosperous as our best dreams, when certain rumours were set afloat touching the solvency of our disinterested friend Mr. Mazard. After two or three days' whispering, a tall black-browed man who "happened in" from Gullsborough, the place which had for some time been honoured as the residence of the Dousterswivel of Montacute, stated boldly that Mr. Mazard had absconded; or, in Western language "cleared." It seemed passing strange that he should run away from the large house which was going on under his auspices; the materials all on the ground and the work in full progress. Still more unaccountable did it appear to us that his workmen should go on so quietly, without so much as expressing any anxiety about their pay.

Mr. Clavers had just been telling me of these things, when the long genius above mentioned, presented himself at the door of the loggery. His *abord* was a singular mixture of coarseness, and an attempt at being civil; and he sat for some minutes looking round and asking various questions before he touched the mainspring of his visit.

At length, after some fumbling in his pocket, he produced a dingy sheet of paper, which he handed to Mr. Clavers.

"There; I want you to read that, and tell me what you think of it."

I did not look at the paper, but at my husband's face, which was black enough. He walked away with the tall man, "and I saw no more of them at that time."

Mr. Clavers did not return until late in the evening, and it was then I learned that Mr. Mazard had been getting large quantities of lumber and other materials on his account, and as his agent; and that the money which had been placed in the agent's hands, for the purchase of certain lands to be flowed by the mill-pond, had gone into government coffers in payment for sundry eighty acre lots, which were intended for his, Mr. Mazard's private behoof and benefit. These items present but a sample of our amiable friends trifling mistakes. I will not fatigue the reader by dwelling on the subject. The results of all this were most unpleasant to us. Mr. Clavers found himself involved to a large amount; and his only remedy seemed to prosecute Mr. Mazard. A consultation with his lawyer, however, convinced him that even by this most disagreeable mode, redress was out of the question, since he had through inadvertence rendered himself liable for whatever that gentleman chose to buy or engage in his name. All that could be done, was to get out of the affair with as little loss as possible, and to take warning against land sharks in future.

An immediate journey to Detroit became necessary, and I was once more left alone, and in no overflowing spirits. I sat,

> "Revolving in *my* altered soul
> The various turns of fate below,"[4]

when a tall damsel, of perhaps twenty-eight or thirty came in to make a visit. She was tastefully attired in a blue gingham dress, with broad cuffs of black morocco, and a black cambric apron edged with orange worsted lace. Her oily black locks were cut quite short round the ears, and confined close to her head by a black ribbon, from one side of which depended, almost in her eye, two very long tassels of black silk, intended to do duty as curls. Prunelle slippers with high heels, and a cotton handkerchief tied under the chin, finished the costume, which I have been thus particular in describing, because I have observed so many that were nearly similar.

The lady greeted me in the usual style, with a familiar nod, and seated herself at once in a chair near the door.

"Well, how do like Michi*gan?*"

This question received the most polite answer which my conscience afforded; and I asked the lady in my turn, if she was one of my neighbours?

"Why, massy, yes!" she replied; "do n't you know me? I tho't every body know'd me. Why, I'm the school ma'am, Simeon Jenkins' sister, Cleory Jenkins."

Thus introduced, I put all my civility in requisition to entertain my guest, but she seemed quite independent, finding amusement for herself, and asking questions on every possible theme.

"You're doing your own work now, a'n't ye?"

This might not be denied; and I asked if she did not know of a girl whom I might be likely to get.

"Well, I do n't know; I'm looking for a place where I can board and do chores myself. I have a good deal of time before school, and after I get back; and I did n't know but I might suit ye for a while."

I was pondering on this proffer, when the sallow damsel arose from her seat, took a short pipe from her bosom, (not "Pan's reedy pipe,"[5] reader) filled it with tobacco, which she carried in her "work-pocket," and reseating herself, began to smoke with the greatest gusto, turning ever and anon to spit at the hearth.

Incredible again? alas, would it were not true! I have since known a girl of seventeen, who was attending a neighbour's sick infant, smoke the live-long day, and take snuff besides; and I can vouch for it, that a large proportion of the married women in the interior of Michigan use tobacco in some form, usually that of the odious pipe.

I took the earliest decent opportunity to decline the offered help, telling the school-ma'am plainly, that an inmate who smoked would make the house uncomfortable to me.

"Why, law!" said she, laughing; "that's nothing but pride now : folks is often too proud to take comfort. For my part, I could n't do without my pipe to please nobody."

Mr. Simeon Jenkins, the brother of this independent young lady now made his appearance on some trifling errand; and his sister repeated to him what I had said.

Mr. Jenkins took his inch of cigar from his mouth, and asked if I really disliked tobacco-smoke, seeming to think it scarcely possible.

"Do n't your old man smoke?" said he.

"No, indeed," said I, with more than my usual energy; "I should hope he never would."

"Well," said neighbour Jenkins, "I tell you what, I'm *boss* at home; and if my old woman was to stick up that fashion, I'd keep the house so blue she could n't see to snuff the candle."

His sister laughed long and loud at this sally, which was uttered rather angrily, and with an air of most manful bravery; and, Mr. Jenkins, picking up his end of cigar from the floor, walked off with an air evidently intended to be as expressive as the celebrated and oft-quoted nod of Lord Burleigh in the Critic.[6]

Miss Jenkins was still arguing on the subject of her pipe, when a gentleman approached, whose dress and manner told me that he did not belong to our neighbourhood. He was a red-faced, jolly-looking person, evidently "well to do in the world," and sufficiently consequential for any meridian. He seated himself quite unceremoniously; for who feels ceremony in a log-house? said he understood Mr. Clavers was absent—then hesitated; and, as Miss Jenkins afterwards observed, "hummed and hawed," and seemed as if he would fain say something, but scarce knew how.

At length Miss Cleora took the hint—a most necessary point of delicacy, where there is no withdrawing room. She gave her parting nod, and disappeared; and the old gentleman proceeded.

He had come to Montacute with the view of settling his son, "a wild chap," he said, a lawyer by profession, and not very fond of work of any sort; but as he himself had a good deal of land in the vicinity, he thought his son might find employment in attending to it, adding such professional business as might occur.

"But what I wished particularly to say, my dear madam," said he, "regards rather my son's wife than himself. She is a charming girl, and accustomed to much indulgence; and I have felt afraid that a removal to a place so new as this might be too trying to her. I knew you must be well able to judge of the difficulties to be encountered here, and took the liberty of calling on that account."

I was so much pleased with the idea of having a neighbour, whose habits might in some respects accord with my own, that I fear I was scarcely impartial in the view which I gave Mr. Rivers, of the possibilities of Montacute. At least, I communicated only such as rises before my own mind, while watching perhaps a glorious sunset reflected in the glassy pond; my hyacinths in all their glory; the evening breeze beginning to sigh in the tree-tops; the children just coming in after a fine frolic with D'Orsay on the grass; and Papa and Prince returning up the lane. At such times, I always conclude, that Montacute is, after all, a dear little world; and I am probably quite as near the truth, as when,

——"on some cold rainy day,
When the birds cannot show a dry feather;"

when Arthur comes in with a pound of mud on each foot, D'Orsay at his heels, bringing in as much more; little Bell crying to go out to play; Charlie prodigiously fretful with his prospective tooth; and some gaunt marauder from "up north," or "out west," sits talking on "bis'ness," and covering my andirons with tobacco juice; I determine sagely, that a life in the woods is worse than no life at all. One view is, I insist, as good as the other; but I told Mr. Rivers he must make due allowance for my desire to have his fair daughter-in-law for a neighbour, with which he departed; and I felt that my gloom had essentially lightened in consequence of his visit.

CHAPTER XVI

Art thou so confident? within what space
Hop'st thou my cure?
  —*All's Well That Ends Well* [1]

MR. CLAVERS at length returned; and the progress of the village, though materially retarded by the obliquities of Mr. Mazard's course, was still not entirely at a stand. If our own operations were slow and doubtful, there were others whose building and improving went on at a rapid rate; and before the close of summer, several small tenements were enclosed and rendered in some sort habitable. A store and a public house were to be ready for business in a very short time.

I had the pleasure of receiving early in the month of September, a visit from a young city friend, a charming lively girl, who unaffectedly enjoyed the pleasures of the country, and whose taste for long walks and rides was insatiable. I curtained off with the unfailing cotton sheets a snow-white bower for her in the loft, and spread a piece of carpeting, a relic of former magnificence, over the loose boards that served for a floor. The foot square window was shaded by a pink curtain, and a bed-side chair and a candle-stand completed a sleeping apartment which she declared was perfectly delightful.

So smoothly flowed our days during that charming visit that I had begun to fear my fair guest would be obliged to return to —— without

a single adventure worth telling, when one morning as we s
Arthur ran in with a prodigious snake-story, to which, though we were
first disposed to pay no attention, we were at length obliged to listen.

"A most beautiful snake," he declared, "was coming up to the
back door."

To the back door we ran; and there, to be sure, was a large rattle-
snake, or massasauga, lazily winding its course towards the house, Alice
standing still to admire it, too ignorant to fear.

My young friend snatched up a long switch, whose ordinary office
was to warn the chickens from the dinner-table, and struck at the reptile
which was not three feet from the door. It reared its head at once, made
several attempts to strike, or spring, as it is called here, though it never
really springs. Fanny continued to strike; and at length the snake turned
for flight, not however without a battle of at least two minutes.

"Here's the axe, cousin Fanny," said Arthur, "don't let him run
away!" and while poor I stood in silent terror, the brave girl followed,
struck once ineffectually, and with another blow divided the snake, whose
writhings turned to the sun as many hues as the windings of Broadway on a
spring morning—and Fanny was a heroine.

It is my opinion that next to having a cougar spring at one, the
absolute killing of a rattle-snake is peculiarly appropriate to constitute a
Michigan heroine;—and the cream of my snake-story is, that it might be
sworn to, chapter and verse, before the nearest justice. What cougar story
can say as much?

But the nobler part of the snake ran away with far more celerity than
it had displayed while it "could a *tail* unfold," and we exalted the *coda* to a
high station on the logs at the corner of the house—for fear none of the
scornful sex would credit our prowess.

That snake absolutely haunted us for a day or two; we felt sure that
there were more near the house, and our ten days of happiness seemed cut
short like those of Seged, and by a cause not very dissimilar. But the gloom
consequent upon confining ourselves, children and all, to the house, in
delicious weather, was too much for our prudence; and we soon began to
venture out a little, warily inspecting every nook, and harassing the poor
children with incessant cautions.

We had been watching the wheelings and flittings of a flock of prairie
hens, which had alighted in Mr. Jenkins's corn-field, turning ever and anon
a delighted glance westward at the masses of purple and crimson which
make sunset so splendid in the region of the great lakes. I felt the dew, and

warning all my conpanions, stepped into the house. I had reached the middle of the room, when I trod full upon something soft, which eluded my foot. I shrieked "a snake! a snake!" and fell senseless on the floor.

When I recovered myself I was on the bed, and well sprinkled with camphor, that never failing specific in the woods.

"Where is it?" said I, as soon as I could utter a word. There was a general smile. "Why, mamma," said Alice, who was exalted to a place on the bed, "dont you recollect that great toad that always sits behind the flour-barrel in the corner?"

I did not repent my fainting though it was not a snake, for if there is anything besides a snake that curdles the blood in my veins it is a toad. The harmless wretch was carried to a great distance from the house, but the next morning, there it sat again in the corner catching flies. I have been told by some persons that they "liked to have toads in the room in fly time." Truly may it be said, "What's one man's meat————" Shade of Chesterfield,[2] forgive me!—but that any body *can* be willing to live with a toad! To my thinking nothing but a *toady* can be more odious.

The next morning I awoke with a severe head-ache, and racking pains in every bone. Dame Jennings said it was the "*agur.*" I insisted that it could be nothing but the toad. The fair Fanny was obliged to leave us this day, or lose her escort home—a thing not to be risked in the wilderness. I thought I should get up to dinner, and in that hope bade her a gay farewell, with a charge to make the most of the snake story for the honour of the woods.

I did *not* get up to dinner, for the simple reason that I could not stand—and Mrs. Jennings consoled me by telling me every ten minutes, "Why, you've got th' agur! woman alive! Why, I know the fever-agur as well as I know beans! It a'n't nothin' else!"

But no chills came. My pains and my fever became intense, and I knew but little about it after the first day, for there was an indistinctness about my perceptions, which almost, although not quite, amounted to delirium.

A physician was sent for, and we expected, of course, some village Galen,[3] who knew just enough to bleed and blister, for all mortal ills. No such thing! A man of first-rate education, who had walked European hospitals, and who had mother-wit in abundance, to enable him to profit by his advantages. It is surprising how many such people one meets in Michigan. Some, indeed, we have been led to suppose, from some traits in their American history, might have "left their country for their country's

good:"—others appear to have forsaken the old world, either in consequence of some temporary disgust, or through romantic notions of the
liberty to be enjoyed in this favoured land. I can at this moment call to
mind, several among our ten-mile neighbours, who can boast University
honours, either European or American, and who are reading men, even
now. Yet one might pass any one of these gentlemen in the road without
distinguishing between him and the Corydon[4] who curries his horses, so
complete is their outward transformation.

Our medical friend, treated me very judiciously; and by his skill, the
severe attack of rheumatic-fever, which my sunset and evening impru-
dences had been kindling in my veins, subsided after a week, into a daily
ague; but Mrs. Jennings was not there to exult in this proof of her sagacity.
She had been called away to visit a daughter, who had been taken ill at a
distance from home, and I was left without a nurse.

My neighbours showed but little sympathy on the occasion. They
had imbibed the idea that we held ourselves above them, and chose to take
it for granted, that we did not need their aid. There were a good many
cases of ague too, and, of course, people had their own troubles to attend
to. The result was, that we were in a sad case enough. Oh! for one of those
feminine men, who can make good gruel, and wash the children's faces!
Mr. Clavers certainly did his best, and who can more? But the hot side of
the bowl always *would* come to his fingers—and the sauce-pan *would* overset, let him balance it ever so nicely. And then—such hungry children!
They wanted to eat all the time. After a day's efforts, he began to complain
that stooping over the fire made him very dizzy. I was quite self-absorbed,
or I should have noticed such a complaint from one who makes none
without cause; but the matter went on, until, when I asked for my gruel, he
had very nearly fallen on the coals, in the attempt to take it from the fire.
He staggered to the bed, and was unable to sit up for many days after.

When matters reached this pitch—when we had, literally, no one to
prepare food, or look after the children—little Bell added to the sick-list,
too—our physician proved our good genius. He procured a nurse from
a considerable distance; and it was through his means that good Mrs.
Danforth heard of our sad condition, and sent us a maiden of all-work,
who materially amended the aspect of our domestic affairs.

Our agues were tremendous. I used to think I should certainly die in
my ten or twelve hours' fever—and Mr. Clavers confidently asserted,
several times, that the upper half of his head was taking leave of the lower.
But the event proved that we were both mistaken; for our physician veri-

fied his own assertion, that an ague was as easily managed as a common cold, by curing us both in a short time after our illness had assumed the intermittent form. There is, however, one important distinction to be observed between a cold and the ague—the former does not recur after every trifling exertion, as the latter is sure to do. Again and again, after we seemed entirely cured, did the insidious enemy renew his attacks. A short ride, a walk, a drive of two or three miles, and we were prostrated for a week or two. Even a slight alarm, or any thing that occasioned an unpleasant surprise, would be followed by a chill and fever.

These things are, it must be conceded, very discouraging. One learns to feel as if the climate must be a wretched one, and it is not till after these first clouds have blown over, that we have resolution to look around us— to estimate the sunny skies of Michigan, and the ruddy countenances of its older inhabitants as they deserve.

The people are obstinately attached to some superstitious notions respecting agues. They hold that it is unlucky to break them. "You should let them run on," say they, "till they wear themselves out." This has probably arisen from some imprudent use of quinine, (or "Queen Ann,") and other powerful tonics, which are often taken before the system is properly prepared. There is also much prejudice against "Doctor's physic;"[5] while Lobelia, and other poisonous plants, which happen to grow wild in the woods are used with the most reckless rashness. The opinion that each region produces the medicines which its own diseases require, prevails extensively,—a notion which, though perhaps theoretically correct to a certain extent, is a most dangerous one for the ignorant to practise upon.

These agues are, as yet, the only diseases of the country. Consumption is almost unknown, as a Michigan evil. Indeed many, who have been induced to forsake the sea-board, by reason of too sensitive lungs, find themselves renovated after a year in the Peninsula. Our sickly season, from August till October, passed over without a single death within our knowledge.

To be sure, a neighbour told me, not long ago, that her old man had a complaint of "the lights," and that "to try to work any, gits his lights all up in a heap." But as this is a disease beyond the bounds of my medical knowledge, I can only "say the tale as 't was said to me," hoping, that none of my emigrating friends may find it contagious;—any disease which is brought on by *working,* being certainly much to be dreaded in this Western country!

CHAPTER XVII

The house's form within was rude and strong,
    Like an huge cave hewn out of rocky clift;
From whose rough vault the ragged breaches hung:—
. . . .
And over them Arachne high did lift
    Her cunning web, and spread her subtle net,
Enwrapped in foul smoke, and clouds more black than jet.
    —Spenser, *The Faery Queene* [1]

It were good that men, in their innovations, would follow the example of time itself, which, indeed, innovateth greatly, but quietly, and by degrees scarce to be perceived.—Bacon [2]

IT WAS on one of our superlatively doleful ague days, when a cold drizzling rain had sent mildew into our unfortunate bones; and I lay in bed, burning with fever, while my stronger half sat by the fire, taking his chill with his great-coat, hat, and boots on, that Mr. Rivers came to introduce his young daughter-in-law. I shall never forget the utterly disconsolate air, which, in spite of the fair lady's politeness, would make itself visible in the pauses of our conversation. She *did* try not to cast a curious glance round the room. She fixed her eyes on the fire-place—but there were the clay-filled sticks, instead of a chimney-piece—the half-consumed wooden *crane,* which had, more than once, let our dinner fall—the Rocky-Mountain hearth, and the reflector, baking biscuits for tea—so she thought it hardly polite to appear to dwell too long there. She turned towards the window: there were the shelves, with our remaining crockery, a grotesque assortment! and, just beneath, the unnameable iron and tin affairs, that are reckoned among the indispensables, even of the half-civilized state. She tried the other side, but there was the ladder, the flour-barrel, and a host of other things—rather odd parlour furniture—and she cast her eyes on the floor, with its gaping cracks, wide enough to admit a massasauga from below, and its inequalities, which might trip any but a sylph. The poor thing looked absolutely confounded, and I exerted all the energy my fever had left me, to try to say something a little encouraging.

"Come to-morrow morning, Mrs. Rivers," said I, "and you shall see the aspect of things quite changed; and I shall be able to tell you a great deal in favour of this wild life."

She smiled faintly, and tried not to look miserable, but I saw plainly that she was sadly depressed, and I could not feel surprised that she should be so. Mr. Rivers spoke very kindly to her, and filled up all the pauses in our forced talk with such cheering observations as he could muster.

He had found lodgings, he said, in a farm-house, not far from us, and his son's house would, ere long, be completed, when we should be quite near neighbours.

I saw tears swelling in the poor girl's eyes, as she took leave, and I longed to be well for her sake. In this newly-formed world, the earlier settler has a feeling of hostess-ship toward the new comer. I speak only of women—men look upon each one, newly arrived, merely as an additional business-automaton—a somebody more with whom to try the race of enterprize, i.e. money-making.

The next day Mrs. Rivers came again, and this time her husband was with her. Then I saw at a glance why it was that life in the wilderness looked so peculiarly gloomy to her. Her husband's face shewed but too plainly the marks of early excess; and there was at intervals, in spite of an evident effort to play the agreeable, an appearance of absence, of indifference, which spoke volumes of domestic history. He made innumerable inquiries, touching the hunting and fishing facilities of the country around us, expressed himself enthusiastically fond of those sports, and said the country was a living death without them, regretting much that Mr. Clavers was not of the same mind.

Meanwhile I had begun to take quite an interest in his little wife. I found that she was as fond of novels and poetry, as her husband was of field-sports. Some of her flights of sentiment were quite beyond my sobered-down views. But I saw we should get on admirably, and so we have done ever since. I did not mistake that pleasant smile, and that soft sweet voice. They are even now as attractive as ever. And I had a neighbour.

Before the winter had quite set in, our little nest was finished, or as nearly finished as anything in Michigan; and Mr. and Mrs. Rivers took possession of their new dwelling, on the very same day that we smiled our adieux to the loggery.

Our new house was merely the beginning of a house, intended for the reception of a front-building, Yankee-fashion, whenever the owner should be able to enlarge his borders. But the contrast with our sometime dwelling, made even this humble cot seem absolutely sumptuous. The children could do nothing but admire the conveniences it afforded. Robinson Crusoe exulted not more warmly in his successive acquisitions than did Alice in "a kitchen, a real kitchen! and a pantry to put the dishes!" while Arthur found much to praise in the wee bed-room which was allotted as his sanctum in the "hic, hæc, hoc,"[3] hours. Mrs. Rivers, who was fresh from "the settlements," often curled her pretty lip at the deficiencies in her little mansion, but we had learned to prize any thing which was even a shade above the wigwam, and dreamed not of two parlours or a piazza.

Other families removed to Montacute in the course of the winter. Our visiting list was considerably enlarged, and I used all my influence with Mrs. Rivers to persuade her that her true happiness lay in making friends of her neighbours. She was very shy, easily shocked by those sins against Chesterfield, which one encounters here at every turn, did not conceal her fatigue when a neighbour happened in after breakfast to make a three hours' call, forgot to ask those who came at one o'clock to take off their things and stay to tea, even though the knitting needles might peep out beneath the shawl. For these and similar omissions I lectured her continually but with little effect. It was with the greatest difficulty I could persuade her to enter any house but ours, although I took especial care to be impartial in my own visiting habits, determined at all sacrifice to live down the impression that I felt *above* my neighbours. In fact, however we may justify certain exclusive habits in populous places, they are strikingly and confessedly ridiculous in the wilderness. What can be more absurd than a feeling of proud distinction, where a stray spark of fire, a sudden illness, or a day's contre-temps, may throw you entirely upon the kindness of your humblest neighbour? If I treat Mrs. Timson with neglect to-day can I with any face borrow her broom to-morrow? And what would become of me, if in revenge for my declining her invitation to tea this afternoon, she should decline coming to do my washing on Monday?

It was as a practical corollary to these my lectures, that I persuaded Mrs. Rivers to accept an invitation that we received for the wedding of a young girl, the sister of our cooper, Mr. Whitefield. I attired myself in white, considered here as the extreme of festal elegance, to do honour to the occasion; and called for Mrs. Rivers in the ox-cart at two o'clock.

I found her in her ordinary neat home-dress; and it required some argument on my part to induce her to exchange it for a gay chally with appropriate ornaments.

"It really seems ridiculous," she said, "to *dress* for such a place! and besides, my dear Mrs. Clavers, I am afraid we shall be suspected of a desire to outshine."

I assured her we were in more danger of that other and far more dangerous suspicion of undervaluing our rustic neighbours.

"I s'pose they did n't think it worth while to put on their best gowns for country-folks!"

I assumed the part of Mentor on this and many similar occasions; considering myself by this time quite an old resident, and of right entitled to speak for the natives.

Mrs. Rivers was a little disposed to laugh at the ox-cart; but I soon convinced her that, with its cushion of straw overspread with a buffalo-robe, it was far preferable to a more ambitious carriage.

"No letting down of steps, no ruining one's dress against a muddy wheel! no gay horses tipping one into the gutter!"

She was obliged to acknowledge the superiority of our vehicle, and we congratulated ourselves upon reclining *à la* Lalla Rookh[4] and Lady Mary Wortley Montague.[5] Certainly a cart is next to a palanquin.

The pretty bride was in white cambric, worn over pink glazed muslin. The prodigiously stiff under-dress with its large cords (not more than three or four years behind the fashion) gave additional slenderness to her taper waist, bound straitly with a sky-blue zone. The fair hair was decorated, not covered, with a cap, the universal adjunct of full dress in the country, placed far behind the ears, and displaying the largest puffs, set off by sundry gilt combs. The unfailing high-heeled prunelle shoes gave the finishing-touch, and the whole was scented, *à l'outrance,*[6] with essence of lemon.

After the ceremony, which occupied perhaps three minutes, fully twice as long as is required by our state laws, tea was served, absolutely handed on a salver, and by the master of the house, a respectable farmer. Mountains of cake followed. I think either pile might have measured a foot in height, and each piece would have furnished a meal for a hungry school-boy. Other things were equally abundant, and much pleasant talk followed the refreshments. I returned home highly delighted, and tried to persuade my companion to look on the rational side of the thing, which she scarcely seemed disposed to do, so *outré* did the whole appear to her. I, who had begun to claim for myself the dignified character of a cosmopolite, a philo-sophical observer of men and things, consoled myself for this deroga-tory view of Montacute gentility, by thinking, "All city people are so cockneyish!"

CHAPTER XVIII

Lend me your *ears.*
—Shakespeare[1]

Grant graciously what you cannot refuse safely.—*Lacon*[2]

"*MOTHER* wants your sifter," said Miss Ianthe Howard, a young lady of six years' standing, attired in a tattered calico, thickened with dirt; her unkempt locks straggling from under that hideous substitute for a bonnet, so universal in the western country, a dirty cotton handkerchief, which is used, *ad nauseam,* for all sorts of purposes.

"Mother wants your sifter, and she says she guesses you can let her have some sugar and tea, 'cause you've got plenty."

This excellent reason, "'cause you've got plenty," is conclusive as to sharing with your neighbours. Whoever comes into Michigan with nothing, will be sure to better his condition; but wo to him that brings with him any thing like an appearance of abundance, whether of money or mere household conveniences. To have them, and not be willing to share them in some sort with the whole community, is an unpardonable crime. You must lend your best horse to *qui que ce soit,*[3] to go ten miles over hill and marsh, in the darkest night, for a doctor; or your team to travel twenty after a "gal;" your wheel-barrows, your shovels, your utensils of all sorts, belong, not to yourself, but to the public, who do not think it necessary even to *ask* a loan, but take it for granted. The two saddles and bridles of Montacute spend most of their time travelling from house to house a-manback; and I have actually known a stray martingale to be traced to four dwellings two miles apart, having been lent from one to another, without a word to the original proprietor, who sat waiting, not very patiently, to commence a journey.

Then within doors, an inventory of your plenishing of all sorts, would scarcely more than include the articles which you are solicited to lend. Not only are all kitchen utensils as much your neighbours as your own, but bedsteads, beds, blankets, sheets, travel from house to house, a pleasant and effectual mode of securing the perpetuity of certain efflorescent peculiarities of the skin, for which Michigan is becoming almost as famous as the land "'twixt Maidenkirk and John o'Groat's."[4] Sieves, smoothing

irons, and churns run about as if they had legs; one brass kettle is enough
for a whole neighbourhood; and I could point to a cradle which has rocked
half the babies in Montacute. For my own part, I have lent my broom, my
thread, my tape, my spoons, my cat, my thimble, my scissors, my shawl,
my shoes; and have been asked for my combs and brushes: and my husband, for his shaving apparatus and his pantaloons.

But the cream of the joke lies in the manner of the thing. It is so
straight-forward and honest, none of your hypocritical civility and servile
gratitude! Your true republican, when he finds that you possess any thing
which would contribute to his convenience, walks in with, "Are you going
to use your horses *to-day?*" if horses happen to be the thing he needs.

"Yes, I shall probably want them."

"Oh, well; if you want them—I was thinking to get 'em to go up
north a piece."

Or perhaps the desired article comes within the female department.

"Mother wants to get some butter: that 'ere butter you bought of
Miss Barton this mornin'."

And away goes your golden store, to be repaid perhaps with some
cheesy, greasy stuff, brought in a dirty pail, with, "Here's your butter!"

A girl came in to borrow a "wash-dish," "because we've got company." Presently she came back: "Mother says you've forgot to send a
towel."

"The pen and ink and a sheet o' paper and a wafer," is no unusual
request; and when the pen is returned, you are generally informed that you
sent "an awful bad pen."

I have been frequently reminded of one of Johnson's humorous
sketches.[5] A man returning a broken wheel-barrow to a Quaker, with,
"Here I've broke your rotten wheel-barrow usin' on't. I wish you'd get it
mended right off, 'cause I want to borrow it again this afternoon." The
Quaker is made to reply, "Friend, it shall be done:" and I wish I possessed
more of his spirit.

But I did not intend to write a chapter on involuntary loans; I have a
story to tell.

One of my best neighbours is Mr. Philo Doubleday, a long, awkward,
honest, hard-working Maine-man, or Mainote I suppose one might say; so
good-natured, that he might be mistaken for a simpleton; but that must be
by those who do not know him. He is quite an old settler, came in four
years ago, bringing with him a wife who is to him as vinegar-bottle to oil-

cruet, or as mustard to the sugar which is used to soften its biting qualities. Mrs. Doubleday has the sharpest eyes, the sharpest nose, the sharpest tongue, the sharpest elbows, and above all, the sharpest voice that ever "penetrated the interior" of Michigan. She has a tall, straight, bony figure, in contour somewhat resembling two hard-oak planks fastened together and stood on end; and, strange to say! she was full five-and-thirty when her mature graces attracted the eye and won the affections of the worthy Philo. What eclipse had come over Mr. Doubleday's usual sagacity when he made choice of his Polly, I am sure I never could guess; but he is certainly the only man in the wide world who could possibly have lived with her; and he makes her a most excellent husband.

She is possessed with a neat devil; I have known many such cases; her floor is scoured every night, after all are in bed but the unlucky scrubber, Betsey, the maid of all work; and wo to the unfortunate "indiffidle," as neighbour Jenkins says, who first sets dirty boot on it in the morning. If men come in to talk over road business, for Philo is much sought when "the public" has any work to do, or school-business, for that being very troublesome, and quite devoid of profit, is often conferred upon Philo, Mrs. Doubleday makes twenty errands into the room, expressing in her visage all the force of Mrs. Raddle's inquiry, "*Is* them wretches going?" And when at length their backs are turned, out comes the bottled vengeance. The sharp eyes, tongue, elbow, and voice, are all in instant requisition.

"Fetch the broom, Betsey! and the scrub-broom, Betsey! and the mop, and that 'ere dish of soap, Betsey; and why on earth did n't you bring some ashes? You did n't expect to clean such a floor as this without ashes, did you?"—"What time are you going to have dinner, my dear?" says the imperturbable Philo, who is getting ready to go out.

"Dinner! I 'm sure I do n't know! there's no time to cook dinner in this house! nothing but slave, slave, slave, from morning till night, cleaning up after a set of nasty, dirty," &c. &c. "Phew!" says Mr. Doubleday, looking at his fuming helpmate with a calm smile, "It 'll all rub out when it 's dry, if you'll only let it alone."

"Yes, yes; and it would be plenty clean enough for you if there had been forty horses in here."

Philo on some such occasion waited till his Polly had stepped out of the room, and then with a bit of chalk wrote on the broad black-walnut mantel-piece:

A New Home, Who'll Follow?

Bolt and bar hold gate of wood,
Gate of iron springs make good,
Bolt nor spring can bind the flame,
Woman's tongue can no man tame

and then took his hat and walked off.

This is his favourite mode of vengeance—"poetical justice" he calls it; and as he is never at a loss for a rhyme of his own or other people's, Mrs. Doubleday stands in no small dread of these efforts of genius. Once, when Philo's crony, James Porter, the blacksmith, had left the print of his blackened knuckles on the outside of the oft-scrubbed door, and was the subject of some rather severe remarks from the gentle Polly, Philo, as he left the house with his friend, turned and wrote over the offended spot:

Knock not here!
Or dread my dear.
P.D.

and the very next person that came was Mrs. Skinner, the merchant's wife, all drest in her red merino, to make a visit. Mrs. Skinner, who did not possess an unusual share of tact, walked gravely round to the back-door, and there was Mrs. Doubleday up to the eyes in soap-making. Dire was the mortification, and point-blank were the questions as to how the visitor came to go round that way; and when the warning couplet was produced in justification, we must draw a veil over what followed—as the novelists say.

Sometimes these poeticals came in aid of poor Betsey; as once, when on hearing a crash in the little shanty-kitchen, Mrs. Doubleday called in her shrillest tones, "Betsy! what on earth 's the matter?" Poor Betsey, knowing what was coming, answered in a deprecatory whine, "The cow 's kicked over the buck-wheat batter!"

When the clear, hilarous voice of Philo from the yard, where he was chopping, instantly completed the triplet—

"Take up the pieces and throw 'em at her!" for once the grim features of his spouse relaxed into a smile, and Betsey escaped her scolding.

Yet, Mrs. Doubleday is not without her excellent qualities as a wife, a friend, and a neighbour. She keeps her husband's house and stockings in unexceptionable trim. Her *emptin's* are the envy of the neighbourhood. Her vinegar is, as how could it fail? the *ne plus ultra* of sharpness; and her pickles are greener than the grass of the field. She will watch night after night with the sick, perform the last sad offices for the dead, or take to her home and heart the little ones whose mother is removed forever from her place at the fireside. All this she can do cheerfully, and she will not repay herself as many good people do by recounting every word of the querulous sick man, or the desolate mourner with added hints of tumbled drawers, closets all in heaps, or *awful* dirty kitchens.

I was sitting one morning with my neighbour Mrs. Jenkins, who is a sister of Mr. Doubleday, when Betsey, Mrs. Doubleday's "hired girl" came in with one of the shingles of Philo's handiwork in her hand, which bore in Mr. Doubleday's well-known chalk marks—

> Come quick, Fanny!
> And bring the granny,
> For Mrs. Double-
> day's in trouble.

And the next intelligence was of a fine new pair of lungs at that hitherto silent mansion. I called very soon after to take a peep at the "latest found;" and if the suppressed delight of the new papa was a treat, how much more was the softened aspect, the womanized tone of the proud and happy mother. I never saw a being so completely transformed. She would almost forget to answer me in her absorbed watching of the breath of the little sleeper. Even when trying to be polite, and to say what the occasion demanded, her eyes would *not* be withdrawn from the tiny face. Conversation on any subject but the ever-new theme of "babies" was out of the question. Whatever we began upon whirled round sooner or later to the one point. The needle may tremble, but it turns not with the less constancy to the pole.

As I pass for an oracle in the matter of paps and possets, I had frequent communication with my now happy neighbour, who had forgotten to scold her husband, learned to let Betsey have time to eat, and omitted the nightly scouring of the floor, lest so much dampness might be bad for the baby. We were in deep consultation one morning on some important point touching the well-being of this sole object of Mrs. Doubleday's thoughts and dreams, when the very same little Ianthe Howard, dirty as ever, presented herself. She sat down and stared awhile without speaking, *à l'ordinaire;* and then informed us that her mother "wanted Miss Doubleday to let her have her baby for a little while, 'cause Benny's mouth 's so sore that"—but she had no time to finish the sentence.

"LEND MY BABY!!!"—and her utterance failed. The new mother's feelings were fortunately too big for speech, and Ianthe wisely disappeared before Mrs. Doubleday found her tongue. Philo, who entered on the instant, burst into one of his electrifying laughs with—

"Ask my Polly,
To lend her dolly!"

—and I could not help thinking that one must come "west" in order to learn a little of every thing.

The identical glass-tube which I offered Mrs. Howard, as a substitute for Mrs. Doubleday's baby, and which had already, frail as it is, threaded the country for miles in all directions, is, even as I write, in demand; a man on horse-back comes from somewhere near Danforth's, and asks in mysterious whispers for—but I shall not tell what he calls it. The reader must come to Michigan.

CHAPTER XIX

Le bonheur et le malheur des hommes ne dépend pas moins de leur humeur que de la fortune.—Rochefoucault [1]

It has been a canker in
Thy heart from the beginning: but for this
We had not felt our poverty, but as
Millions of myriads feel it,—cheerfully;—
. . . .
Thou might'st have earn'd thy bread as thousands earn it;
Or, if that seem too humble, tried by commerce,
Or other civic means, to mend thy fortunes.
—Byron, *Werner* [2]

THE WINTER—the much dreaded winter in the woods, strange to tell, flew away more rapidly than any previous winter of my life. One has so much to do in the country. The division of labour is almost unknown. If in absolutely savage life, each man is of necessity "his own tailor, tent-maker, carpenter, cook, huntsman, and fisherman;"—so in the state of society which I am attempting to describe, each woman is, at times at least, her own cook, chamber-maid and waiter; nurse, seamstress and school-ma'am; not to mention various occasional callings to any one of which she must be able to turn her hand at a moment's notice. And every man, whatever his circumstances or resources, must be qualified to play groom, teamster, or boot-black, as the case may be; besides "tending the baby" at odd times, and cutting wood to cook his dinner with. If he has good sense, good nature, and a little spice of practical philosophy, all this goes exceedingly well. He will find neither his mind less cheerful, nor his body less vigorous for these little sacrifices. If he is too proud or too indolent to submit to such infringements upon his dignity and ease, most essential deductions from the daily comfort of his family will be the mortifying and vexatious result of his obstinate adherence to early habits.

We witnessed by accident so striking a lesson on this subject, not long after our removal to Montacute, that I must be allowed to record the impression it made upon my mind. A business errand called Mr. Clavers some miles from home; and having heard much of the loveliness of the scenery in that direction, I packed the children into the great waggon and went with him.

The drive was a charming one. The time, mid-summer, and the wilderness literally "blossoming as the rose." In a tour of ten miles we saw three lovely lakes, each a lonely gem set deep in masses of emerald green, which shut it in completely from all but its own bright beauty. The road was a most intricate one "thorough bush—thorough brier,"[3] and the ascents, the "pitches," the "sidlings" in some places quite terrific. At one of the latter points, where the road wound, as so many Michigan roads do, round the edge of a broad green marsh, I insisted upon getting out, as usual. The place was quite damp; but I thought I could pick my way over the green spots better than trust myself in the waggon, which went along for some rods at an angle (*I* said so at least,) of forty-five. Two men were mowing on the marsh, and seemed highly amused at my perplexity, when after watching the receding vehicle till it ascended a steep bank on the farther side, I began my course. For a few steps I made out tolerably, but then I began to sink most inconveniently. Silly thin shoes again. Nobody should ever go one mile from home in thin shoes in this country, but old Broadway habits are *so* hard to forget.

At length, my case became desperate. One shoe had provokingly disappeared. I had stood on one foot as long as ever goose did, but no trace of the missing Broqua could I find, and down went the stocking six inches into the black mud. I cried out for help; and the mowers, with "a lang and a loud guffaw," came leisurely towards me. Just then appeared Mr. Clavers on the green slope above mentioned. It seems his high mightiness had concluded by this time that I had been sufficiently punished for my folly, (all husbands are so tyrannical!) and condescended to come to my rescue. I should have been very sulky; but then, there were the children. However, my spouse did try to find a road which should less frequently give rise to those troublesome terrors of mine. So we drove on and on, through ancient woods, which I could not help admiring; and, at length, missing our way, we came suddenly upon a log-house, very different from that which was the object of our search. It was embowered in oaks of the largest size; and one glance told us that the hand of refined taste had been there. The under-brush had been entirely cleared away, and the broad expanse before the house looked like a smooth-shaven lawn, deep-shadowed by the fine trees I have mentioned. Gleams of sunset fell on beds of flowers of every hue; curtains of French muslin shaded the narrow windows, and on a rustic seat near the door lay a Spanish guitar, with its broad scarf of blue silk. I could not think of exhibiting my inky stocking to the inmates of such a cottage, though I longed for a peep; and Mr. Clavers went alone to the house to inquire the way, while I played *tiger* and held the horses.

I might have remained undiscovered, but for the delighted exclamations of the children, who were in raptures with the beautiful flowers, and the lake which shone, a silver mirror, immediately beneath the bank on which we were standing. Their merry talk echoed through the trees, and presently out came a young lady in a *demi-suisse*[4] costume; her dark hair closely braided and tied with ribbons, and the pockets of her rustic apron full of mosses and wild flowers. With the air rather of Paris than of Michigan, she insisted on my alighting; and though in awkward plight, I suffered myself to be persuaded. The interior of the house corresponded in part with the impressions I had received from my first glance at the exterior. There was a harp in a recess, and the white-washed log-walls were hung with a variety of cabinet pictures. A tasteful drapery of French chintz partly concealed another recess, closely filled with books; a fowling-piece hung over the chimney, and before a large old-fashioned looking-glass stood a French pier-table, on which were piled fossil specimens, mosses, vases of flowers, books, pictures, and music. So far all was well; and two young ladies seated on a small sofa near the table, with netting and needle-work were in keeping with the romantic side of the picture. But there was more than all this.

The bare floor was marked in every direction with that detestable yellow dye which mars every thing in this country, although a great box filled with sand stood near the hearth, melancholy and fruitless provision against this filthy visitation. Two great dirty dogs lay near a large rocking-chair, and this rocking-chair sustained the tall person of the master of the house, a man of perhaps forty years or thereabouts, the lines of whose face were such, as he who runs may read.[5] Pride and passion, and reckless self-indulgence were there, and fierce discontent and determined indolence. An enormous pair of whiskers, which surrounded the whole lower part of the countenance, afforded incessant employment for the long slender fingers, which showed no marks of labour, except very dirty nails. This gentleman had, after all, something of a high-bred air, if one did not look at the floor, and could forget certain indications of excessive carelessness discernible in his dress and person.

We had not yet seen the lady of the cottage; the young girl who had ushered me in so politely was her sister, now on a summer visit Mrs. B——— shortly after entered in an undress, but with a very lady-like grace of manner, and the step of a queen. Her face, which bore the traces of beauty, struck me as one of the most melancholy I had ever seen; and it was over-spread with a sort of painful flush, which did not conceal its habitual paleness.

We had been conversing but a few moments, when a shriek from the children called every one out of doors in an instant. One of Mr. B———'s sons had ventured too near the horses, and received from our "old Tom," who is a little roguish, a kick on the arm. He roared most lustily, and every body was very much frightened, and ran in all directions seeking remedies. I called upon a boy, who seemed to be a domestic, to get some salt and vinegar, (for the mother was disabled by terror) but as he only grinned and stared at me, I ran into the kitchen to procure it myself. I opened a closet door, but the place seemed empty or nearly so; I sought every where within ken, but all was equally desolate. I opened the door of a small bed-room, but I saw in a moment that I ought not to have gone there, and shut it again instantly. Hopeless of finding what I sought, I returned to the parlour, and there the little boy was holding a vinaigrette to his mother's nose, while the young ladies were chafing her hands. She had swooned in excessive alarm, and the kick had, after all, produced only a trifling bruise.

After Mrs. B——— had recovered herself a little, she entered at some length, and with a good deal of animation on a detail of her Michigan *experiences;* not, as I had hoped at the beginning,

In equal scale weighing delight and dole;[6]

But giving so depressing a view of the difficulties of the country, that I felt almost disposed for the moment to regret my determination of trying a woodland life. She had found all barren. They had no neighbours, or worse than none—could get no domestics—found every one disposed to deal unfairly, in all possible transactions; and though last not least, could get nothing fit to eat.

Mr. B———'s account, though given with a careless, off-hand air, had a strong dash of bitterness in it—a sort of fierce defiance of earth and heaven, which is apt to be the resource of those who have wilfully thrown away their chances of happiness. His remarks upon the disagreeables which we had to encounter, were carried at least as far as those of his wife; and he asserted that there was but one alternative in Michigan—cheat or be cheated.

We were not invited to remain to tea; but took our leave with many polite hopes of further acquaintance. Mr. Clavers found the spot he had been seeking, and then, taking another road home, we called to see Mrs. Danforth; whom we considered even then in the light of the very good friend which she has since so often proved herself. I told of our accidental visit and learned from the good lady some particulars respecting this family, whose condition seemed so strange and contradictory, even in the western country, where every element enters into the composition of that anomalous mass called society.

Mr. B———, was born to a large fortune, a lot which certainly seems in our country to carry a curse with it in a large proportion of instances. Feeling quite above the laborious calling by which his father had amassed wealth, the son's only aim had been to spend his money, like a gentleman; and in this he had succeeded so well that by the time he had established himself, at the head of the ton in one of our great Eastern cities, and been set down as an irreclaimable *roué* by his sober friends, he found that a few more losses at play would leave him stranded. But he had been quite the idol of the "good society" into which he had purchased admission, and the one never-failing resource in such cases—a rich wife, was still perhaps in his power. Before his altered fortunes were more than whispered by his very particular friends, he had secured the hand of an orphan heiress, a really amiable and well-bred girl; and it was not until she had been his wife for a year or more, that she knew that her thousands had done no more than prop a falling house.

Many efforts were made by the friends on both sides, to aid Mr.
B——— in establishing himself in business, but his pride and his indolence proved insuperable difficulties; and after some years of those painful
struggles between pride and poverty, which so many of the devotees of
fashion can appreciate from their own bitter experience, a retreat to the
West was chosen as the least of prospective evils.

Here the whole country was before him "where to choose." He
could have bought at government price any land in the region to which he
had directed his steps. Water-power of all capabilities was at his command,
for there was scarce a settler in the neighbourhood. But he scorned the
idea of a place for *business.* What he wanted was a charming spot for a
gentlemanly residence. There, with his gun and his fishing rod he was to
live; a small income which still remained of his wife's fortune furnishing
the only dependance.

And this income, small as it was, would have been, in prudent and
industrious hands, a subsistence at least; so small is the amount really
requisite for a frugal way of life in these isolated situations. But unfortunately Mr. B———'s character had by no means changed with his place
of residence. His land, which by cultivation would have yielded abundant
supplies for his table, was suffered to lie unimproved, because he had not
money to pay labourers. Even a garden was too much trouble; the flower-
beds I had seen were made by the hands of Mrs. B———, and her sisters;
and it was asserted that the comforts of life were often lacking in this
unfortunate household, and would have been always deficient but for constant aid from Mrs. B———'s friends.

Mrs. B——— had done as women so often do in similar situations,
making always a great effort to keep up a certain appearance, and allowing
her neighbours to discover that she considered them far beneath her; she
had still not forgotten her delicate habits, and that they were delicate and
lady-like, no one can doubt who had ever seen her, and laboured with all
her little strength for the comfort of her family. She had brought up five
children on little else beside Indian meal and potatoes; and at one time the
neighbours had known the whole family live for weeks upon bread and tea
without sugar or milk;—Mr. B——— sitting in the house smoking
cigars, and playing the flute, as much of a gentleman as ever.

And these people, bringing with them such views and feelings as
make straitened means productive of absolute wretchedness any where,
abuse Michigan, and visit upon their homely neighbours the bitter feelings
which spring from that fountain of gall, mortified yet indomitable pride.

Finding themselves growing poorer and poorer, they persuade themselves that all who thrive, do so by dishonest gains, or by mean sacrifices; and they are teaching their children, by the irresistible power of daily example, to despise plodding industry, and to indulge in repining and feverish longings after unearned enjoyments.

But I am running into an absolute homily! I set out to say only that we had been warned at the beginning against indulging in certain habits which darken the whole course of country life; and here I have been betrayed into a chapter of sermonizing. I can only beg pardon and resume my broken thread.

CHAPTER XX

I come, I come! ye have called me long,
I come o'er the mountains with light and song!
Away from the chamber and sullen hearth!
The young leaves are dancing in breezy mirth.
—Mrs. Hemans, *Voice of Spring* [1]

And because the breath of flowers is far sweeter in the air (where it comes and goes like the warbling of music,) therefore nothing is more fit for that delight than to know what be the flowers and plants that do best perfume the air.—Bacon [2]

I BELIEVE I was recurring to the rapidity with which our first winter in the wilds slipped away. We found that when the spring came we were not half prepared to take advantage of it; but armed with the "American Gardener," [3] and quantities of choice seeds received in a box of treasures from home during the previous Autumn, we set about making something like a garden. It would seem that in our generous soil this could not be a difficult task; but our experience has taught us quite differently. Besides the eradication of stumps, which is a work of time and labour any where, the "grubs" present a most formidable hindrance to all gardening efforts in the "oak-openings." I dare say my reader imagines a "grub" to be a worm, a destructive wretch that spoils peach trees. In Michigan, it is quite another affair. Grubs are, in western parlance, the gnarled roots of small trees and shrubs, with which our soil is interlaced in some places almost to absolute solidity. When these are disturbed by the immense "breaking up" plough, with its three or four yoke of oxen, the surface of the ground wears every where the appearance of chevaux-de-frise;[4] and to pile in heaps for burning, such of these serried files as have been fairly loosened by the plough, is a work of much time and labour. And after this is done in the best way, your *potagerie*[5] will still seem to be full of grubs; and it will take two or three years to get rid of these troublesome proofs of the fertility of your soil. But your incipient Eden will afford much of interest and comfort before this work is accomplished, and I sincerely pity those who lack a taste for this primitive source of pleasure.

On the opening of our first spring, the snow had scarcely disappeared ere the green tops of my early bulbs were peeping above the black soil in which they had been buried on our first arrival; and the interest with which I watched each day's development of these lovely children of the sun, might almost compare with that which I felt in the daily increasing perfections of my six months' old Charlie, whose rosy cheeks alone, could, in my view at least, outblush my splendid double hyacinths.

Whatever of a perennial kind we could procure, we planted at once, without waiting until our garden should be permanently arranged. All that we have since regretted on this point is that we had not made far greater efforts to increase our variety; since one year's time is well worth gaining, where such valuables are in question.

On the subject of flowers, I scarcely dare trust my pen with a word, so sure am I that my enthusiastic love for them would, to most readers, seem absolutely silly or affected. But where the earth produces spontaneously such myriads of splendid specimens, it would seem really ungrateful to spare the little time and pains required for their cultivation. This is a sin which I at least shall avoid; and I lose no opportunity of attempting to inspire my neighbours with some small portion of my love for every thing which can be called a flower, whether exotic or home-bred.

The ordinary name with us for a rose is "a rosy-flower;" our vase of flowers usually a broken-nosed pitcher, is a "posy-pot;" and "yaller lilies" are among the most dearly-prized of all the gifts of Flora. A neighbour after looking approvingly at a glass of splendid tulips, of which I was vainglorious beyond all justification, asked me if I got "them blossoms out of these here woods." Another coolly broke off a spike of my finest hyacinths, and after putting it to his undiscriminating nose, threw it on the ground with a "pah!" as contemptuous as Hamlet's. But I revenged myself when I set him sniffing at a crown imperial—so we are at quits now.

A lady to whom I offered a cutting of my noble balm geranium, with leaves larger than Charlie's hand, declined the gift, saying, "she never know'd nobody make nothin' by raisin' sich things." One might have enlightened her a little as to their moneyed value, but I held my peace and gave her some sage-seed.

Yet, oddly enough, if any thing could be odd in Michigan—there is, within three miles of us, a gardener and florist of no mean rank, and one whose aid can be obtained at any time for some small consideration of "rascal counters;" so that a hot-bed, or even a greenhouse is within our reach.

I have sometimes thought that there could scarcely be a trade or profession which is not largely represented among the farmers of Michigan, judging from the somewhat extensive portion of the state with which we have become familiar. I was regretting the necessity of a journey to Detroit for the sake of a gold filling; when lo! a dentist at my elbow, with his case of instruments, his gold foil, and his skill, all very much at my service.

Montacute, half-fledged as it is, affords facilities that one could scarce expect. Besides the blacksmith, the cooper, the chair maker, the collar maker, and sundry carpenters and masons, and three stores, there is the mantua-maker for your dresses, the milliner for your bonnets, not mine, the "hen tailor" for your little boy's pantaloons; the plain seamstress, plain enough sometimes, for all the sewing you can't possibly get time for, and

"The spinners and the knitters in the sun,"

or in the chimney-corner, for all your needs in the winter hosiery line. Is one of your guests dependent upon a barber? Mr. Jenkins can shave. Does your husband get *too* shaggy? Mr. Jenkins cuts hair. Does he demolish his boot upon a *grub?* Mr. Jenkins is great at a *rifacciamento.*[6] Does Billy lose his cap in the pond? Mr. Jenkins makes caps *comme il y en a peu.*[7] Does your bellows get the asthma? Mr. Jenkins is a famous Francis Flute.[8] Then there is Philemon Greenly has been apprenticed to a baker, and he can make you crackers, baker's-bread and round-hearts, the like of which—, but you should get *his* story. And I certainly can make long digressions, if nothing else. Here I am wandering like another Eve from my dearly beloved garden.

A bed of asparagus—I mean a dozen of them, should be among the very first cares of spring; for you must recollect, as did the Cardinal De Retz at Vincennes,[9] that asparagus takes three years to come to the beginnings of perfection. Ours, seeded down after the Shaker fashion, promise to be invaluable. They grew so nobly the first year that the *haulm* [10] was almost worth mowing, like the fondly-prized down on the chin of sixteen. Then, what majestic palm-leaf rhubarb, and what egg-plants! Nobody can deny that our soil amply repays whatever trouble we may bestow upon it. Even on the first turning up, it furnishes you with all the humbler luxuries in the vegetable way, from the earliest pea to the most delicate cauliflower, and the golden pumpkin, larger than Cinderella's grandmother ever saw in her dreams. Enrich it properly, and you need lack nothing that will grow north of Charleston.

Melons, which attain a delicious perfection in our rich sandy loam, are no despicable substitute for the peaches of the older world; at least during the six or seven summers which must elapse before the latter can be abundant. I advise a prodigious melon-patch.

A fruit sometimes despised elsewhere, is here among the highly-prized treasures of the summer. The whortle-berry of Michigan, is a different affair from the little half-starved thing which bears the name elsewhere. It is of a deep rich blue, something near the size of a rifle bullet, and of a delicious sweetness. The Indians bring in immense quantities slung in panniers or mococks of bark on the sides of their wild-looking ponies; a squaw, with any quantity of pappooses, usually ridng *à l'Espagnole* [11] on the ridge between them.

"Schwap? Nappanee?" is the question of the queen of the forest; which means, "will you exchange, or *swap,* for flour:" and you take the whortle-berries in whatever vessel you choose, returning the same measured quantity of flour.

The spirit in which the Indians buy and sell is much the same now as in the days of the renowned Wouter Van Twiller,[12] when "the hand of a Dutchman weighed a pound, and his foot two pounds." The largest haunch of venison goes for two fingers, viz. twenty-five cents, and an entire deer for one hand, one dollar. Wild strawberries of rare size and flavour, "schwap-nappanee," which always means equal quantities. A pony, whatever be his age or qualities, two hands held up twice, with the fingers extended, twenty dollars. If you add to the price an old garment, or a blanket, or a string of glass-beads, the treasure is at once put on and worn with *such* an air of "look at me." Broadway could hardly exceed it.

The Indians bring in cranberries too; and here again Michigan excels. The wild plum, so little prized elsewhere, is valued where its civilized namesake is unattainable; and the assertion frequently made, that "it makes excellent *saase,*" is undeniably true. But grapes! One must see the loads of grapes in order to believe.

The practical conclusion I wish to draw from all this wandering talk is, that it is well worth while to make garden in Michigan. I hope my reader will not be disposed to reply in that terse and forceful style which is cultivated at Montacute, and which has more than once been employed in answer to my enthusiastic lectures on this subject. "Taters grow in the field, and 'taters is good enough for me."

CHAPTER XXI

Les hommes ne vivraient pas long-temps en société, s' ils n' etaient pas les dupes les uns des autres.—La Rochefoucault[1]

I HAVE NOT said a single word as yet of our neighbour Tinkerville; a village whose rising fortunes have given occasion for more discussion in the select circles of Montacute than any thing but the plan of the new school-house. I know this rambling gossiping style, this going back to take up dropped stitches, is not the orthodox way of telling one's story; and if I thought I could do any better, I would certainly go back and begin at the very beginning; but I feel conscious that the truly feminine sin of talking "about it and about it," the unconquerable partiality for wandering wordiness would cleave to me still; so I proceed in despair of improvement to touch upon such points in the history of Tinkerville as have seemed of vital and absorbing interest to the citizens of Montacute.

Tinkerville was originally one of the many speculations of the enterprising Mr. Mazard, and it differed from most of his landed property, in having been purchased at second hand. This fact was often mentioned in his proffers of sale, as a reason why the tract could not be afforded *quite* so low as was his general practice. He omitted to state, that he bought of a person who, having purchased at the land-office without viewing, was so entirely discouraged when he saw the woody swamp in which he was to pitch his tent, that he was glad to sell out to our speculator at a large discount, and try elsewhere on the old and sound principle of "look before you leap." The tract contained, as Mr. Mazard's advertisement fairly set forth, "almost every variety of land;" and as he did not say which kind predominated, nobody could complain if imagination played tricks, as is sometimes the case in land-purchases.

An old gentleman of some property in Massachusetts became the fortunate owner of the emblazoned chart, which Mr. Mazard had caused to set forth the advantages of his choice location. There were canals and rail-roads, with boats and cars at full speed. There was a steam-mill, a wind-mill or two; for even a land-shark did not dare to put a stream where there was scarce running water for the cattle; and a state-road, which had at least been talked of, and a court-house and other county buildings, "all very grand;" for, as the spot was not more than ten miles from the centre of the county, it might some day become the county-seat. Besides all this, there was a large and elegantly-decorated space for the name of the happy pur-chaser, if he chose thus to dignify his future capital.

Mr. Tinker was easily persuaded that the cherished surname of his ancestors would blend most musically with the modern and very genteel termination in which so many of our western villages glory; so Tinkerville was appointed to fill the trump of fame and the blank on the chart; and Mr. Mazard, furnished with full powers, took out the charter, staked out the streets, where he could get at them, and peddled out the lots, and laid out the money, all very much to his own satisfaction; Mr. Tinker rejoicing that he had happened to obtain so "enterprising" an agent.

We are not informed what were the internal sensations of the lot-holders, when they brought their families, and came to take possession of their various "stands for business." They were wise men; and having no money to carry them back, they set about making the best of what they could find. And it is to be doubted whether Mr. Mazard's multifarious avocations permitted him to visit Tinkerville after the settlers began to come in. Many of them expressed themselves quite satisfied that there was abundance of water there to duck a land-shark, if they could catch him near it; and Mr. Mazard was a wise man too.

While the little settlement was gradually increasing, and a store had been, as we were told, added to its many advantages and attractions, we heard that the padroon of Tinkerville had sold out; but whether from the fear that the income from his Michigan property would scarce become tangible before his great grandson's time, or whether some Bangor Mr.

Mazard had offered him a tempting bargain nearer home, remains to us unknown. It was enough for Montacute to discover that the new owners were "enterprising men." This put us all upon the alert.

The Tinkervillians, who were obliged to come to us for grinding until their wind-mills could be erected, talked much of a new hotel, a school-house, and a tannery; all which, they averred, were "going up" imme-diately. They turned up their noses at our squint-eyed "Montacute house," expressing themselves certain of getting the county honours, and ended by trying to entice away our blacksmith. But our Mr. Porter, who "had a soul above buttons,"[2] scorned their arts, and would none of their counsel. Mr. Simeon Jenkins did, I fear, favourably incline to their side; but on its being whispered to him that Montacute had determined upon employing a singing-master next winter; he informed the ambassadors, who were no doubt spies in disguise, that he would never be so selfish as to prefer his own interest to the public good. No one thought of analyzing so patriotic a sentiment, or it might have been doubted whether Mr. Jenkins sacrificed much in remaining to exercise his many trades, where there were twice as many people to profit by them as he would find at Tinkerville.

CHAPTER XXII

🦋🦋🦋🦋🦋🦋

Ignorance lies at the bottom of all human knowledge, and the deeper we penetrate, the nearer we arrive unto it.—*Lacon*[1]

MRS. RIVERS and I had long been planning a ride on horse-back; and when the good stars were in conjunction, so that two horses and two saddles were to be had at one time, we determined to wend our resolute way as far as Tinkerville, to judge for ourselves of the state of the enemy's prepara-tions. We set out soon after breakfast in high style; my Eclipse being Mr. Jenkin's old Governor, seventeen last grass; and my fair companion's a twenty-dollar Indian pony, age undecided—men's saddles of course, for the settlement boasts no other as yet; and, by way of luxury, a large long-woolled sheep-skin strapped over each.

We jogged on charmingly, now through woods cool and moist as the grotto of Undine,[2] and carpeted every where with strawberry vines and thousands of flowers; now across strips of open land where you could look through the straight-stemmed and scattered groves for miles on each side.

A marsh or two were to be passed, so said our most minute directions, and then we should come to the trail through deep woods, which would lead us in a short time to the emerging glories of our boastful neighbour.

We found the marshes, without difficulty, and soon afterwards the trail, and D'Orsay's joyous bark, as he ran far before us, told that he had made some discovery. "Deer, perhaps," said I. It was only an Indian, and when I stopped and tried to inquire whether we were in the right track, he could not be made to understand but gave the usual assenting grunt and passed on.

When I turned to speak to my companion she was so ashy pale that I feared she must fall from her horse.

"What *is* the matter, my dearest madam!" said I, going as near her as I could coax old Governor.

"The Indian! the Indian!" was all she could utter. I was terribly puzzled. It had never occurred to me that the Indians would naturally be objects of terror to a young lady who had scarcely ever seen one; and I knew we should probably meet dozens of them in the course of our short ride.

I said all I could, and she tried her best to seem courageous, and, after she had rallied her spirits a little, we proceeded, thinking the end of our journey could not be distant, especially as we saw several log-houses at intervals which we supposed were the outskirts of Tinkerville.

But we were disappointed in this; for the road led through a marsh, and then through woods again, and such tangled woods, that I began to fear, in my secret soul, that we had wandered far from our track, betrayed by D'Orsay's frolics.

I was at length constrained to hint to my pale companion my misgivings, and to propose a return to the nearest log hut for information. Without a word she wheeled her shaggy pony, and, in a few minutes, we found ourselves at the bars belonging to the last log house we had passed.

A wretched looking woman was washing at the door.

"Can you tell us which is the road to Tinkerville?"

"Well, I guess you can't miss it if you follow your own tracks. It a'n't long since you came through it. That big stump is the middle of the public square."

CHAPTER XXIII

I boast no song in magic wonders rife,
But yet, oh nature! is there nought to prize
Familiar in thy bosom-scenes of life?
And dwells in day-light truth's salubrious skies
No form with which the soul may sympathize?
—Campbell[1]

WE RETURNED by a different and less lonely route, the Tinkervillians having very civilly directed us to one on which we should not at any point be far distant from a dwelling. The single Indian we had encountered in the morning had been quite sufficient to spoil Mrs. Rivers' ride; and we hurried on at the best pace of our sober steeds.

The country through which we were passing was so really lovely that even my timid little friend forgot her fears at times and exclaimed like a very enthusiast. At least two small lakes lay near our way; and these, of winding outline, and most dazzling brightness, seemed, as we espied them now and then through the arched vistas of the deep woods, multiplied to a dozen or more. We saw grape-vines which had so embraced large trees that the long waving pennons flared over their very tops; while the lower branches of the sturdy oaks were one undistinguishable mass of light green foliage, without an inch of bark to be seen. The road side was piled like an exaggerated velvet with exquisitely beautiful ferns of almost every variety; and some open spots gleamed scarlet with those wild strawberries so abundant with us, and which might challenge the world for flavour.

Birds of every variety of song and hue, were not wanting, nor the lively squirrel, that most joyous of nature's pensioners; and it cost us some little care to keep D'Orsay in his post of honour as sole escort through these lonely passes. But alack! "'t was ever thus!" We had scarcely sauntered two miles when a scattered drop or two foretold that we were probably to try the melting mood. We had not noticed a cloud, but thus warned we saw portentious gatherings of these bug-bears of life.

Now if our poneys would only have gone a little faster! But they would not, so we were wet to the skin—travelling *jets d' eau*[2]—looking doubtless very much like the western settler taking his stirrup-cup in one of Mrs. Trollope's[3] true pictures.

A New Home, Who'll Follow?

When we could be no further soaked we reached a farm-house—not a Michigan farm-house, but a great, noble, yankee "palace of pine boards," looking like a cantle of Massachusetts or Western New-York dropped *par hazard,*⁺ in these remote wilds. To me who had for a long while seen nothing of dwelling kind larger than a good sized chicken-coop, the scene was quite one of *Eastern* enchantment. A large barn with shed and stables and poultry-yard and all! Fields of grain, well fenced and stumpless, surrounded this happy dwelling; and a most inviting door-yard, filled to profusion with shrubs and flowers, seemed to invite our entrance.

"A honey-suckle! absolutely a honey-suckle on the porch!" Mrs. Rivers was almost too forlorn to sympathize with me: but then she had not been quite so long from home. I have been troubled with a sort of home calenture at times since we removed westward.

As we were about to dismount, the sun shone out most provokingly: and I was afraid there would be scarce the shadow of an excuse for a visit to the interesting inmates, for such I had decided they must be, of this delicious home-like spot; but, as we wavered, a young man as wet as ourselves, came up the road, and, opening the gate at once, invited us to enter and dry our dripping garments.

We stayed not for urging, but turned our graceless steeds into the shady lane, and dismounting, not at the front entrance, but, *à la Michigan,* at the kitchen door, we were received with much grave but cordial politeness by the comely mistress of the mansion, who was sharing with her pretty daughter the after-dinner cares of the day. Our upper garments were spread to dry, and when we were equipped, with urgent hospitality, in others belonging to our hostesses, we were ushered into the parlor or "keeping room."

Here, writing at an old-fashioned *secretary,* sat the master of the house, a hearty, cheerful-looking, middle-aged man; evidently a person of less refinement than his wife, but still of a most prepossessing exterior. He fell no whit behind in doing the honours, and we soon found ourselves quite at ease. We recounted the adventures of our tiny journey, and laughed at our unlucky over-running of the game.

"Ah! Tinkerville! yes, I think it will be some time yet before those dreams will come to pass. I have told Mr. Jephson there was nothing there to make a village out of."

"You are acquainted then with the present proprietors?"

"With one of them I have been acquainted since we were boys; and he has been a speculator all that time, and is now at least as poor as ever. He has been very urgent with me to sell out here and locate in his village, as he calls it; but we knew rather too much of him at home for that," and he glanced at his fair spouse with some archness. I could scarcely believe that any man could have been impudent enough to propose such an exchange, but nothing is incredible in Michigan.

Mrs. Beckworth was now engaged in getting tea, in spite of our hollow-hearted declarations that we did not wish it. With us, be it known to new comers, whatever be the hour of the day, a cup of tea with *trimmings,* is always in season; and is considered as the orthodox mode of welcoming any guest, from the clergyman to "the maid that does the meanest chores." We were soon seated at a delicately-furnished table.

The countenance of the good lady had something of peculiar interest for me. It was mild, intelligent, and very pleasing. No envious silver streaked the rich brown locks which were folded with no little elegance above the fair brow. A slight depression of the outer extremity of the eyelid, and of the delicately-pencilled arch above it, seemed to tell of sorrow and meek endurance. I was sure that like so many western settlers, the fair and pensive matron had a story; and when I had once arrived at this conclusion, I determined to make a brave push to ascertain the truth of my conjecture.

I began, while Mrs. Beckworth was absent from the parlour, by telling every thing I could think of; this being the established mode of getting knowledge in this country. Mr. Beckworth did not bite.

"Is this young lady your daughter, Mr. Beckworth?"

"A daughter of my wife's—Mary Jane Harrington?"

"Oh! ah! a former marriage; and the fine young man who brought us into such good quarters is a brother of Miss Harrington's I am sure."

"A half brother—Charles Boon."

"Mrs. Beckworth thrice married! impossible!" was my not very civil but quite natural exclamation.

Our host smiled quietly, a smile which enticed me still further. He was, fortunately for my reputation for civility, too kindly polite not to consent to gratify my curiosity, which I told him sincerely had been awakened by the charming countenance of his wife, who was evidently the object of his highest admiration.

As we rode through the freshened woods with Mr. Beckworth, who had, with ready politeness, offered to see us safely a part of the way, he gave us the particulars of his early history; and to establish my claim to the character of a physiognomist, I shall here recount what he told me; and, as I cannot recollect his words, I must give this romance of rustic life in my own, taking a new chapter for it.

CHAPTER XXIV

Sudden partings, such as press,
The life from out young hearts; and choking sighs
Which ne'er might be repeated, who could guess
If ever more should meet those mutual eyes—
—Byron[1]

HENRY BECKWORTH, the eldest son of a Massachusetts farmer, of small means and many mouths, was glad to accept a situation as clerk in the comprehensive "variety store" of his cousin Ellis Irving, who was called a great merchant in the neighbouring town of Langton. This cousin Ellis had fallen into the dangerous and not very usual predicament of having every body's good word; and it was not until he had failed in business, that any one discovered that he had a fault in the world.

While he was yet in his hey-day, and before the world knew that he had been so good-natured as to endorse for his wife's harum-scarum brother, his clerk, Henry Beckworth, had never dared to acknowledge, even in his dreams, that he loved to very dizziness his sweet cousin Agnes Irving. But when mortification and apoplexy had done their work upon Mr. Irving, and his delicate wife had ascertained that the remnant of her days must pass in absolute poverty, dependant for food and raiment upon her daughter's needle, Henry found his wits and his tongue, and made so good use of both, that, ere long, his cousin Agnes did not deny that she liked him very well.

Now young ladies who have been at boarding-school and learned to paint water-melons in water colours, and work Rebecca at the well in chenille and gold thread, find real, thrifty, housewifely sewing, very slow and hard work, to earn even bread and salt by; but the dove-eyed Agnes had been the sole care and pride of a genuine New England housewife, who could make hard gingerbread as well as soft, and who had plumed herself on being able to put every stitch into six fine shirts between Sunday evening and Saturday night. And so the fair child, though delicately bred, earned her mother's living and her own, with cheerful and ungrudging industry; and Henry sent all the surplus of his clerkly gains to his father, who sometimes found the cry of "crowdie, crowdie, a' the day," rather difficult to pacify.

But by-and-bye, Mrs. Irving became so feeble that Agnes was obliged to nurse her instead of plying her skilful needle; and then matters went far astray, so that after a while the kind neighbours brought in almost all that was consumed in that sad little household; Henry Beckworth being then out of employ, and unable for the time to find any way of aiding his cousin, save by his personal services in the sick-room.

He grew almost mad under his distress, and the anxious, careful love which is the nursling of poverty, and at length seeing Mrs. Irving's health a little amended, he gave a long, sad, farewell kiss to his Agnes, and left her with an assurance that she should hear from him soon. He dared not tell her that he was quitting her to go to sea, in order that he might have immediate command of a trifling sum which he could devote to her service.

He made his way to the nearest sea-port, secured a berth before the mast in a vessel about to sail for the East Indies; and then put into a letter all the love, and hope, and fear, and caution, and encouragement, and resolution, and devotedness, that one poor sheet could carry, giving the precious document into the care of a Langton man, who was returning "direct," as he said, to the spot where poor Henry had left his senses.

This said letter told Agnes, among other things, how and when to draw on Messrs. ———, for Henry's wages, which were left subject to her order—and the lover went to sea, with a heavy heart indeed, but with a comforting security that he had done all that poverty would let him, for the idol of his heart.

An East India voyage is very long, and most people experience many a changing mood and many a wayward moment during its course; but Henry Beckworth's heart beat as if it would burst his blue jacket, when he found himself on shore again, and thought of what awaited him at Langton.

He called on Messrs. ———, to ascertain whether any thing remained of his pay, and found that every dollar was untouched. At first this angered him a little; "for," as he justly argued, "if Agnes loved me as I love her— but, never mind!" This I give as a fair specimen of his thoughts on his homeward journey. All his contemplations, however incoherent or wide of the mark, came invariably to one conclusion—that Agnes would surely be willing to marry him, poor as he was, rather than he should go to sea again.

It was evening, and a very dull, lead-coloured evening, when the stage that contained our lover stopped at the only public-house in Langton. The True Blue Hotel, kept, as the oval sign which creaked by its side informed the grateful public, by Job Jephson, (at this moment J. Jephson, Esquire, of Tinkerville, in Michigan,) the very Job Jephson to whose kindly care Henry had committed his parting letter. The stage passed on, and Mr. Beckworth paced the tesselated floor of Mr. Jephson's bar-room, until the worthy proprietor and himself were left its sole occupants.

"Why, Henry, my boy, is that you? Do tell! Why your hat was slouched over your eyes so, that I did not know you! Why, man! where on *airth* have you sprung from!"

Henry asked after every body, and then after Agnes Irving and her mother.

"Agnes Irving!"

"Dead!" said Henry, wildly enough.

"Dead! no, married to be sure! three months ago; and this very day a week ago, her mother was buried."

It is really surprising how instantaneously pride comes to one's aid on some occasions. The flashing thought of the loved one's death, had been anguish intolerable and inconcealable; the certainty of what was far worse only blanched Henry's cheek, and set his teeth firmly together while his lips questioned on, and the loquacious host of the True Blue proceeded.

"Poor Agnes saw hard times after you went away. She had to give up the house you left her in, and take a room at Mr. Truesdell's. And then Mrs. Irving did nothing but pine after the comforts she had lost, for her mind was kind o' broke up by trouble. And Agnes tried to find some other place to board, because her mother took such an awful dislike to Mrs. Truesdell; but there was n't nobody willing to take them in, because the old lady was so particular. And so, John Harrington—you know John?—made up to her again, though she'd refused him two or three times before; and said he loved her better than ever, and that he would take her mother home and do for her as if she was his own. Now, you see, the neighbours had got pretty much tired of sending in things, because they thought Aggy ought n't to refuse such a good offer, and so after a while John got her. After all the poor old lady did not seem to enjoy her new home, but pined away faster than ever, and said she knew Aggy had sold herself for her sake, but that was only a notion you know, for John was an excellent match for a poor ——"

"Did you give my cousin the letter I handed you?" interrupted Henry.

"I'll just tell you all about that," responded Mr. Jephson, complacently drawing a chair for Henry, and inviting him to sit, as if for a long story. "I'll just tell you how that was. When you and I parted that time, I thought I was all ready for a start home; but there was a chance turned up to spekilate a little, and arter that I went down South to trade away some notions, so that when I got back to Langton it was quite cold weather, and I took off my best coat and laid it away, for where's the use of wearing good clothes under a great coat, you know? and there, to be sure was your letter in the pocket of it. Well, before I found it again Agnes was getting ready to be married; and, thinks I to myself, like enough it's a love-letter, and might break off the match if she got it, gals are so foolish! so I just locked up the letter and said nothing to nobody and"—there lay Mr. Jephson on his bar-room floor.

Henry turned from the place with some glimmering of an intention to seek his lost love and tell her all, but one moment's lapse cured this madness; so he only sat down and looked at Job, who was picking himself up and talking all the while.

"Man alive! what do you put yourself into such a plaguy passion for? I done it all for the best; and as to forgetting, who does not forget sometimes? Plague take you! you've given my back such a wrench I sha'n't be able to go to trainin' to-morrow, and tore my pantaloons besides; and, arter all, you may likely thank me for it as long as you live. There's as good fish in the sea as ever was caught—but I swan! you're as white as the wall, and no mistake," and he caught the poor soul as he was falling from his chair.

"Well, now, if this does n't beat cock-fighting!" muttered he, as he laid his insensible guest at full length on the floor and ran to the bar for some "camphire," which he administered in all haste, "to take on so about a gal without a cent, but he wont come to after all, and I shall have to bleed him:" saying which he pulled off one sleeve of Henry's jacket and proceeded in due form to the operation.

"He wont bleed, I vow! Hang the fellow! if he dies, I shall be took up for manslaughter. Why, Harry, I say!" shaking him soundly, and dragging at his arm with no gentle force. At last blood came slowly, and Beckworth became once more conscious of misery, and Mr. Jephson's tongue set out as if fresh oiled by the relief of his fears for his own safety.

"Now, Henry, do n't make such a fool of yourself! You always used to be a fellow of some sconce. What can't be cured must be endured." But as Henry's lips resumed their colour, and he raised himself from the floor, Mr. Jephson's habitual prudence urged him farther and farther from the reach of the well arm. His fears were groundless, however, for all that Henry now wanted was to be alone, that he might weep like a woman.

"Promise me that you will never tell any one that I have been here this night," said he at length; "this is all I ask. Since Agnes is another man's wife, God forbid I should wish my name mentioned in her presence."

"Why, law! I'll promise that, to be sure; but you should n't make so much out o' nothing: Aggy has got the best house in town, and every thing comfortable; and it a' n't no ways likely she would fret after *you.*" And with this comforting assurance Henry prepared for departure.

"I say, Beckworth!" said Mr. Jephson as his guest left the room with his valise; "I sha'n't charge you anything for the bleeding."

CHAPTER XXV

> Now I will believe
> That there are unicorns; that in Arabia
> There is one tree the Phœnix' throne; one Phœnix
> At this hour reigning there. *** I'll believe both,
> And what else doth want credit, come to me
> And I'll be sworn 't is true.
> —Shakespeare, *The Tempest.*[1]

THE WINDOWS of heaven were opened that night. The rain descended in sheets instead of drops; and it was only by an occasional flash of pale lightning that our unfortunate was able to find the house which he well recollected for John Harrington's. There it was in all its fresh whiteness and greenness, and its deep masses of foliage, and its rich screens of honeysuckle and sweet-briar, meet residence for a happy bridegroom and his new-found treasure. The upper half of the parlour shutters was unclosed, and plainly by the clear bright lamp-light could Henry see the delicate papering of the walls, and the pretty French clock under its glass shade on the mantel-piece. Oh! for one glance at the table, near which he felt sure Agnes was sitting. Wild thoughts of the old song—

> We took but ae kiss, an' we tore ourselves away,

Were coursing through his brain, and he was deliberating upon the chance that the end window, which looked on a piazza, might be free from the envious shutter, when a man ran against him in the dark. The next flash showed a great-coated figure entering the pretty rural gate to the little shrubbery; and in another moment the hall-door opened. Henry saw the interior, light and cheerful; and again all was dark.

It would have been very wrong to set the house on fire and then go and murder Job Jephson; and as Henry could not at the moment decide upon any other course of conduct, which would be at all in unison with his feelings, he set out, a human loco-motive at the top-speed, in the very teeth of the storm, on his way towards the sea-port again. The worse one feels, the faster one travels, hoping to outrun sorrow; so it did not take Henry Beckworth long to reach a neighbouring town, where he could find a stage-coach; and he was far at sea again in the course of a very few days.

His *outre-mer* [2] adventures are of no importance to my story—how, as he stood with two or three messmates, staring, like a true Yankee, at the Tower of London, a press-gang seized them all, and rowed them to a vessel which lay off the Traitors' Gate, the Americans protesting themselves such, and the John Bulls laughing at them;—how, when they got on board the man o' war, they showed their protections, and the officer of his Majesty's recruiting service said he could do nothing in the case till the ship returned from her cruize—and how the ship did not return from her cruize, but after cruizing about for some three years or more, was taken by a French first-rate and carried into Brest. All this is but little to the purpose. But when Henry was thrown into a French prison, his American certificate procured his release through the consul's good offices, and he shipped at once for New-York, somewhat weary of a sea life.

At New-York he learned from a townsman whom he met there that Agnes Harrington had been two years a widow.

"Is she rich?" asked Henry. A strange question for a true lover.

"Rich!—Lord bless ye! John Harrington was n't worth *that;*" snapping his fingers most expressively. His property was under mortgage to such an extent, that all it would sell for would n't clear it. His widow and child will not have a cent after old Horner forecloses, as he is now about doing. And Mrs. Harrington's health is very poor, though to my thinking she's prettier than ever."

Henry's movements were but little impeded by baggage, and the journey to Langton was performed in a short time. Once more was he set down at Job Jephson's; and there was day-light enough this time to see, besides the oval sign before hinted at, which had for years held out hopes of "Entertainment for man and beast," a legend over the door in great white characters, "Post Office,"—"good business for Job," thought Henry Beckworth,—a board in one window setting forth, "Drugs and Medicines," and a card in the other, "Tailoring done here."

Slight salutation contented Henry, when the man of letters made his appearance, and he requested a horse to carry him as far as his father's, saying he would send for his trunk in the morning. Mr. Jephson made some little difficulty and delay, but Henry seemed in fiery haste. In truth he hated the sight of Job beyond all reason; but that complacent personage seemed to have forgotten, very conveniently, all former passages in that memorable bar-room.

"You do n't ask after your old friends, Harry," said he. "A good many things has altered here since I see you last. You came that time a little too late."

Henry looked dirks at the fellow, but he went on as coldly as ever.

"Now this time, to my thinkin', you've come a *leetle* too soon."

Henry tried not to ask him what he meant; but for his life he could not help it.

"Why, I mean, if John Harrington's widow has not more sense than I think she has, you've come in time to spoil a good match."

"A match!" was all Henry could say.

"Aye, a match; for Colonel Boon came from there yesterday, and sent for old Horner here to this blessed house, and took up the mortgage on Harrington's property; and every body knows he has been after Aggy this twelvemonth, offering to marry her and clear the property, and do well by the child. And if there's a good man on airth, Boon is that man, and every body knows it."

What did Henry Beckworth now? He un-ordered his horse, and went quietly to bed.

CHAPTER XXVI

There are thoughts that our burden can lighten,
Though toilsome and steep be the way,
And dreams that like moon-light can brighten
With a lustre far clearer than day.

Love nursed amid pleasures is faithless as they,
But the love born of sorrow, like sorrow, is true.
—Moore[1]

HENRY BECKWORTH came from the hand of Nature abundantly furnished with that excellent qualification known and revered throughout New England, under the expressive name of "spunk." This quality at first prompted him, spite of the croakings of the ill-omened Job, to present himself before the one and only object of his constant soul, to tell her all, and to ask her to share with him the weal or wo which might yet be in store for him. But he had now seen a good deal of this excellent world, and the very indifferent people who transact its affairs. He had tasted the tender mercies of a British man of war, and the various *agrémens*[2] of a French prison; and the practical conclusion which had gradually possessed itself of his mind, was, that money is, beyond all dispute, one of the necessaries of life.

No way of making money off-hand occurred to him as he tossed and groaned through the endless hours of that weary night. He had neither house nor land, nor yet a lottery ticket—nor a place under government—and the chest which stood at his bed-side, though it contained enough of this world's goods to keep his fair proportions from the weather; and a sea-journal—a love-log—which he hoped might one day, by some romantic chance, come into the fair hands of his beloved, and give her to guess how his sad life had passed—held as he well knew, nothing which she could in anywise eat, or that she would be probably willing, under any contingency to put on.

I feel proud of my hero. He was "a man of deeds, not words." He loved Agnes so well, that before morning shone on his haggard cheek, he had determined to turn his back forever on the home of his youth, the scene of his first love-dream; and to seek his dark fortune far away from the place which held all that his heart prized on earth.

This resolution once taken, he arose and addressed himself to his sad journey, waiting only the earliest beam of light before he awakened Mr. Jephson. This worthy commended much his prudent course, and recommended a long voyage; an attempt to discover the North-West Passage, or to ascertain the truth of Capt. Symmes' theory; to take the nonsense out of him and make a little money.

For five long years did Henry Beckworth box the compass; five years of whaling voyages and all their attendant hardships—and when at the end of that time he retouched his native shore, richer than he had ever been before in his life, he heard, as the reader will no doubt anticipate, that Agnes Boon was again unmated; her worthy Colonel having been killed by a fall from his horse in less than two years from his marriage.

Yet did our phœnix of lovers approach the village which he had vowed never to see again, with many more misgivings than he had experienced on former occasions. Years and a rough life he was well aware had changed him much. He thought of his Agnes, fair and graceful as a snow-drop, and feared lest his weather-beaten visage might find no favour in her eyes. Yet he determined that this time nothing, not even that screech-owl Job Jephson, should prevent him from seeing her, face to face, and learning his fate from her own lips.

He approached Langton by a road that passed not near the detested house of man and horse entertainment, and was just emerging from a thick grove which skirted the village on that side, when he came near riding over a man who seemed crouched on the ground as if in search of something, and muttering to himself the while. The face that turned hastily round was Job Jephson's.

"Why, it a'n't! Yes, I'll be switched if it is n't Harry Beckworth rose from the dead!" said this fated tormentor; and he fastened himself on the bridle-rein in such sort, that Henry could not rid himself of his company without switching him in good earnest.

"Here was I, lookin' up some little things for my steam doctorin' business," said Mr. Jephson, "and little thinkin' of any body in the world; and you must come along jist like a sperrit. But I've a notion you 've hit it about right this time. I s'pose you know Aggy 's a rich widow by this time, do n't ye?"

Henry vouchsafed no reply, though he found it very difficult to maintain a dignified reserve, when so many questions were clustering on his lips. But it was all one to Job—question or no question, answer or no answer, he would talk on, and on, and on.

"I'll tell ye what," he continued, "I should n't wonder if Aggy looked higher now, for she's a good spec for any man. I see you've smarted up a good deal, but don't be cock-sure—for there's others that would be glad to take her and her two children. I've been a thinkin' myself—"

And now Henry gave Job such a switch across the knuckles as effectually cleared the bridle, and changed the current of the steam-doctor's thoughts. In half an hour he rang at Mrs. Boon's door, and was ushered at once into her presence.

"Mr. Beckworth, ma'am," said the little waiting-maid as she threw open the parlour door.

Agnes, the beloved, rose from her seat—sat down again—tried to speak, and burst into tears; while Henry looked on her countenance—changed indeed, but still lovely in matronly dignity—more fondly than in the days of his lighter youthful love; and seating himself beside her, began at the wrong end of the story, as most people do in such cases, talking as if it were a thing of course that his twice-widowed love should become his wife.

"Marry again! oh, never!"—that was entirely out of the question; and she wiped her eyes and asked her cousin to stay to dinner. But Henry deferred his ultimatum on this important point, till he should have ravelled out the whole web of his past life before the dewy eyes of his still fair mistress, till he should tell her all his love—no, that he could never fully tell, but some of the proofs of it at least, and that first horrible forget of Job Jephson's. And when this was told in many words, Agnes, all sighs and tears, still said no, but so much more faintly that Mr. Beckworth thought he would stay to dinner. And then—but why should I tell the rest, when the reader of my true-love story has already seen Mrs. Beckworth like a fair though full-blown China-rose—Mr. Beckworth with *bien content*[3] written on every line of his handsome middle-aged face—Mary Jane Harrington a comely marriageable lass, and George Boon a strapping youth of eighteen—all flourishing on an oak opening in the depths of Michigan?

Let none imagine that this tale of man's constancy must be the mere dream of my fancy. I acknowledge nothing but the prettinesses. To Henry Beckworth himself I refer the incredulous, and if they do not recognize my story in his, I cannot help it. Even a woman can do no more than her best.

CHAPTER XXVII

Smelling so sweetly (all musk), and so rushling, I warrant you, in silk and gold; and in such alligant terms.—Shakespeare, *The Merry Wives of Windsor.*[1]

Art thou not Romeo, and a Montague?
—Shakespeare[2]

My brain's in a fever, my pulses beat quick
I shall die, or at least be exceedingly sick!
Oh what do you think! after all my romancing
My visions of glory, my sighing, my glancing—
—Miss Biddy Fudge.[3]

AN ADDITION to our Montacute first circle had lately appeared in the person of Miss Eloise Fidler, an elder sister of Mrs. Rivers, who was to spend some months "in this peaceful retreat,"—to borrow one of her favourite expressions.

This young lady was not as handsome as she would fain have been, if I may judge by the cataracts of ash-coloured ringlets which shaded her cheeks, and the exceeding straitness of the stays which restrained her somewhat exuberant proportions. Her age was at a stand; but I could never discover exactly where, for this point proved an exception to the general communicativeness of her disposition. I guessed it at eight-and-twenty; but perhaps she would have judged this uncharitable, so I will not insist. Certain it is that it must have taken a good while to read as many novels and commit to memory as much poetry, as lined the head and exalted the sensibilities of our fair visitant.

Her dress was in the height of fashion, and all her accoutrements *point de vice.*[4] A gold pencil-case of the most delicate proportions was suspended by a kindred chain round a neck which might be called whity-brown; and a note-book of corresponding lady-like-ness was peeping from the pocket of her highly-useful apron of blue silk—ever ready to secure a passing thought or an elegant quotation. Her album—she was just the person to have an album—was resplendent in gold and satin, and the verses which meandered over its emblazoned pages were of the most unexceptionable quality, overlaid with flowers and gems—love and despair. To find any degree of appropriateness in these various offerings, one must allow the fortunate possessor of the purple volume, at least all the various perfections of an Admirable Crichton,[5] allayed in some small measure by the trifling faults of coldness, fickleness, and deceit; and to judge of Miss Fidler's friends by their handwriting, they must have been able to offer an edifying variety of bumps to the fingers of the phrenologist. But here is the very book itself at my elbow, waiting these three months, I blush to say, for a contribution which has yet to be pumped up from my unwilling brains; and I have a mind to steal a few specimens from its already loaded pages, for the benefit of the distressed, who may, like myself, be at their wits' end for something to put in just such a book.

The first page, rich with embossed lilies, bears the invocation, written in a great black spattering hand, and wearing the air of a defiance. It runs thus:

> If among the names of the stainless few
>   Thine own hath maintain'd a place,
> Come dip thy pen in the sable dew
>   And with it this volume grace.
>
> But oh! if thy soul e'er encouraged a thought
>   Which purity's self might blame,
> Close quickly the volume, and venture not
>   To sully its snows with thy name.

Then we come to a wreath of flowers of gorgeous hues, within whose circle appears in a *miminee piminee*[6] hand, evidently a young lady's—

THE WREATH OF SLEEP

> Oh let me twine this glowing wreath
>   Amid those rings of golden hair,
> 'T will soothe thee with its odorous breath
>   To sweet forgetfulness of care.
>
> 'T is form'd of every scented flower
>   That flings its fragrance o'er the night;
> And gifted with a fairy power
>   To fill thy dreams with forms of light.
>
> 'T was braided by an angel boy
>   When fresh from Paradise he came

A New Home, Who'll Follow?

To fill our earth-born hearts with joy—
Ah! need I tell the cherub's name?

This contributor I have settled in my own mind to be a descendant of Anna Matilda, the high-priestess of the Della Cruscan order.[7] The next blazon is an interesting view of a young lady, combing her hair. As she seems not to have been long out of bed, the lines which follow are rather appropriate, though I feel quite sure they come from the expert fingers of a merchant's clerk—from the finished elegance, and very sweeping tails of the chirography.

MORNING

Awake! arise! art thou slumbering still?
When the sun is above the mapled hill,
And the shadows are flitting fast away,
And the dews are diamond beneath his ray,
And every bird in our vine-roofed bower
Is waked into song by the joyous hour;
Come, banish sleep from thy gentle eyes,
Sister! sweet sister! awake! arise!

Yet I love to gaze on thy lids of pearl,
And to mark the wave of the single curl
That shades in its beauty thy brow of snow,
And the cheek that lies like a rose below;
And to list to the murmuring notes that fall
From thy lips, like music in fairy hall.
But it must not be—the sweet morning flies
Ere thou hast enjoyed it; awake! arise!

There is balm on the wings of this freshen'd air;
'T will make thine eye brighter, thy brow more fair,
And a deep, deep rose on thy cheek shall be
The meed of an early walk with me.
We will seek the shade by the green hill side,
Or follow the clear brook's whispering tide;
And brush the dew from the violet's eyes—
Sister! sweet sister! awake! arise!

This I transcribe for the good advice which it contains. And what have we here? It is tastefully headed by an engraving of Hero and Ursula in

101

the "pleached bower," and Beatrice running "like a lap-wing" in the background.[8] It begins ominously.

TO ——

Oh, look upon this pallid brow!
 Say, canst thou there discern one trace
Of that proud soul which oft ere now
 Thou'st sworn shed radiance o'er my face?
Chill'd is that soul—its darling themes,
 Thy manly honour, virtue, truth
Prove now to be but fleeting dreams,
 Like other lovely thoughts of youth.

Meet, if thy coward spirit dare,
 This sunken eye; say, dost thou see
The rays thou saidst were sparkling there
 When first its gaze was turn'd on thee?
That eye's young light is quench'd forever;
 No change its radiance can repair:
Will Joy's keen touch relume it? Never!
 It gleams the watch-light of Despair.

  I find myself growing hoarse by sympathy, and I shall venture only a
single extract more, and this because Miss Fidler declares it, without exception, the sweetest thing she ever read. It is written with a crow-quill,
and has other marks of femininity. Its vignette is a little girl and boy playing
at battle-door.[9]

BALLAD

The deadly strife was over, and across the field of fame,
With anguish in his haughty eye, the Moor Almanzor came;
He prick'd his fiery courser on among the scatter'd dead,
Till he came at last to what he sought, a sever'd human head.

It might have seem'd a maiden's, so pale it was, and fair;
But the lip and chin were shaded till they match'd the raven hair.
There lingered yet upon the brow a spirit bold and high,
And the stroke of death had scarcely closed the piercing eagle eye.

Almanzor grasp'd the flowing locks, and he staid not in his flight,
Till he reach'd a lonely castle's gate where stood a lady bright.

"Inez! behold thy paramour!" he loud and sternly cried,
And threw his ghastly burden down, close at the lady's side.

"I sought thy bower at even-tide, thou syren, false as fair!
"And, would that I had rather died! I found yon stripling there.
"I turn'd me from the hated spot, but I swore by yon dread Heaven,
"To know no rest until my sword the traitor's life had riven."

The lady stood like stone until he turn'd to ride away,
And then she oped her marble lips, and wildly thus did say:
"Alas, alas! thou cruel Moor, what is it thou hast done!
"This was my brother Rodriguez, my father's only son."

And then before his frenzied eyes, like a crush'd lily bell,
Lifeless upon the bleeding head, the gentle Inez fell.
He drew his glittering ataghan—he sheath'd it in his side—
And for his Spanish ladye-love the Moor Almanzor died.

This is not a very novel incident, but young ladies like stories of love and murder, and Miss Fidler's tastes were peculiarly young-lady-like. She praised Ainsworth and James,[10] but thought Bulwer's [11] works "very immoral," though I never could discover that she had more than skimmed the story from any of them. Cooper [12] she found "pretty;" Miss Sedgwick,[13] "pretty well, only her characters are such common sort of people."

Miss Fidler wrote her own poetry, so that she had ample employment for her time while with us in the woods. It was unfortunate that she could not walk out much on account of her shoes. She was obliged to make out with diluted inspiration. The nearest approach she usually made to the study of Nature, was to sit on the wood-pile, under a girdled tree, and there, with her gold pencil in hand, and her "eyne, grey as glas," rolled upwards, poefy by the hour. Several people, and especially one marriageable lady of a certain age, felt afraid Miss Fidler was "kind o' crazy."

And, standing marvel of Montacute, no guest at morning or night ever found the fair Eloise ungloved. Think of it! In the very wilds to be always like a cat in nutshells, alone useless where all are so busy! I do not wonder our good neighbours thought the damsel a little touched. And then her shoes! "Saint Crispin Crispianus" [14] never had so self-sacrificing a votary. No shoemaker this side of New-York could make a sole papery enough; no tannery out of France could produce materials for this piece of exquisite feminine foppery. Eternal imprisonment within doors, except in the warmest and driest weather, was indeed somewhat of a price to pay, but it was ungrudged. The sofa and its footstool, finery and novels, *would* have made a delicious world for Miss Eloise Fidler, *if*——

But, alas! "all this availeth me nothing," has been ever the song of poor human nature. The mention of that unfortunate name includes the only real, personal, pungent distress which had as yet shaded the lot of my interesting heroine. Fidler! In the mortification adhering to so unpoetical, so unromantic, so inelegant a surname—a name irredeemable even by the highly classical elegance of the Eloise, or as the fair lady herself pronounced it, "Elovees;" in this lay all her wo; and the grand study of her life had been to sink this hated cognomen in one more congenial to her taste. Perhaps this very anxiety had defeated itself; at any rate, here she was at—I did not mean to touch on the ungrateful guess again, but at least at mateable years; neither married, nor particularly likely to be married.

Mrs. Rivers was the object of absolute envy to the pining Eloise. "Anna had been so fortunate," she said; "Rivers was the sweetest name! and Harley was such an elegant fellow!"

We thought poor Anna had been any thing but fortunate. She might better have been Fidler or Fiddlestring all her life than to have taken the name of an indifferent and dissipated husband. But not so thought Miss Fidler. It was not long after the arrival of the elegant Eloise, that the Montacute Lyceum held its first meeting in Mr. Simeon Jenkins's shop, lighted by three candles, supported by a candelabra of scooped potatoes; Mr. Jenkins himself sitting on the head of a barrel, as president. At first the debates of the institute were held with closed doors; but after the youthful or less practised speakers had tried their powers for a few evenings, the Lyceum was thrown open to the world every Tuesday evening, at six o'clock. The list of members was not very select as to age, character, or standing; and it soon included the entire gentility of the town, and some who scarce claimed rank elsewhere. The attendance of the ladies was particularly requested; and the whole fair sex of Montacute made a point of showing occasionally the interest they undoubtedly felt in the gallant knights who tilted in this field of honour.

But I must not be too diffuse—I was speaking of Miss Fidler. One evening—I hope that beginning prepares the reader for something highly interesting—one evening the question to be debated was the equally novel and striking one which regards the comparative mental capacity of the sexes; and as it was expected that some of the best speakers on both sides would be drawn out by the interesting nature of the subject, every body was anxious to attend.

Among the rest was Miss Fidler, much to the surprise of her sister and myself, who had hitherto been so unfashionable as to deny ourselves this gratification.

"What new whim posseses you, Eloise?" said Mrs. Rivers; "you who never go out in the day-time."

"Oh, just *per passy le tong*,"[15] said the young lady, who was a great French scholar; and go she would and did.

The debate was interesting to absolute breathlessness, both of speakers and hearers, and was gallantly decided in favour of the fair by a youthful member who occupied the barrel as president for the evening. He gave it as his decided opinion, that if the natural and social disadvantages under which woman laboured and must ever continue to labour, could be removed; if their education could be entirely different, and their position in society the reverse of what it is at present, they would be very nearly, if not quite, equal to the nobler sex, in all but strength of mind, in which very useful quality it was his opinion that man would still have the advantage, especially in those communities whose energies were developed by the aid of debating societies.

This decision was hailed with acclamations, and as soon as the question for the ensuing debate, "which is the more useful animal the ox or the ass?" was announced, Miss Eloise Fielder returned home to rave of the elegant young man who sat on the barrel, whom she had decided to be one of "Nature's aristocracy," and whom she had discovered to bear the splendid appellative of Dacre. "Edward Dacre," said she, "for I heard the rude creature Jenkins call him Ed."

The next morning witnessed another departure from Miss Fidler's usual habits. She proposed a walk; and observed that she had never yet bought an article at the store, and really felt as if she ought to purchase something. Mrs. Rivers chancing to be somewhat occupied, Miss Fidler did me the honour of a call, as she could not think of walking without a chaperon.

Behind the counter at Skinner's I saw for the first time a spruce clerk, a really well-looking young man, who made his very best bow to Miss Fidler, and served us with much assiduity. The young lady's purchases occupied some time, and I was obliged gently to hint home-affairs before she could decide between two pieces of muslin, which she declared to be so nearly alike, that it was almost impossible to say which was the best.

When we were at length on our return, I was closely questioned as to my knowledge of "that gentleman," and on my observing that he seemed to be a very decent young man, Miss Fidler warmly justified him from any such opinion, and after a glowing eulogium on his firm countenance, his elegant manners and his grace as a debater, concluded by informing me, as if to cap the climax, that his name was Edward Dacre.

I had thought no more of the matter for some time, though I knew Mr. Darce had become a frequent visitor at Mr. Rivers', when Mrs. Rivers came to me one morning with a perplexed brow, and confided to me her sisterly fears that Eloise was about to make a fool of herself, as she had done more than once before.

"My father," she said, "hoped in this remote corner of creation Eloise might forget her nonsense and act like other people; but I verily believe she is bent upon encouraging this low fellow, whose principal charm in her bewildered eyes is his name."

"His name?" said I, "pray explain;" for I had not then learned all the boundless absurdity of this new Cherubina's fancies.

"Edward Dacre?" said my friend, "this is what enchants my sister, who is absolutely mad on the subject of her own homely appellation."

"Oh, is that all?" said I, "send her to me, then; and I engage to dismiss her cured."

And Miss Fidler came to spend the day. We talked of all novels without exception, and all poetry of all magazines, and Miss Fidler asked me if I had read the "Young Duke." [16] Upon my confessing as much, she asked my opinion of the heroine, and then if I had ever heard so sweet a name. "May Dacre—May Dacre," she repeated, as if to solace her delighted ears.

"Only think how such names are murdered in this country," said I, tossing carelessly before her an account of Mr. Skinner's which bore, "Edkins Daker" below the receipt. I never saw a change equal to that which seemed to "come o'er the spirit of her dream." I went on with my citations of murdered names, telling how Rogers was turned into Rudgers, Conway into Coniway, and Montague into Montaig, but poor Miss Fidler was no longer in talking mood; and, long before the day was out, she complained of a head-ache and returned to her sister's. Mr. Daker found her "not at home" that evening; and when I called next morning, the young lady was in bed, steeping her long ringlets in tears, real tears.

To hasten to the catastrophe: it was discovered ere long that Mr. Edkins Daker's handsome face, and really pleasant manners, had fairly vanquished Miss Fidler's romance, and she had responded to his professions of attachment with a truth and sincerity, which while it vexed her family inexpressibly, seemed to me to atone for all her follies. Mr. Daker's prospects were by no means despicable, since a small capital employed in merchandize in Michigan, is very apt to confer upon the industrious and fortunate possesser that crowning charm, without which handsome faces, and even handsome names, are quite worthless in our Western eyes.

Some little disparity of age existed between Miss Fidler and her adorer; but this was conceded by all to be abundantly made up by the superabounding gentility of the lady; and when Mr. Daker returned from New-York with his new stock of goods and his stylish bride, I thought I had seldom seen a happier or better mated couple. And at this present writing, I do not believe Eloise, with all her whims, would exchange her very nice Edkins for the proudest Dacre of the British Peerage.

CHAPTER XXVIII

By sports like these are all their cares beguiled,
The sports of children satisfy the child;
Each nobler aim, repress'd by long control,
Now sinks at last, or feebly mans the soul;
While low delights succeeding fast behind,
In happier meanness occupy the mind.
—Goldsmith, *The Traveller* [1]

THERE IS in our vicinity one class of settlers whose condition has always been inexplicable to me. They seem to work hard, to dress wretchedly, and to live in the most uncomfortable style in all respects, apparently denying themselves and their families every thing beyond the absolute necessaries of life. They complain most bitterly of poverty. They perform the severe labour which is shunned by their neighbours; they purchase the coarsest food, and are not too proud to ask for an old coat or a pair of cast boots, though it is always with the peculiar air of dignity and "dont care," which is characteristic of the country.

Yet instead of increasing their means by these penurious habits, they grow poorer every day. Their dwellings are more and more out of repair. There are more and more shingles in the windows, old hats and red petticoats cannot be spared; and an increasing dearth of cows, pigs, and chickens. The daughters go to service, and the sons "chore round" for every body and any body; and even the mamma, the centre of dignity, is fain to go out washing by the day.

A family of this description had fallen much under our notice. The father and his stout sons had performed a good deal of hard work in our service, and the females of the family had been employed on many occasions when "help" was scarce. Many requests for cast articles, or those of trifling value had been proffered during the course of our acquaintance; and in several attacks of illness, such comforts as our house afforded had been frequently sought, though no visit was ever requested.

They had been living through the summer in a shanty, built against a sloping bank, with a fire-place dug in the hill-side, and a hole pierced through the turf by way of chimney. In this den of some twelve feet square, the whole family had burrowed since April; but in October, a log-house of the ordinary size was roofed in, and though it had neither door nor window, nor chimney, nor hearth, they removed, and felt much elated with the change. Something like a door was soon after swinging on its leathern hinges, and the old man said they were now quite comfortable, though he *should* like to get a window!

The first intelligence we received from them after this, was that Mr. Newland, the father, was dangerously ill with inflammation of the lungs. This was not surprising, for a quilt is but a poor substitute for a window during a Michigan November. A window was supplied, and such alleviations as might be collected, were contributed by several of the neighbours. The old man lingered on, much to my surprise, and after two or three weeks we heard that he was better, and would be able to "kick round" pretty soon.

It was not long after, that we were enjoying the fine sleighing, which is usually so short-lived in this lakey region. The roads were not yet much beaten, and we had small choice in our drives, not desiring the troublesome honour of leading the way. It so happened that we found ourselves in the neighbourhood of Mr. Newland's clearing; and though the sun was low, we thought we might stop a moment to ask how the old man did.

We drove to the door, and so noiseless was our approach, guiltless of bells, that no one seemed aware of our coming. We tapped, and heard the usual reply, "Walk!" which I used to think must mean "Walk off."

I opened the door very softly, fearing to disturb the sick man; but I found this caution quite mal-apropos. Mrs. Newland was evidently in high holiday trim. The quilts had been removed from their stations round the bed, and the old man, shrunken and miserable-looking enough, sat on a chair in the corner. The whole apartment bore the marks of expected hilarity. The logs over-head were completely shrouded by broad hemlock boughs fastened against them; and evergreens of various kinds were disposed in all directions, while three tall slender candles, with the usual potato supporters, were placed on the cupboard shelf.

On the table, a cloth seemed to cover a variety of refreshments; and in front of this cloth stood a tin pail, nearly full of a liquid whose odour was but too discernible; and on the whiskey, for such it seemed, swam a small tin cup. But I forget the more striking part of the picture, the sons and daughters of the house. The former flaming in green stocks and scarlet watchguards, while the cut of their long dangling coats showed that whoever they might once have fitted, they were now exceedingly out of place; the latter decked in tawdry, dirty finery, and wearing any look but that of the modest country maiden, who, "in choosing her garments, counts no bravery in the world like decency."

The eldest girl, Amelia, who had lived with me at one time, had been lately at a hotel in a large village at some distance, and had returned but a short time before, not improved either in manners or reputation. Her tall commanding person was arrayed in far better taste than her sisters', and by contrast with the place and circumstances, she wore really a splendid air. Her dress was of rich silk, made in the extreme mode, and set off by elegant jewelry. Her black locks were drest with scarlet berries; most elaborate pendants of wrought gold hung almost to her shoulders; and above her glittering basilisk eyes, was a gold chain with a handsome clasp of cut coral. The large hands were covered with elegant gloves, and an embroidered handkerchief was carefully arranged in her lap.

I have attempted to give some idea of the appearance of things in this wretched log-hut, but I cannot pretend to paint the confusion into which our ill-timed visit threw the family, who had always appeared before us in such different characters. The mother asked us to sit down, however, and Mr. Newland muttered something, from which I gathered, that "the girls thought they must have a kind of a house-warmin' like."

We made our visit very short, of course; but before we could make our escape, an old fellow came in with a violin, and an ox-sled approached the door, loaded with young people of both sexes, who were all "spilt" into the deep snow, by a "mistake on purpose" of the driver. In the scramble which ensued, we took leave; wondering no longer at the destitution of the Newlands, or of the other families of the same class, whose young people we had recognized in the mêlée.

The Newland family did not visit us as usual after this. There was a certain consciousness in their appearance when we met, and the old man more than once alluded to our accidental discovery with evident uneasiness. He was a person not devoid of shrewdness, and he was aware that the utter discrepancy between his complaints, and the appearances we had witnessed, had given us but slight opinion of his veracity; and for some time we were almost strangers to each other.

How was I surprised some two months after at being called out of bed by a most urgent message from Mrs. Newland, that Amelia, her eldest daughter, was dying! The messenger could give no account of her condition, but that she was now in convulsions, and her mother despairing of her life.

I lost not a moment, but the way was long, and ere I entered the house, the shrieks of the mother and her children, told me I had come too late. Struck with horror I almost hesitated whether to proceed, but the door was opened, and I went in. Two or three neighbours with terrified countenances stood near the bed, and on it lay the remains of the poor girl, swollen and discoloured, and already so changed in appearance that I should not have recognized it elsewhere.

I asked for particulars, but the person whom I addressed, shook her head and declined answering; and there was altogether an air of horror and mystery which I was entirely unable to understand. Mrs. Newland, in her lamentations, alluded to the suddenness of the blow, and when I saw her a little calmed, I begged to know how long Amelia had been ill, expressing my surprise that I had heard nothing of it. She turned upon me as if I had stung her.

"What, you've heard their lies too, have ye!" she exclaimed fiercely, and she cursed in no measured terms those who meddled with what did not concern them. I felt much shocked: and disclaiming all intention of wounding her feelings, I offered the needful aid, and when all was finished, returned home uninformed as to the manner of Amelia Newland's death.

Yet I could not avoid noticing that all was not right.

> Oft have I seen a timely-parted ghost
> Of ashy semblance, meagre, pale and bloodless—[2]

but the whole appearance of this sad wreck was quite different from that of any corpse I had ever viewed before. Nothing was done, but much said or hinted on all sides. Rumour was busy as usual; and I have been assured by those who ought to have warrant for their assertions, that this was but one

fatal instance out of the *many cases,* wherein life was perilled in the desperate effort to elude the "slow unmoving finger" of public scorn.

That the class of settlers to which the Newlands belong, a class but
too numerous in Michigan, is a vicious and degraded one, I cannot doubt:
but whether the charge to which I have but alluded, is in any degree just, I
am unable to determine. I can only repeat, "I say the tale as 't was said to
me," and I may add that more than one instance of a similar kind, though
with results less evidently fatal, has since come under my knowledge.

The Newlands have since left this part of the country, driving off
with their own, as many of their neighbours' cattle and hogs as they could
persuade to accompany them; and not forgetting one of the train of fierce
dogs which have not only shown ample sagacity in getting their own living,
but, "gin a' tales be true," assisted in supporting the family by their habits
of nightly prowling.

I passed by their deserted dwelling. They had carried off the door and
window, and some boys were busy pulling the shingles from the roof to
make quail-traps. I trust we have few such neighbours left. Texas and the
Canada war have done much for us in this way; and the wide west is rapidly
drafting off those whom we shall regret as little as the Newlands.

CHAPTER XXIX

Something that mellows and that glorifies,
Ev'n like the soft and spiritual glow
Kindling rich woods whereon th' ethereal bow
Sleeps lovingly the while.
. . . .
Swift and high
The arrowy pillars of the fire-light grew.—
—Mrs. Hemans [1]

AS I HAVE NEVER made any remarkable progress in the heights and depths
of meteorology, I am unable to speak with confidence as to the concatena-
tion of causes which may withhold from this fertile peninsula the treasures
of the clouds, in the early spring-time, when our land elsewhere, is satu-
rated even to repletion with the "milky nutriment." In plain terms, I
cannot tell any thing about the reason why we have such dry Springs in

Michigan, I can only advert to the fact as occasioning scenes rather striking to the new comer.

In April, instead of the "misty-moisty morning," which proverbially heralds the "uncertain glory" of the day in that much belied month, the sun, day after day, and week after week, shows his jolly red face, at the proper hour, little by little above the horizon, casting a scarlet glory on the leafless trees, and investing the well-pile brush-heaps with a burning splendour before their time. Now and then a brisk shower occurs, but it is short-lived, and not very abundant; and after being here through a season or two, one begins to wonder that the soil is so fertile. My own private theory is, that when the peninsula was covered with water, as it doubtless was before the Niagara met with such a fall, the porous mass became so throughly soaked, that the sun performs the office of rain, by drawing from below to the rich surface, the supplies of moisture which, under ordinary circumstances, are necessarily furnished from the aerial reservoirs. Such are my views, which I offer with the diffidence becoming a tyro; but at the same time avowing frankly that I shall not even consider an opposing hypothesis, until my antagonist shall have traversed the entire state, and counted the marshes and cat-holes from which I triumphantly draw my conclusion.

Leaving this question, then, I will make an effort to regain the float-ing end of my broken thread. These exceedingly dry Spring-times—all sun and a very little east-wind—leave every tree, bush, brier and blade of grass, dry as new tinder. They are as combustible as the heart of a Sopho-more; as ready for a blaze as a conclave of ancient ladies who have swal-lowed the first cup of Hyson,[2] and only wait one single word to begin.

At this very suitable time, it is one of the customs of the country for every man that has an acre of marsh, to burn it over, in order to prepare for a new crop of grass; and a handful of fire thus applied, wants but a cap-full of wind, to send it miles in any or all directions. The decayed trees, and those which may have been some time felled, catch the swift destruction, and aid the roaring flame; and while the earth seems covered with writhing serpents of living fire, ever and anon an undulating pyramid flares wildly upward, as if threatening the very skies, only to fall the next moment in crashing fragments, which serve to further the spreading ruin.

These scenes have a terrible splendour by night; but the effect by day is particularly curious. The air is so filled with the widely-diffused smoke, that the soft sunshine of April is mellowed into the ruddy glow of Autumn, and the mist which seems to hang heavy over the distant hills and woods, completes the illusion. One's associations are those of approaching winter, and it seems really a solecism to be making garden under such a sky. But this is not all.

We were all busy in the rough, pole-fenced acre, which we had begun to call our garden;—one with a spade, another with a hoe or rake, and the least useful,—videlicet, I,—with a trowel and a paper of celery-seed, when a rough neighbour of ours shouted over the fence:—

"What be you a potterin' there for? You 'd a plaguy sight better be a fighting fire, *I* tell ye! The wind is this way, and that fire 'll be on your haystacks in less than no time, if you don't mind."

Thus warned, we gazed at the dark smoke which had been wavering over the north-west all day, and saw that it had indeed made fearful advances. But two well-travelled roads still lay between us and the burning marshes, and these generally prove tolerably effectual barriers when the wind is low. So our operatives took their way toward the scene of action, carrying with them the gardening implements, as the most efficient weapons in "fighting fire."

They had to walk a long distance, but the fire was very obliging and advanced more than two steps to meet them. In short, the first barrier was overleapt before they reached the second, and the air had become so heated that they could only use the hoes and spades in widening the road nearest our dwelling, by scraping away the leaves and bushes; and even there they found it necessary to retreat more rapidly than was consistent with a thorough performance of the work. The winds, though light, favoured the destroyer, and the more experienced of the neighbours, who had turned out for the general good, declared there was nothing now but to make a "back-fire!" So homeward all ran, and set about kindling an opposing serpent which should "swallow up the rest;" but it proved too late. The flames only reached our stable and haystacks the sooner, and all that we could now accomplish was to preserve the cottage and its immediate appurtenances.

I scarce remember a blanker hour. I could not be glad that the house and horses were safe, so vexed did I feel to think that a rational attention to the advance of that black threatening column, would have prevented the disaster. I sat gazing out of the back window, watching the gradual blackening of the remains of our stores of hay—scolding the while most vehemently, at myself and every body else, for having been so stupidly negligent; declaring that I should not take the slightest interest in the garden which had so engrossed us, and wishing most heartily that the fellow who set the marsh on fire, could be detected and fined "not more than one thousand dollars," as the law directs; when our neighbour, long Sam Jennings, the slowest talker in Michigan, came sauntering across the yard with his rusty fowling-piece on his shoulder, and drawled out—

"I should think your dam was broke some; I see the water in the creek look dreadful muddy." And while Sam took his leisurely way to the woods, the tired fire-fighters raced, one and all, to the dam, where they found the water pouring through a hole near the head-gate, at a rate which seemed likely to carry off the entire structure in a very short time.

But I have purposely refrained from troubling the reader with a detail of any of the various accidents which attended our own particular début, in the back-woods. I mentioned the fire because it is an annual occurrence throughout the country, and often consumes wheat-stacks, and even solitary dwellings; and I was drawn in to record the first breach in the mill-dam, as occurring on the very day of the disaster by fire.

I shall spare my friends any account of the many troubles and vexatious delays attendant on repairing that necessary evil, the dam; and even a transcript of the three astounding figures which footed the account of expenses on the occasion. I shall only observe, that if long Sam Jennings did not get a ducking for not giving intelligence of the impending evil a full half-hour before it suited his convenience to stroll our way, it was not because he did not richly deserve it—and so I close my chapter of accidents.

CHAPTER XXX

Qu'ay je oublié? dere is some simples in my closet, dat I vill not for de varld I shall leave behind.

***

Shal. The Council shall hear it: it is a riot.

Evans. It is petter that friends is the sword, and end it; and there is another device in my prain which, peradventure, prings goot discretions with it. ** We will afterwards 'ork upon the cause with as great discreetly as we can.—Shakespeare, The Merry Wives of Windsor [1]

"AH! who can tell how hard it is to" say—any thing about an unpretending village like ours, in terms suited to the delicate organization of "ears

114

polite." How can one hope to find any thing of interest about such common-place people? Where is the aristocratic distinction which makes the kind visit of the great lady at the sick-bed of suffering indigence so great a favour, that all the inmates of the cottage behave picturesquely out of gratitude—form themselves into *tableaux,* and make speeches worth recording? Here are neither great ladies nor humble cottagers. I cannot bring to my aid either the exquisite boudoir of the one class, with its captivating *bijouterie*—its velvet couches and its draperies of rose-coloured satin, so becoming to the complexions of one's young-lady characters—nor yet the cot of the other more simple but not less elegant, surrounded with clustering eglantine and clematis, and inhabited by goodness, grace, and beauty. These materials are denied me; but yet I must try to describe something of Michigan cottage life, taking care to avail myself of such delicate periphrasis as may best veil the true homeliness of my subject.

Moonlight and the ague are, however, the same every where. At least I meet with no description in any of the poets of my acquaintance which might not be applied, without reservation, to Michigan moonlight; and as for the ague, did not great Cæsar shake "when the fit was on him?"

> T'is true, this god did shake:
> His coward lips did from their colour fly—[2]

And in this important particular poor Lorenzo Titmouse was just like the inventor of the laurel crown. We—Mrs. Rivers and I—went to his father's, at his urgent request, on just such a night as is usually chosen for romantic walks by a certain class of lovers. We waited not for escort, although the night had already fallen, and there was a narrow strip of forest to pass in our way; but leaving word whither we had gone, we accompanied the poor shivering boy, each carrying what we could. And what does the gentle reader think we carried? A custard or a glass of jelly each, perhaps; and a nice sponge-cake, or something equally delicate, and likely to tempt the faint appetite of the invalid. No such thing. We had learned better than to offer such nick-nacks to people who "a' n't us'd to sweetnin'." My companion was "doubly arm'd:" a small tin pail of cranberry sauce in one hand, a bottle of vinegar in the other. I carried a modicum of "hop 'east," and a little bag of crackers; a scrap of Hyson, and a box of quinine pills. Odd enough; but we had been at such places before.

We had a delicious walk; though poor Lorenzo, who had a bag of flour on his shoulders, was fain to rest often. This was his "well day," to be sure; but he had had some eight or ten fits of ague, enough to wither any body's pith and marrow, as those will say who have tried it. That innate politeness which young rustics, out of books as well as in them, are apt to exhibit when they are in good humour, made Lorenzo decline, most vehemently, our offers of assistance. But we at length fairly took his bag from him, and passing a stick through the string, carried it between us; while the boy disposed of our various small articles by the aid of his capacious pockets. And a short half mile from the bridge brought us to his father's.

It was an ordinary log house, but quite old and dilapidated: the great open chimney occupying most of one end of the single apartment, and two double-beds with a trundle-bed, the other. In one of the large beds lay the father and the eldest son; in the other, the mother and two little daughters, all ill with ague, and all sad and silent, save my friend Mrs. Titmouse, whose untameable tongue was too much even for the ague. Mrs. Titmouse is one of those fortunate beings who can talk all day without saying any thing. She is the only person whom I have met in these regions who appears to have paid her devoirs at Castle Blarney.³

"How d'ye do, ladies,—how d'ye do? Bless my soul! if ever I thought to be catch'd in sitch a condition, and by sich grand ladies too! Not a chair for you to sit down on. I often tell Titmouse that we live jist like the pigs; but he ha' n't no ambition. I'm sure I'm under a thousand compliments to ye for coming to see me. We're expecting a mother of his'n to come and stay with us, but she ha' n't come yet—and I in sitch a condition; can't show ye no civility. Do sit down, ladies, if you *can* sit upon a chest—ladies like you. I'm sure I'm under a thousand compliments—" and so the poor soul ran on till she was fairly out of breath, in spite of our efforts to out-talk her with our assurances that we could accommodate ourselves very well, and could stay but a few minutes.

"And now, Mrs. Titmouse," said Mrs. Rivers, in her sweet, pleasant voice, "tell us what we can do for you."

"Do for me! Oh, massy! Oh, nothing, I thank ye. There a' n't nothing that ladies like you can do for me. We make out very well, and—"

"What do you say so for!" growled her husband from the other bed. "You know we ha' n't tasted a mouthful since morning, nor had n't it, and I sent Lorenzo myself—"

"Well, I never!" responded his help-mate; "you're always doing just so: troubling people. You never had no ambition, Titmouse; you know I always said so. To be sure, we ha' n't had no tea this good while, and tea *does* taste dreadful good when a body's got the agur; and my bread is gone, and I ha' n't been able to set no emptins; but—"

Here we told what we had brought, and prepared at once to make some bread; but Mrs. Titmouse seemed quite horrified, and insisted upon getting out of bed, though she staggered, and would have fallen if we had not supported her to a seat.

"Now tell *me* where the water is, and I will get it myself," said Mrs. Rivers, "and do you sit still and see how soon I will make a loaf."

"Water!" said the poor soul; "I'm afraid we have not water enough to make a loaf. Mr. Grimes brought us a barrel day before yesterday, and we 've been dreadful careful of it, but the agur is so dreadful thirsty—I'm afraid there a' n't none."

"Have you no spring?"

"No, ma'am; but we have always got plenty of water down by the *mash* till this dry summer."

"I should think that was enough to give you the ague. Do n't you think the marsh water unwholesome?"

"Well, I do n't know but it is; but you see *he* was always a-going to dig a well; but he ha' n't no ambition, nor never had, and I always told him so. And as to the agur, if you 've got to have it, why you can't get clear of it."

There was, fortunately, water enough left in the barrel to set the bread and half-fill the tea-kettle; and we soon made a little blaze with sticks, which served to boil the kettle to make that luxury of the woods, a cup of green tea.

Mrs. Titmouse did not need the tea to help her talking powers, for she was an independent talker, whose gush of words knew no ebb nor exhaustion.

> Alike to her was tide or time,
> Moonless midnight or matin prime.

Her few remaining teeth chattered no faster when she had the ague than at any other time. The stream flowed on

> In one weak, washy, everlasting flood.

When we had done what little we could, and were about to depart, glad to escape her overwhelming protestations of eternal gratitude, her husband reminded her that the cow had not been milked since the evening before, when "Miss Grimes" had been there. Here was a dilemma! How we regretted our defective education, which prevented our rendering so simple yet so necessary a service to the sick poor.

We remembered the gentleman who did not know whether he could read Greek, as he had never tried; and set ourselves resolutely at work to ascertain our powers in the milking line.

But alas! the "milky mother of the herd" had small respect for timid and useless town ladies.

> Crummie kick'd, and Crummie flounced,
> And Crummie whisk'd her tail.

In vain did Mrs. Rivers hold the pail with both hands, while I essayed the arduous task. So sure as I succeeded in bringing ever so tiny a stream, the ill-mannered beast would almost put out my eyes with her tail, and oblige us both to jump up and run away; and after a protracted struggle, the cow gained the victory, as might have been expected, and we were fain to retreat into the house.

The next expedient was to support Mrs. Titmouse on the little bench, while she tried to accomplish the mighty work; and having been partially successful in this, we at length took our leave, promising aid for the morrow, and hearing the poor woman's tongue at intervals till we were far in the wood.

"Lord bless ye! I'm sure I'm under an everlastin' compliment to ye; I wish I know'd how I could pay ye. Such ladies to be a waitin' on the likes of me; I'm sure I never see nothing like it," &c. &c.

And now we began to wonder how long it would be before we should see our respected spouses, as poor Lorenzo had fallen exhausted on the bed, and was in no condition to see us even a part of the way home. The wood was very dark, though we could see glimpses of the mill-pond lying like liquid diamonds in the moon-light.

We had advanced near the brow of the hill which descends toward the pond, when strange sounds met our ears. Strange sounds for our peaceful village! Shouts and howling—eldrich screams—Indian yells— the braying of tin horns, and the violent clashing of various noisy articles.

We hurried on, and soon came in sight of a crowd of persons, who seemed coming from the village to the pond. And now loud talking, threats—"Duck him! duck the impudent rascal!" what could it be?

Here was a mob! a Montacute mob! and the cause? I believe all mobs pretend to have causes. Could the choice spirits have caught an abolitionist? which they thought, as I had heard, meant nothing less than a monster.

But now I recollected having heard that a ventriloquist, which I believe most of our citizens considered a beast of the same nature, had sent notices of an exhibition for the evening; and the truth flashed upon us at once.

"In with him! in with him!" they shouted as they approached the water, just as we began to descend the hill. And then the clear fine voice of the dealer in voice was distinctly audible above the hideous din—

"Gentlemen, I have warned you; I possess the means of defending myself, you will force me to use them."

"Stop his mouth," shouted a well-known bully, "he lies; he ha' n't got nothing! in with him!" and a violent struggle followed, some few of our sober citizens striving to protect the stranger.

One word to Mrs. Rivers, and we set up a united shriek, a screech like an army of sea-gulls. "Help! help!" and we stopped on the hill-side, our white dresses distinctly visible in the clear, dazzling moon-light.

We "stinted not nor staid" till a diversion was fairly effected. A dozen forms seceded at once from the crowd, and the spirit of the thing was at an end.

We waited on the spot where our artifice began, certain of knowing every individual who should approach; and the very first proved those we most wished to see. And now came the very awkward business of explaining our *ruse,* and Mrs. Rivers was rather sharply reproved for *her* part of it. Harley Rivers was not the man to object to any thing like a *lark,* and he had only attempted to effect the release of the ventriloquist, after Mr. Clavers had joined him on the way to Mr. Titmouse's. The boobies who had been most active in the outrage, would fain have renewed the sport; but the ventriloquist had wisely taken advantage of our diversion in his favour, and was no where to be found. The person at whose house he had put up told afterwards that he had gone out with loaded pistols in his pocket; so even a woman's shrieks, hated of gods and men, may sometimes be of service.

Montacute is far above mobbing now. This was the first and last exhibition of the spirit of the age. The most mobbish of our neighbours have flitted westward, seeking more congenial association. I trust they may be so well satisfied that they will not think of returning; for it is not pleasant to find a dead pig in one's well, or a favourite dog hung up at the gate-post; to say nothing of cows milked on the marshes, hen-roosts rifled, or melon-patches cleared in the course of the night.

We learned afterwards the "head and front" of the ventriloquist's offence. He had asked twenty-five cents a-head for the admission of the sovereign people.

CHAPTER XXXI

Bah! bah!—not a bit magic in it at all—not a bit. It is all founded on de planetary influence, and de sympathy and force of numbers. I will show you much finer dan dis.—*The Antiquary*[1]

THE VERY NEXT intelligence from our urban rival came in the shape of a polite note to Mr. Clavers, offering him any amount of stock in the "Merchants' and Manufacturers' Bank of Tinkerville." My honoured spouse—I acknowledge it with regret—is any thing but "an enterprising man." But our neighbour, Mr. Rivers, or his astute father for him, thought this chance for turning paper into gold and silver too tempting to be slighted, and entered at once into the business of making money on a large scale.

I looked at first upon the whole matter with unfeigned indifference, for money has never seemed so valueless to me as since I have experienced how little it will buy in the woods; but I was most unpleasantly surprised when I heard that Harley Rivers, the husband of my friend, was to be exalted to the office of President of the new bank.

"Just as we were beginning to be so comfortable, to think you should leave us," said I to Mrs. Rivers.

"Oh! dear no," she replied; "Harley says it will not be necessary for us to remove at present. The business can be transacted just as well here, and we shall not go until the banking-house and our own can be erected."

This seemed odd to a novice like myself; but I rejoiced that arrangements were so easily made which would allow me to retain for a while so pleasant a companion.

As I make not the least pretension to regularity, but only an attempt to "body forth" an unvarnished picture of the times, I may as well proceed in this place to give the uninitiated reader so much of the history of the Tinkerville Bank, as has become the property of the public; supposing that the effects of our "General Banking Law" may not be as familiarly known elsewhere as they unfortunately are in this vicinity.

When our speculators in land found that the glamour had departed, that the community had seen the ridicule of the delusion which had so long made

> "The cobwebs on a cottage wall
> Seem tapestry in lordly hall;
> A nutshell seem a gilded barge,
> A sheeling seem a palace large,
> And youth seem age and age seem youth."

And poverty seem riches, and idleness industry, and fraud enterprise; some of these cunning magicians set themselves about concocting a new species of gramarye, by means of which the millions of acres of wild land which were left on their hands might be turned into *bonâ fide* cash—paper cash at least, to meet certain times of payment of certain moneys borrowed at certain rates of interest during the fervour of the speculating mania. The "General Banking Law" of enviable notoriety, which allowed any dozen of men who could pledge real estate to a nominal amount, to assume the power of making money of rags; this was the magic cauldron, whose powers were destined to transmute these acres of wood and meadow into splendid metropolitan residences, with equipages of corresponding elegance. It was only "bubble-bubble," and burr-oaks were turned into marble tables, tall tamaracks into draperied bedsteads, lakes into looking-glasses, and huge expanses of wet marsh into velvet couches, and carpets from the looms of Agra and of Ind.

It is not to be denied that this necromantic power had its limits. Many of these successful wizards seemed after all a little out of place in their palaces of enchantment; and one could hardly help thinking, that some of them would have been more suitably employed in tramping, with cow-hide boot, the slippery marshes on which their greatness was based, than in treading mincingly the piled carpets which were the magical product of those marshes. But that was nobody's business but their own. They considered themselves as fulfilling their destiny.

Some thirty banks or more were the fungous growth of the new political hot-bed; and many of these were of course without a "local habitation," though they might boast the "name," it may be, of some part of the deep woods, where the wild cat had hitherto been the most formidable foe to the unwary and defenceless. Hence the celebrated term "Wild Cat," justified fully by the course of these cunning and stealthy blood-suckers; more fatal in their treacherous spring than ever was their forest prototype. A stout farmer might hope to "whip" a wild cat or two; but once in the grasp of a "wild cat bank," his struggles were unavailing. Hopeless ruin has been the consequence in numerous instances, and every day adds new names to the list.

But I have fallen into the sin of generalizing, instead of journalizing, as I promised. The interesting nature of the subject will be deemed a sufficient justification, by such of my readers as may have enjoyed the pleasure of making alumets of bank-notes, as so many Michiganians have done, or might have done if they had not been too angry.

Of the *locale* of the Merchants' and Manufacturers' Bank of Tinkerville, I have already attempted to give some faint idea; and I doubt not one might have ridden over many of the new banks in a similar manner, without suspecting their existence. The rubicand and smooth-spoken father-in-law of my friend was the main-spring of the institution in question; and his son Harley, who "did not love work," was placed in a conspicuous part of the panorama as President. I thought our Caleb Quotem[2] neighbour, Mr. Simeon Jenkins, would have found time to fulfil the duties of cashier, and he can write "S. Jenkins" very legibly; so there would have been no objection on that score: but it was thought prudent to give the office to a Tinkervillian—a man of straw, for aught I know to the contrary; for all I saw or heard of him was his name, "A. Bite," on the bills. A fatal mistake this, according to Mr. Jenkins. He can demonstrate, to any body who feels an interest in the facts of the case, that the bank never would have "flatted out," if he had had a finger in the pie.

Just as our Wild Cat was ready for a spring, the only obstacle in her path was removed, by the abolition of the old-fashioned-and-troublesome-but-now-exploded plan of specie payments; and our neighbours went up like the best rocket from Vauxhall. The Tinkerville Astor House, the County Offices, the Banking House, were all begun simultaneously, as at the waving of a wand of power. Montacute came at once to a dead stand; for not a workman could be had for love or flour. Those beautifully engraved bills were too much for the public spirit of most of us, and we forgot our Montacute patriotism for a time. "Real estate pledged;" of course, the notes were better than gold or silver, because they were lighter in the pocket.

Time's whirligig went round. Meanwhile all was prosperous at the incipient capital of our rising county. Mr. President Rivers talked much of removing to the bank; and in preparation, sent to New-York for a complete outfit of furniture, and a pretty carriage; while Mrs. Rivers astonished the natives in our log meeting-house, and the wood-chucks in our forest strolls, by a Parisian bonnet of the most exquisite rose-colour, her husband's taste. Mr. Rivers, senior, and sundry other gentlemen, some ruddy-gilled and full-pocketed like himself, others looking so lean and hungry, that I wondered any body would trust them in a bank—a place where, as I supposed in my greenness,

In bright confusion open rouleaux lie,[3]

Made frequent and closetted sojourn at Montacute. Our mill whirred merrily, and toll-wheat is a currency that never depreciates; but in other respects, we were only moderately prosperous. Our first merchant, Mr. Skinner, did not clear above three thousand dollars the first year. Slow work for Michigan; and somehow, Mr. Jenkins was far from getting rich as fast as he expected.

One bright morning, as I stood looking down Main-street, thinking I certainly saw a deer's tail at intervals flying through the woods, two gentlemen on horseback rode deliberately into town. They had the air of men who were on serious business; and as they dismounted at the door of the Montacute House, a messenger was despatched in an instant to Mr. Rivers. Ere long, I discovered the ruddy papa wending his dignified way towards the Hotel, while the President, on his famous trotter Greenhorn, emerged from the back-gate, and cleared the ground in fine style towards Tinkerville.

A full hour elapsed before the elder Mr. Rivers was ready to accompany the gentlemen on their ride. He happened to be going that way, which was very convenient, since the Bank Commissioners, for our portly strangers were none other, did not know in what part of the unsurveyed lands the new city lay. The day was far spent when the party returned to take tea with Mrs. Rivers. All seemed in high good humour. The examination prescribed by our severe laws had been exceedingly satisfactory. The books of the Bank were in apple-pie order. Specie certificates, a newly-invented kind of gold and silver, were abundant. A long row of boxes, which contained the sinews of peace as well as of war, had been viewed and "hefted" by the Commissioners. The liabilities seemed as nothing compared with the resources; and the securities were as substantial as earth and stone could make them.

If the height of prosperity could have been heightened, Tinkerville would have gone on faster than ever after this beneficent visitation. Mr. Rivers' new furniture arrived, and passed through our humble village in triumphal procession, pile after pile of huge boxes, provokingly impervious to the public eye; and, last of all, the new carriage, covered as closely from the vulgar gaze as a celebrated belle whose charms are on the wane. The public buildings at the county seat were proclaimed finished, or *nearly* finished, a school-house begun, a meeting-house talked of; but for the latter, it was supposed to be *too early*—rather premature.

CHAPTER XXXII

And whare is your honours gaun the day wi' a' your picks and shules?—*The Antiquary* [1]

On peut être plus fin qu'un autre, mais non pas plus fin que tous les autres.—Rochefoucault [2]

ALL TOO SOON came the period when I must part with my pleasant neighbour Mrs. Rivers, the opening brilliancy of whose lot seemed to threaten a lasting separation, from those whose way led rather through the "cool, sequestered vale," [3] so much praised, and so little coveted.

Mr. Rivers had for some time found abundant leisure for his favourite occupations of hunting and fishing. The signing of bills took up but little time, and an occasional ride to the scene of future glories, for the purpose of superintending the various improvements, was all that had necessarily called him away. But now, final preparations for a removal were absolutely in progress; and I had begun to feel really sad at the thought of losing the gentle Anna, when the Bank Commissioners again paced in official dignity up Main-street, and, this time, alighted at Mr. Rivers' door.

The President and Greenhorn had trotted to Tinkerville that morning, and the old gentleman was not in town; so our men of power gravely wended their way towards the newly-painted and pine-pillared honours of the Merchants' and Manufacturers' Banking-house, not without leaving behind them many a surmise as to the probable object of this new visitation.

It was Mr. Skinner's opinion, and Mr. Skinner is a long-headed Yankee, that the Bank had issued too many bills; and for the sincerity of his judgment, he referred his hearers to the fact, that he had for some time been turning the splendid notes of the Merchants' and Manufacturers' Bank of Tinkerville into wheat and corn as fast as he conveniently could.

A sly old farmer, who had sold several hundred bushels of wheat to Mr. Skinner, at one dollar twenty-five cents a bushel, winked knowingly as the merchant mentioned this proof of his own far-seeing astuteness; and informed the company that he had paid out the last dollar long ago on certain outstanding debts.

Mr. Porter knew that the Tinkerville blacksmith had run up a most unconscionable bill for the iron doors, &c. &c., which were necessary to secure the immense vaults of the Bank; that would give, as he presumed, some hint of the probable object of the Commissioners.

Mr. Simeon Jenkins, if not the greatest, certainly the most grandiloquent man in Montacute, did 'nt want to know any better than he did know, that the Cashier of the Bank was a thick-skull; and he felt very much afraid that the said Cashier had been getting his principals into trouble. Mr. Bite's manner of writing his name was, in Mr. Jenkins' view, proof positive of his lack of capacity; since "nobody in the universal world" as Mr. Jenkins averred, "ever wrote such a hand as that, that know'd any thing worth knowing."

But conjectures, however positively advanced, are, after all, not quite satisfactory; and the return of the commissioners was most anxiously awaited even by the very worthies who knew their business so well.

The sun set most perversely soon, and the light would not stay long after him; and thick darkness settled upon this mundane sphere, and no word transpired from Tinkerville. Morning came, and with it the men of office, but oh! with what lengthened faces!

There were whispers of "an injunction"—horrid sound!—upon the Merchants' and Manufacturers' Bank of Tinkerville.

To picture the dismay which drew into all sorts of shapes the universal face of Montacute, would require a dozen Wilkies.[4] I shall content myself with saying that there was no joking about the matter.

The commissioners were not very communicative, but in spite of their dignified mystification, something about broken glass and tenpenny nails did leak out before their track was fairly cold.

And where was Harley Rivers? "Echo answers, where!" His dear little wife watered her pillow with her tears for many a night before he returned to Montacute.

It seemed, as we afterwards learned, that the commissioners had seen some suspicious circumstances about the management of the Bank, and returned with a determination to examine into matters a little more scrupulously. It had been found in other cases that certain "specie-certificates" had been locomotive. It had been rumoured, since the new batch of Banks had come into operation, that

> Thirty steeds both fleet and wight
> Stood saddled in the stables day and night—

ready to effect at short notice certain transfers of assets and specie. And in the course of the Tinkerville investigation the commissioners had ascertained by the aid of hammer and chisel, that the boxes of the "real stuff" which had been so loudly vaunted, contained a heavy charge of broken glass and tenpenny nails, covered above and below with half-dollars, principally *"bogus."* Alas! for Tinkerville, and alas, for poor Michigan!

The distress among the poorer classes of farmers which was the immediate consequence of this and other Bank failures, was indescribable. Those who have seen only a city panic, can form no idea of the extent and severity of the sufferings on these occasions. And how many small farmers are there in Michigan who have *not* suffered from this cause?

The only adequate punishment which I should prescribe for this class of heartless adventurers, would be to behold at one glance all the misery they have occasioned; to be gifted with an Asmodean[5] power, and forced to use it. The hardiest among them, could scarcely, I think, endure to witness the unroofing of the humble log-huts of Michigan, after the bursting of one of these Dead-sea apples. Bitter indeed were the ashes which they scattered!

How many settlers who came in from the deep woods many miles distant where no grain had yet grown, after travelling perhaps two or three days and nights, with a half-starved ox-team, and living on a few crusts by the way, were told when they offered their splendid-looking bank-notes, their hard-earned all, for the flour which was to be the sole food of wife and babes through the long winter, that these hoarded treasures were valueless as the ragged paper which wrapped them! Can we blame them if they cursed in their agony, the soul-less wretches who had thus drained their best blood for the furtherance of their own schemes of low ambition? Can we wonder that the poor, feeling such wrongs as these, learn to hate the rich, and to fancy them natural enemies?

Could one of these heart-wrung beings have been introduced, just as he was, with the trembling yet in his heart, and the curses on his lips, into the gilded saloon of his betrayer, methinks the dance would have flagged, the song wavered, the wine palled, for the moment at least.

Light is the dance and doubly sweet the lays
When for the dear delight another pays—

But the uninvited presence of the involuntary pay-master, would have
been "the hand on the wall" to many a successful (!) banker.

After public indignation had in some measure subsided, and indeed
such occurrences as I have described became too common to stir the
surface of society very rudely, Mr. Harley Rivers returned to Montacute,
and prepared at once for the removal of his family. I took leave of his wife
with most sincere regret, and I felt at the time as if we should never meet
again. But I have heard frequently from them until quite lately; and they
have been living very handsomely (Mr. Rivers always boasted that he *would*
live like a gentleman) in one of the Eastern cities on the spoils of the
Tinkerville Wild-cat.

CHAPTER XXXIII

I say the pulpit, (and I name it, filled
With solemn awe, that bids me well beware
With what intent I touch that holy thing.)
    —Cowper[1]

ONE of the greatest deficiencies and disadvantages of the settler in the new
world, is the lack of the ordinary means of public religious instruction.
This is felt, not only when the Sabbath morn recurs without its call for
public worship, and children ask longingly for that mild and pleasing form
of religious and moral training, to which they are all attached as if by an
intuition of nature; but it makes itself but too evident throughout the
entire structure and condition of society. Those who consider Religion a
gloom and a burden, have only to reside for a while where Religion is
habitually forgotten or wilfully set aside. They will soon learn at least to
appreciate the practical value of the injunction, "Forsake not the assem-
bling of yourselves together."

We have never indeed been entirely destitute for any length of time
of the semblance of public worship. Preachers belonging to various denominations have, from the beginning, occasionally called meetings in the
little log school-house, and many of the neighbours always make a point of

being present, although a far greater proportion reserve the Sunday for fishing and gunning. And it must be confessed that there has generally been but little that was attractive in the attempts at public service. A bare, cold room, the wind whistling through a thousand crevices in the unplastered walls, and pouring down through as many more in the shrunken roof, seats formed by laying rough boards on rougher blocks, and the whole covered thick with the week's dirt of the district school; these are scarcely the appliances which draw the indolent, the careless, the indifferent, the self-indulgent, to the house of worship. And the preacher, "the messenger of Heaven," "the legate of the skies,"[2]—Alas! I dare not trust my pen to draw the portraits of *some* of these well-meaning, but most incompetent persons. I can only say that a large part of them seem to me grievously to have mistaken their vocation.

"All are not such." We have occasionally a preacher whose language and manner, though plain, are far from being either coarse or vulgar, and whose sermons, though generally quite curious in their way, have nothing that is either ridiculous or disgusting. If we suffer ourselves to be driven from the humble meeting-house by one preacher with the dress and air of a horse-jockey, who will rant and scream till he is obliged to have incessant recourse to his handkerchief to dry the tears which are the natural result of the excitement into which he has lashed himself, we may perhaps lose a good plain practical discourse from another, who with only tolerable worldly advantages, has yet studied his Bible with profit, and offers with gentle persuasiveness its message of mercy. Yet to sit from two to three hours trying to listen to the blubberer, is a trial of one's nerves and patience which is almost too much to ask; greater I confess, than I am often willing to endure, well convinced as I am, that the best good of all, requires the support of some form of public worship.

I have often been a little amused not only at the very characteristic style of the illustrations which are freely made use of, by all who are in the habit of preaching in the new settlements, but at the extreme politeness with which certain rather too common classes of sins, are touched upon by these pioneers among us. They belong to various denominations, and they are well aware that a still greater number of differing sects are represented in their audience; and each is naturally desirous to secure as many adherents as possible to his own view of religious truth. It becomes therefore particularly necessary to avoid giving personal offence. Does the speaker wish to show the evils and penalties of Sabbath-breaking, of profanity, of falsehood, of slander, of dishonest dealings, or any other offence which he knows is practised by some at least among his auditors, he generally begins with observing that he is quite a stranger, very little acquainted in the neighbourhood, entirely ignorant whether what he is going to say may or may not be especially applicable to any of his hearers, and that he only judges from the general condition of human nature, that such cautions or exhortations may be necessary, &c., exhibiting a constant struggle between his sense of duty and his fear of making enemies.

The illustrative style to which I have alluded, is certainly much better calculated to excite the attention, and keep alive the interest of an un-lettered audience, than the most powerful argument could possibly be, but it is sometimes carried so far that the younger part of the congregation find it hard to maintain the gravity befitting the time. It is not long since I heard a good man preach from the text "Behold how great a matter a little fire kindleth."[3] He began by saying that it could not be necessary to show the literal truth of this observation of the Apostle; "For you yourselves know, my friends, especially at this time of year, when most of you have had to fight fire more or less, how easy it is to kindle what is so difficult to put out. You know that what fire a man can carry in his hand, applied to the dry grass on the marshes, will grow so, that in ten minutes a hundred men could not put it out, and, if you do n't take care, it will burn up your haystacks and your barns too, aye, and your houses, if the wind happens to be pretty strong. And if you get a cannon loaded up with powder, it wont take but a leetle grain of fire to produce a great explosion, and maybe kill somebody. And I dare say that some of you have seen the way they get along in making rail-roads in the winter, when the ground's froze so hard that they can't dig a bit; they blast off great bodies of the hard ground, just as they blast rocks. And it do n't take any more than a spark to set it a-going. Even so, a *woman's tongue,* can set a whole neighbourhood together by the ears, and do more mischief in a minute, than she can undo in a month." At this all the young folks looked at each other and smiled, and as the preacher went on in a similar strain, the smile was frequently repeated; and such scenes are not very uncommon.

It was some little time before we could learn the rules of etiquette which are observed among these itinerant or voluntary preachers. We supposed that if a meeting was given out for Sunday morning at the school-house by a Baptist, any other room might be obtained and occupied at the same hour by a Presbyterian or Methodist, leaving it to the people to chose which they would hear. But this is considered a most ungenerous usurpa-tion, and such things are indignantly frowned upon by all the meeting-goers in the community. If a minister of any denomination has appointed a meeting, no other must preach at the same hour in the neighbourhood; and this singular notion gives rise to much of the petty squabbling and ill-will which torments Montacute as well as other small places.

This is one of the many cases wherein it is easier to waive one's rights than to quarrel for them. I hope, as our numbers increase rapidly, the evil will soon cure itself, since one room will not long be elastic enough to contain all the church-goers.

Of the state of religion, a light work like this affords no fitting opportunity to speak; but I may say that the really devoted Christian can find no fairer or ampler field. None but the truly devoted will endure the difficulties and discouragements of the way. "Pride, sloth, and silken ease," find no favour in the eyes of the fierce, reckless, hard-handed Wolverine. He needs

A preacher such as Paul,
Were he on earth, would hear, approve and own.[4]

Ministers who cannot or will not conform themselves to the manners of the country, do more harm than good. PRIDE is, as I have elsewhere observed, the bug-bear of the western country; and the appearance of it, or a suspicion of it, in a clergyman, not only destroys his personal influence, but depreciates his office.

It takes one a long while to become accustomed to the unceremonious manner in which the meetings of all sorts are conducted. Many people go in and out whenever they feel disposed; and the young men, who soon tire, give unequivocal symptoms of their weariness, and generally walk off with a *nonchalant* air, at any time during the exercises. Women usually carry their babies, and sometimes two or three who can scarcely walk; and the restlessness of these youthful members, together with an occasional display of their musical talents, sometimes interrupts in no small measure the progress of the speaker. The stove is always in the centre of the room, with benches arranged in a hollow square around it; and the area thus formed is the scene of infantile operations. I have seen a dozen people kept on a stretch during a whole long sermon, by a little, tottering, rosy-cheeked urchin, who chose to approach within a few inches of the stove every minute or two, and to fall at every third step, at the imminent danger of lodging against the hot iron. And the mamma sat looking on with an air of entire complacency, picking up the chubby rogue occasionally, and varying the scene by the performance of the maternal office.

I fancy it would somewhat disconcert a city clergym
his sumptuous pulpit, to find it already occupied by a d
his tin ear-trumpet ready to catch every word. This I ha
again; and however embarrassing to the preacher, an obj
strance on the subject would be very ill-received. And after all, I must
confess, I have heard sermons preached in such circumstances, which
would have reflected no disgrace on certain gorgeous draperies of velvet
and gold.

The meliorating influence of the Sunday school is felt here as every-
where else, and perhaps here more evidently than in places where society
is farther advanced. When books are provided, the children flock to obtain
them, with a zest proportioned to the scarcity of those sweeteners of
solitude. Our little Montacute library has been well-thumbed already, by
old and young; and there is nothing I long for so much as a public library of
works better suited to "children of a larger growth."[5] But *"le bon temps
viendra."*[6]

CHAPTER XXXIV

$$\maltese\maltese\maltese\maltese\maltese\maltese$$

There is a cunning which we in England call "the turning of the
cat in the pan;" which is, when that which a man says to another, he
lays it as if another had said it to him.—Bacon

MY NEAR NEIGHBOUR, Mrs. Nippers, whose garden joins ours, and whose
"keepin' room," I regret to say it, looks into my kitchen, was most cruelly
mortified that she was not elected President of the Montacute Female
Beneficent Society. It would have been an office *so* congenial to her character, condition, and habits! 'T was cruel to give it to Mrs. Skinner, "merely,"
as Mrs. Nippers declares, "because the society wanted to get remnants
from the store!"

Mrs. Campaspe Nippers is a widow lady of some thirty-five, or thereabouts, who lives with her niece alone in a small house, in the midst of a
small garden, in the heart of the village. I have never noticed any thing peculiar in the construction of the house. There are not, that I can discover, any
contrivances resembling ears; or those ingenious funnels of sail-cloth
which are employed on board-ship to coax fresh air down between-decks.
Nor are there large mirrors, nor a telescope, within doors, nor yet a *camera*

obscura.[1] I have never detected any telegraphic signals from without. Yet no man sneezes at opening his front door in the morning; no woman sweeps her steps after breakfast; no child goes late to school; no damsel slips into the store; no bottle out of it; no family has fried onions for dinner; no hen lays an egg in the afternoon; no horse slips his bridle; no cow is missing at milking-time; and no young couple after tea; but Mrs. Nippers, and her niece, Miss Artemisia Clinch, know all about it, and tell it to everybody who will listen to them.

A sad rumour was raised last winter, by some spiteful gossip, against a poor woman who had taken lodgers to gain bread for her family; and when Mrs. Nippers found it rather difficult to gain credence for her view of the story, she nailed the matter, as she supposed, by whispering with mysterious meaning, while her large light eyes dilated with energy and enjoyment—"I have myself seen a light there after eleven o'clock at night!"

In vain did the poor woman's poor husband, a man who worked hard, but would make a beast of himself at times, protest that malice itself might let his wife escape; and dare any *man* to come forward and say aught against her. Mrs. Nippers only smiled, and stretched her eye-lids so far apart, that the sky-blue whites of her light-grey eyes were visible both above and below the scarce distinguishable iris, and then looked at Miss Artemisia Clinch with such triumphant certainty; observing, that a drunkard's word was not worth much. It is impossible ever to convince her, in any body's favour.

But this is mere wandering. Association led me from my intent, which was only to speak of Mrs. Nippers as connected with the Montacute Female Beneficent Society. This Association is the prime dissipation of our village, the magic circle within which lies all our cherished exclusiveness, the strong hold of *caste,* the test of gentility, the temple of emulation, the hive of industry, the mart of fashion, and I must add, though reluctantly, the fountain of village scandal, the hot-bed from which springs every root of bitterness among the petticoated denizens of Montacute. I trust the importance of the Society will be enhanced in the reader's estimation, by the variety of figures I have been compelled to use in describing it. Perhaps it would have been enough to have said it is a Ladies' Sewing Society, and so saved all this wordiness; but I like to amplify.

When the idea was first started, by I know not what fortunate individual,—Mrs. Nippers does, I dare say,—this same widow-lady espoused the thing warmly, donned her India-rubbers, and went all over through the sticky mud, breakfasted with me, dined with Mrs. Rivers, took tea with Mrs. Skinner, and spent the intervals and the evening with half-a-dozen other people, not only to recommend the plan, but to give her opinion of how the affair ought to be conducted, to what benevolent uses applied, and under what laws and by-laws; and though last, far from least, who ought to be its *officers*. Five Directresses did she select, two Secretaries, and a Treasurer, Managers and Auditors,—like the military play of my three brothers, who always had "fore-captain," "hind-captain," and "middle-captain," but no privates. But in all this Mrs. Campaspe never once hinted the name of a Lady President. She said, to be sure, that she should be very glad to be of any sort of service to the Society; and that from her position she should be more at leisure to devote time to its business, than almost any other person; and that both herself and her niece had been concerned in a sewing-society in a certain village at "the East," whose doings were often quoted by both ladies, and concluded by inquiring who her hearer thought would be the most suitable president.

In spite of all this industrious canvassing, when the meeting for forming the society took place at Mrs. Skinner's, Mrs. Campaspe Nippers' name was perversely omitted in the animated ballot for dignities. No one said a word, but every one had a sort of undefined dread of so active a member, and, by tacit consent, every office which she had herself contrived, was filled, without calling upon her. Her eyes grew preternaturally pale, and her lips wan as whit-leather, when the result was known; but she did not trust herself to speak. She placed her name on the list of members with as much composure as could be looked for, under such trying circumstances, and soon after departed with Miss Artemisia Clinch, giving a parting glance which seemed to say, with Sir Peter Teazle,[2] "I leave my character behind me."

A pawkie smile dawned on two or three of the sober visages of our village dames, as the all-knowing widow and her submissive niece closed the door, but no one ventured a remark on the killing frost which had fallen upon Mrs. Nippers' anticipated "budding honours," and after agreeing upon a meeting at our house, the ladies dispersed.

The next morning, as I drew my window curtain, to see whether the sun had aired the world enough to make it safe for me to get up to breakfast,—I do not often dispute the *pas* with Aurora,—I saw Mrs. Nippers emerge from the little front door of her tiny mansion, unattended by her niece for a marvel, and pace majestically down Main-street. I watched her in something of her own prying spirit, to see whither she could be going so early; but she disappeared in the woods, and I turned to my combs and brushes, and thought no more of the matter.

But the next day, and the next, and the day after, almost as early each morning, out trotted my busy neighbour; and although she disappeared in different directions—sometimes P.S. and sometimes O.P.—she never returned till late in the afternoon. My curiosity began to be troublesome.

At length came the much-desired Tuesday, whose destined event was the first meeting of the society. I had made preparations for such plain and simple cheer as is usual at such feminine gatherings, and began to think of arranging my dress with the decorum required by the occasion, when about one hour before the appointed time, came Mrs. Nippers and Miss Clinch, and ere they were unshawled and unhooded, Mrs. Flyter and her three children—the eldest four years, and the youngest six months. Then Mrs. Muggles and her crimson baby, four weeks old. Close on her heels, Mrs. Briggs and her little boy of about three years' standing, in a long-tailed coat, with vest and decencies of scarlet circassian. And there I stood in my gingham wrapper, and kitchen apron; much to my discomfiture, and the undisguised surprise of the Female Beneficent Society.

"I always calculate to be ready to begin at the time appointed," remarked the gristle-lipped widow.

"So do I," responded Mrs. Flyter, and Mrs. Muggles, both of whom sat the whole afternoon with baby on knee, and did not sew a stitch.

"What! is n't there any work ready?" continued Mrs. Nippers, with an astonished aspect; "well, I *did* suppose that such smart officers as *we* have, would have prepared all beforehand. We always used to, at the East."

Mrs. Skinner, who is really quite a pattern-woman in all that makes woman indispensable, viz. cookery and sewing, took up the matter quite warmly, just as I slipped away in disgrace to make the requisite reform in my costume.

When I returned, the work was distributed, and the company broken up into little knots or coteries; every head bowed, and every tongue in full play. I took my seat at as great a distance from the sharp widow as might be, though it is vain to think of eluding a person of her ubiquity, and reconnoitred the company who were "done off" (indigenous,) "in first-rate style," for this important occasion. There were nineteen women with thirteen babies—or at least "young 'uns" (indigenous,) who were not above gingerbread. Of these thirteen, nine held large chunks of gingerbread, or dough-nuts, in trust, for the benefit of the gowns of the society; the remaining four were supplied with bunches of maple sugar, tied in bits of rag, and pinned to their shoulders, or held dripping in the fingers of their mammas.

Mrs. Flyter was "slicked up" for the occasion, in the snuff-coloured silk she was married in, curiously enlarged in the back and not as voluminous in the floating part as is the wasteful custom of the present day. Her three immense children, white-haired and blubber-lipped like their amiable parent, were in pink ginghams and blue glass beads. Mrs. Nippers wore her unfailing brown merino, and black apron; Miss Clinch her inevitable scarlet calico; Mrs. Skinner her red merino with baby of the same; Mrs. Daker shone out in her very choicest city finery (where else could she show it, poor thing) and a dozen other Mistresses shone in their "'tother gowns," and their tamboured collars. Mrs. Doubleday's pretty black-eyed Dolly was neatly stowed in a small willow-basket, where it lay looking about with eyes full of sweet wonder, behaving itself with marvellous quietness and discretion, as did most of the other little torments, to do them justice.

Much consultation, deep and solemn, was held as to the most profitable kinds of work to be undertaken by the society. Many were in favour of making up linen, cotton linen of course, but Mrs. Nippers assured the company that shirts never used to sell well at the East, and she was therefore perfectly certain that they would not do here. Pincushions and such like feminilities were then proposed; but at these Mrs. Nippers held up both hands, and showed a double share of blue-white around her eyes. Nobody about here needed pincushions, and besides where should we get the materials? Aprons, capes, caps, collars, were all proposed with the same ill success. At length Mrs. Doubleday, with an air of great deference, inquired what Mrs. Nippers would recommend.

The good lady hesitated a little at this. It was more her forte to object to other people's plans, than to suggest better; but after a moment's consideration she said she should think fancy-boxes, watch-cases, and alum-baskets would be very pretty.

A dead silence fell on the assembly, but of course it did not last long. Mrs. Skinner went on quietly cutting out shirts, and in a very short time furnished each member with a good supply of work, stating that any lady might take work home to finish if she liked.

Mrs. Nippers took her work and edged herself into a coterie of which Mrs. Flyter had seemed till then the magnet. Very soon I heard, "I declare it's a shame!" "I don't know what'll be done about it;" "She told me so with her own mouth;" "Oh but I was there myself!" etc. etc., in many different voices; the interstices well filled with undistinguishable whispers "not loud but deep."

It was not long before the active widow transferred her seat to another corner;—Miss Clinch plying her tongue, not her needle, in a third. The whispers and the exclamations seemed to be gaining ground. The few silent members were inquiring for more work.

"Mrs. Nippers has the sleeve! Mrs. Nippers, have you finished that sleeve?"

Mrs. Nippers coloured, said "No," and sewed four stitches. At length "the storm grew loud apace." "It will break up the society——"

"What *is* that?" asked Mrs. Doubleday, in her sharp treble. "What is it, Mrs. Nippers? *You* know all about it."

Mrs. Nippers replied that she only knew what she had heard, etc. etc., but, after a little urging, consented to inform the company in general, that there was great dissatisfaction in the neighbourhood; that those who lived in *log-houses* at a little distance from the village, had not been invited to join the society; and also that many people thought twenty-five cents quite too high, for a yearly subscription.

Many looked aghast at this. Public opinion is no-where so strongly felt as in this country, among new settlers. And as many of the present company still lived in log-houses, a tender string was touched.

At length, an old lady who had sat quietly in a corner all the afternoon, looked up from behind the great woollen sock she was knitting—

"Well now! that's queer!" said she, addressing Mrs. Nippers with an air of simplicity simplified. "Miss Turner told me you went round her neighbourhood last Friday, and told how that Miss Clavers and Miss Skinner despised every body that lived in log-houses; and you know you told Miss Briggs that you thought twenty-five cents was too much; did n't she, Miss Briggs?" Mrs. Briggs nodded.

The widow blushed to the very centre of her pale eyes, but, "e'en though vanquished,"[3] she lost not her assurance. "Why, I'm sure I only said that we only paid twelve-and-a-half cents at the East; and as to log-houses, I do n't know, I can't just recollect, but I did n't say more than others did."

But human nature could not bear up against the mortification; and it had, after all, the scarce credible effect of making Mrs. Nippers sew in silence for some time, and carry her colours at half-mast for the remainder of the afternoon.

At tea each lady took one or more of her babies into her lap and much grabbing ensued. Those who wore calicoes seemed in good spirits and appetite, for green tea at least, but those who had unwarily sported silks and other unwashables, looked acid and uncomfortable. Cake flew about at a great rate, and the milk and water which ought to have gone quietly down sundry juvenile throats, was spurted without mercy into various wry faces. But we got through. The astringent refreshment produced its usual crisping effect upon the vivacity of the company. Talk ran high upon almost all Montacutian themes.

"Do you have any butter now?" "When are you going to raise your barn?" "Is your man a going to kill, this week?" "I ha' n't seen a bit of meat these six weeks." "Was you to meetin' last Sabbath?" "Has Miss White got any wool to sell?" "Do tell if you 've been to Detroit!" "Are you out o' candles?" "Well I *should* think Sarah Teals wanted a new gown!" "I hope we shall have milk in a week or two," and so on; for, be it known, that in a state of society like ours, the bare necessaries of life are subjects of sufficient interest for a good deal of conversation. More than one truly respectable woman of our neighbourhood has told me, that it is not very many years since a moderate allowance of Indian meal and potatoes, was literally all that fell to their share of this rich world for weeks together.

"Is your daughter Isabella well?" asked Mrs. Nippers of me solemnly, pointing to little Bell who sat munching her bread and butter, half asleep, at the fragmentious table.

"Yes, I believe so, look at her cheeks."

"Ah yes! it was her cheeks I was looking at. They are so *very* rosy. I have a little niece who is the very image of her. I never see Isabella without thinking of Jerushy; and Jerushy is most dreadfully scrofulous!"

Satisfied at having made me uncomfortable, Mrs. Nippers turned to Mrs. Doubleday, who was trotting her pretty babe with her usual proud fondness.

"Do n't you think your baby breathes rather strangely?" said the tormentor.

"Breathes! how!" said the poor thing, off her guard in an instant.

"Why rather croupish, I think, if *I* am any judge. I have never had any

children of my own to be sure, but I was with Mrs. Green's baby when it
died, and—

"Come, we 'll be off!" said Mr. Doubleday, who had come for his
spouse. "Do n't mind the envious vixen"—aside to his Polly.

Just then, somebody on the opposite side of the room happened to
say, speaking of some cloth affair, "Mrs. Nippers says it ought to be
sponged."

"Well, sponge it then, by all means," said Mr. Doubleday, "nobody
else knows half as much about sponging;" and with wife and baby in tow,
off walked the laughing Philo, leaving the widow absolutely transfixed.

"What *could* Mr. Doubleday mean by that?" was at length her indignant exclamation.

Nobody spoke.

"I am sure," continued the crest-fallen Mrs. Campaspe, with an
attempt at a scornful giggle, "I am sure if any body understood him, I
would be glad to know what he *did* mean."

"Well now, I can tell you;" said the same simple old lady in the
corner, who had let out the secret of Mrs. Nippers' morning walks. "Some
folks calls that *sponging,* when you go about getting your dinner here and
your tea there, and sich like; as you know you and Meesy there does. That
was what he meant I guess." And the old lady quietly put up her knitting,
and prepared to go home.

There have been times when I have thought that almost any degree of
courtly duplicity would be preferable to the *brusquerie* of some of my
neighbours: but on this occasion I gave all due credit to a simple and
downright way of stating the plain truth. The scrofulous hint probably
brightened my mental and moral vision somewhat.

Mrs. Nippers' claret cloak and green bonnet, and Miss Clinch's ditto
ditto, were in earnest requisition, and I do not think either of them spent a
day out that week.

CHAPTER XXXV

We will rear new homes under trees which glow
As if gems were the fruitage of every bough;
O'er our white walls we will train the vine
And sit in its shadow at day's decline.
    —Mrs. Hemans

Alas! they had been friends in youth
But whispering tongues will poison truth.
. . . .
They stood aloof, the scars remaining,—
A dreary sea now flows between.
    —Coleridge, *Christabel* [1]

MANY ENGLISH FAMILIES reside in our vicinity, some of them well calculated to make their way any where; close, penurious, grasping and
indefatigable; denying themselves all but the necessaries of life, in order to
add to their lands, and make the most of their crops; and somewhat apt in
bargaining to overreach even the wary pumpkin-eaters, their neighbours;
others to whom all these things seem so foreign and so unsuitable, that one
cannot but wonder that the vagaries of fortune should have sent them into
so uncongenial an atmosphere. The class last mentioned, generally live
retired, and show little inclination to mingle with their rustic neighbours;
and of course, they become at once the objects of suspicion and dislike.
The principle of "let-a-be for let-a-be" holds not with us. Whoever exhibits any desire for privacy is set down as "praoud," or something worse;
no matter how inoffensive, or even how benevolent he may be; and of all
places in the world in which to live on the shady side of public opinion, an
American back-woods settlement is the very worst, as many of these unfortunately mistaken emigrants have been made to feel.

The better classes of English settlers seem to have left their own
country with high-wrought notions of the unbounded freedom to be enjoyed in this; and it is with feelings of angry surprise that they learn after a
short residence here, that this very universal freedom abridges their own
liberty to do as they please in their individual capacity; that the absolute
democracy which prevails in country places, imposes as heavy restraints

upon one's free-will in some particulars, as do the over-bearing pride and haughty distinctions of the old world in others; and after one has changed one's whole plan of life, and crossed the wide ocean to find a Utopia, the waking to reality is attended with feelings of no slight bitterness. In some instances within my knowledge these feelings of disappointment have been so severe as to neutralize all that was good in American life, and to produce a degree of sour discontent which increased every real evil and went far towards alienating the few who were kindly inclined toward the stranger.

I ever regarded our very intelligent neighbours the Brents, as belonging to the class who have emigrated by mistake, they seemed so well-bred, so well-off, so amiable and so unhappy. They lived a few miles from us, and we saw them but seldom, far less frequently than I could have wished, for there were few whose society was so agreeable. Mr. Brent was a handsome, noble-looking man of thirty or perhaps a little more, well-read, and passionately fond of literary pursuits; no more fit to be a Michigan farmer than to figure as President of the Texan republic; and his wife a gentle and timid woman, very dependent and very lovely, was as ill fitted to bear the household part of a farmer's lot. But all this seemed well-arranged, for the farm was managed "on shares" by a stout husband-man and his family, tolerably honest and trustworthy people as times go; and Mr. Brent and his pale and delicate Catherine disposed of their hours as they thought proper; not however without many secret and some very audible surmises and wonderings on the part of their immediate neighbours, which were duly reported, devoutly believed, and invariably added to, in the course of their diffusion in Montacute.

I might repeat what I heard at a Montacute tea-party; I might give Mrs. Flyter's views of the probable duration of Mr. Brent's means of living on the occasion of having learned from Mrs. Holbrook that Mrs. Brent did not see to the butter-making, and had never milked a cow in her life. I might repeat Mrs. Allerton's estimate of the cost of Mrs. Brent's dress at meeting on a certain Sunday. But I shall only tell what Mrs. Nippers said, for I consider her as unimpeachable authority in such matters. Her decided and solemn assertion was that Mrs. Brent was jealous.

"Jealous of whom?"

"Why of Mr. Brent to be sure!"

"But it is to be supposed that there is somebody else concerned."

"Ah yes! but I do n't know. Mrs. Barton did n't know."

"Oh, it was Mrs. Barton who told you then."

Mrs. Nippers had declined giving her authority, and Mrs. Barton was the wife of Mr. Brent's farmer. So she coloured a little, and said that she did not wish it repeated, as Mrs. Barton had mentioned it to her in confidence. But since it *had* come out by mere chance, she did n't know but she might just as well tell that Mrs. Barton was sure that Mrs. Brent was jealous of somebody in England, or somebody that was dead, she did n't know which. She hoped that none of the ladies would mention it.

There were some fourteen or so in company, and they had not yet had tea. After tea the poor Brents were completely "used up," to borrow a phrase much in vogue with us, and the next day I was not much surprised at being asked by a lady who made me a three hours' morning call beginning at nine o'clock, if I had heard that Mr. and Mrs. Brent were going to "part."

I declared my ignorance of any thing so terrible, and tried to trace back the news, but it must have passed through several able hands before it came to me.

We rode over to see the Brents that afternoon, found them as usual, save that Mrs. Brent seemed wasting, but she always declared herself quite well; and her husband, whose manner towards her is that of great tenderness, yet not exactly that of husbands in general, a little constrained, was reading aloud to her as she lay on the sofa. They seemed pleased to see us, and promised an afternoon next week, to meet "a few friends,'—that is the term, I believe,—but not Mrs. Nippers.

Among those whom I invited to partake our strawberries and cream on the occasion, were Mr. Cathcart and his beautiful wife, English neighbours from a little vine-clad cottage on the hill west of our village; much older residents than the Brents, who had not yet been a year in our vicinity. Mrs. Cathcart is one of the most beautiful women I have ever seen, and certainly a very charming one in all respects, at least to me, who do not dislike a good share of spirit and energy in a lady. Her spouse, though far different, has his good points, and can make himself agreeable enough when he is in the humour; which sometimes occurs, though not often. He is at least twenty years older than his lady, and as ugly as she is handsome, and horribly jealous, I say it myself, of every thing and every body which or whom Mrs. Cathcart may chance to look at or speak to, or take an interest in, gentle or simple, animate or inanimate. It is really pitiable sometimes to see the poor man grin in the effort to suppress the overboiling of his wrath, for he is a very polite person, and generally says the most disagreeable things with a smile.

These neighbours of ours are persons of taste—taste in pictures, in music, in books, in flowers; and thus far they are well mated enough. But there are certain glances and tones which betray to the most careless observer that there *are* points of difference, behind the scenes at least; and little birds have whispered that after Mrs. Cathcart had spent the morning in transplanting flowers, training her honeysuckles and eglantines, and trimming the turf seats which are tastefully disposed round their pretty cottage, Mr. Cathcart has been seen to come out and destroy all she had been doing; ploughing up the neat flower-beds with his knife, tearing down the vines, and covering the turf sofas with gravel. And the same little birds have added, that when Mr. Cathcart, sated with mischief, turned to go into the house again, he found the front-door fastened, and then the back-door fastened; and after striding about for some time till his bald head was well nigh fried, he was fain to crawl in at the little latticed window, and then—but further these deponents say not.

Well! our little strawberry party was to consist of these English neighbours and some others, and I made due provision of the fragrant rubies, and all the et-ceteras of a rural tea-visit. Roses of all hues blushed in my vases—a-hem! they were not pitchers, for the handles were broken off,—and forests of asparagus filled the fire-place. Alice and Arthur figured in their Sundays, little Bell had a new calico apron, and Charlie a shining clean face; so we were all ready.

First of all came the Cathcarts, and their one only and odd son of three years old; a child who looked as old as his father, and walked and talked most ludicrously like him. It did seem really a pity that the uncommonly fine eyes of his beautiful mamma had not descended to him; those large-pupilled grey eyes, with their long black lashes! and her richest of complexions, brighter in bloom and contrast than the sunniest side of a ripe peach; and her thousand graces of face and person. But there he was, a frightful little dwarf, just what his father would seem, looked at through a reversed telescope, or in a convex mirror. And Mr. Cathcart was all smiles and politeness, and brought a whole pocket full of literary novelties lately received from "home." And Mrs. Cathcart, always charming, looked lovelier than usual, in a pale-coloured silk and very delicate ornaments.

She was sitting at the piano, playing some brilliant waltzes for the children, and Mr. Cathcart looking over some New-York papers which lay on the table, when Mrs. Brent, wan and feeble as usual, glided into the room. I introduced her to my guests, with whom she was evidently unacquainted, and in the next moment Mr. Brent entered.

A New Home, Who'll Follow?

It needed but one glance to convince me that, to Mrs. Cathcart at least, there was no occasion to introduce the latest comer. She half rose from her seat, painful blushes overspread her beautiful countenance, and instantly subsiding left it deathly pale, while Mr. Brent seemed equally discomposed, and Mr. Cathcart gazed in undisguised and most angry astonishment. I went through with the ceremony of presentation as well as I could, awkwardly enough, and an embarrassed pause succeeded, when in walked Mrs. Nippers and Miss Clinch.

"Well, good folks," said the widow, fanning herself with a wide expanse of turkeys' feathers, which generally hung on her arm in warm weather; "this is what you may call toiling for pleasure. Mrs. Cathcart, how *do* you manage to get out in such melting weather? Well! I declare you *do* all look as if you *was* overcome by the weather or something else!" and she laughed very pleasantly at her own wit.

"Warm or cool, I believe we had better return home, Mrs. Cathcart," said her amiable spouse with one of his ineffable grins. She obeyed mechanically, and began putting her own straw bonnet on little Algernon.

"I declare," said the agreeable Mrs. Campaspe, "I thought—I was in hopes you were going to stay, and we could have had such a nice sociable time;" for Mrs. Nippers was very fond of inviting company—to other people's houses.

"No, Madam!" said Mr. Cathcart, "we must go instantly. Fanny, what are you doing? Can't you tie the child's hat?"

"One word, Sir!" said Mr. Brent, whose fine countenance had undergone a thousand changes in the few moments which have taken so many lines in telling; and he stepped into the garden path, with a bow which Mr. Cathcart returned very stiffly. He followed, however, and, in less than one minute, returned, wished us a very good day with more than the usual proportion of smiles—rather grinnish ones, 'tis true; but very polite; and almost lifting his trembling wife into the vehicle, which still stood at the gate, drove off at a furious rate.

And how looked the pale and gentle Catherine during this brief scene? As one who feels the death-stroke; like a frail blighted lily.

> And beside her stood in silence
> One with a brow as pale,
> And white lips rigidly compress'd
> Lest the strong heart should fail.

"Your ride has been too much for you, Mrs. Brent," said I; "you must rest awhile;" and I drew her into a small room adjoining the parlour, to avoid the industrious eyes of Mrs. Nippers.

She spoke not, but her eyes thanked me, and I left her, to receive other guests. Mrs. Nippers made a very faint move to depart when she began to perceive that company had been invited.

"Remain to tea, Mrs. Nippers," I said,—could one say less,—and she simpered, and said she was hardly decent, but—and added in a stage-whisper, "If you could lend me a smart cap and cape, I do n't know but I would." So she was ushered in due form to my room, with unbounded choice in a very narrow circle of caps and capes, and a pair of thin shoes, and then clean stockings, were successively added as decided improvements to her array. And when she made her appearance in the state-apartments, she looked, as she said herself, "pretty scrumptious;" but took an early opportunity to whisper, "I did n't know where you kept your pocket-handkerchiefs." So Alice was despatched for one, and the lady was complete.

Mr. Brent, with Bella in his arms, paced the garden walk, pretending to amuse the child, but evidently agitated and unhappy.

"Did you ever see any thing so odd?" whispered Mrs. Nippers, darting a glance toward the garden.

But, fortunately, the person honoured by her notice was all unconscious; and happening to observe his wife as he passed the low window in the little west-room, he stopped a few moments in low and earnest conversation with her. It was not long before Mrs. Brent appeared, and, apologizing with much grace, said, that feeling a little better, she would prefer returning home. I took leave of her with regretful presentiments.

In less than a week, Mrs. Nippers had more than she could attend to. The Brents had left the country, and Mrs. Cathcart was alarmingly ill. The unfortunate strawberry-party so unexpectedly marred by this *rencontre,* was the theme of every convention within five miles, to speak moderately; and by the time the story reached home again, its own mother could not have recognized it.

A letter from Mr. Brent to say farewell and a little more, gave us in few words the outlines of a sad story; and while all Montacute is ringing with one of which not the smallest particular is lacking, I am not at liberty to disclose more of the "OWRE TRUE TALE," than the reader will already have conjectured—"a priory 'tachment."

The way Mrs. Nippers rolls up her eyes when the English are mentioned is certainly "a caution."

CHAPTER XXXVI

Away with these! true wisdom's world will be
Within its own creation, or in thine,
Maternal Nature! ***
Are not the mountains, waves and skies a part
Of me and of my soul, as I of them?
Is not the love of these deep in my heart
With a pure passion?
    —*Childe Harold,* Canto III [1]

WHEN we first took our delighted abode in the "framed house," a palace of some twenty by thirty feet, flanked by a shanty kitchen, and thatched with oak shingles,—a sober neighbour, who having passed most of his life in the country, is extremely philosophical on the follies of civilization, took my husband to task on the appearance of the ghost of a departed parlour carpet, which he was was "introducing luxury." Whether from this bad example, I cannot tell, but it is certain that our neighbours are many of them beginning to perceive that carpets "save trouble." Women are the most reasonable beings in the world; at least, I am sure nobody ever catches a woman without an unanswerable reason for anything she wishes to do. Mrs. Micah Balwhidder only wanted a silver tea-pot, because, as all the world knows, tea tastes better out of silver; and Mrs. Primrose loved her crimson paduasoy, merely because her husband had happened to say it became her.

Of the mingled mass of our country population, a goodly and handsome proportion—goodly as to numbers, and handsome as to cheeks and lips, and thews and sinews, consists of young married people just beginning the world; simple in their habits, moderate in their aspirations, and hoarding a little of old-fashioned romance, unconsciously enough, in the secret nooks of their rustic hearts. These find no fault with their bare loggeries. With a shelter and a handful of furniture they have enough. If there is the wherewithal to spread a warm supper for "th' old man" when

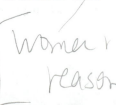

he comes in from work, the young wife forgets the long, solitary, *wordless* day, and asks no greater happiness than preparing it by the help of such materials and such utensils as would be looked at with utter contempt in a comfortable kitchen; and then the youthful pair sit down and enjoy it together, with a zest that the *"orgies parfaites"* of the epicure can never awaken. What lack they that this world can bestow? They have youth, and health, and love and hope, occupation and amusement, and when you have added "meat, clothes, and fire," what more has England's fair young queen? These people are contented, of course.

There is another class of settlers neither so numerous nor so happy; people, who have left small farms in the eastward states, and come to Michigan with the hope of acquiring property at a more rapid rate. They have sold off, perhaps at considerable pecuniary disadvantage the home of their early married life; sacrificed the convenient furniture which had become necessary to daily comfort, and only awake when it is too late, to the fact that it kills old vines to tear them from their clinging-places. These people are much to be pitied, the women especially.

The ladies first
'Gin murmur—as becomes the softer sex.[2]

Woman's little world is overclouded for lack of the old familiar means and appliances. The husband goes to his work with the same axe or hoe which fitted his hand in his old woods and fields, he tills the same soil, or perhaps a far richer and more hopeful one—he gazes on the same book of nature which he has read from his infancy, and sees only a fresher and more glowing page; and he returns to his home with the sun, strong in heart and full of self-gratulation on the favourable change in his lot. But he finds the homebird drooping and disconsolate. *She* has been looking in vain for the reflection of any of the cherished features of her own dear fire-side. She has found a thousand deficiencies which her rougher mate can scarce be taught to feel as evils. What cares he if the time-honoured cupboard is meagerly represented by a few oak-boards lying on pegs and called shelves? His tea-equipage shines as it was wont—the biscuits can hardly stay on the brightly glistening plates. Will he find fault with the clay-built oven, or even the tin "reflector?" His bread never was better baked. What does he want with the great old cushioned rocking-chair? When he is tired he goes to bed, for he is never tired till bed-time. Women are the grumblers in Michigan, and they have some apology. Many of them have made sacrifices for which they were not at all prepared, and which detract largely from their every day stores of comfort. The conviction of good accruing on a large scale does not prevent the wearing sense of minor deprivations.

Another large class of emigrants is composed of people of broken fortunes, or who have been unsuccessful in past undertakings. These like or dislike the country on various grounds, as their peculiar condition may vary. Those who are fortunate or industrious look at their new home with a kindly eye. Those who learn by experience that idlers are no better off in Michigan than elsewhere, can find no terms too virulent in which to express their angry disappointment. The profligate and unprincipled lead stormy and uncomfortable lives any where; and Michigan, *now* at least, begins to regard such characters among her adopted children, with a stern and unfriendly eye, so that the few who may have come among us, hoping for the unwatched and unbridled license which we read of in regions nearer to the setting sun, find themselves marked and shunned as in the older world.

As women feel sensibly the deficiencies of the "salvage" state, so they are the first to attempt the refining process, the introduction of those important nothings on which so much depends. Small additions to the more delicate or showy part of the household gear are accomplished by the aid of some little extra personal exertion. "Spinning-money" buys a looking-glass perhaps, or "butter-money" a nice cherry table. Eglantines and wood-vine, or wild-cucumber, are sought and transplanted to shade the windows. Narrow beds round the house are bright with Balsams and Sweet Williams, Four o'clocks, Poppies and Marigolds; and if "th' old man" is good natured, a little gate takes the place of the great awkward *bars* before the door. By and bye a few apple-trees are set out; sweet briars grace the door yard, and lilacs and currant-bushes; all by female effort—at least I have never yet happened to see it otherwise where these improvements have been made at all. They are not all accomplished by her own hand indeed, but hers is the moving spirit, and if she do her "spiriting gently," and has anything but a Caliban[3] for a minister, she can scarcely fail to throw over the real homeliness of her lot something of the magic of that IDEAL which has been truly sung—

> Nymph of our soul, and brightener of our being;
> She makes the common waters musical—
> Binds the rude night-winds in a silver thrall,
> Bids Hybla's thyme and Tempe's violet dwell
> Round the green marge of her moon-haunted cell.

This shadowy power, or power of shadows is the "arch-vanquisher of time and care" every where; but most of all needed in the waveless calm of a strictly wood-land life, and there most enjoyed. The lovers of "un-written poetry" may find it in the daily talk of our rustic neighbours—in their superstitions—in the remedies which they propose for every ill of human-ity, the ideal makes the charm of their life as it does that of all the world's, peer and poet, wood-cutter and serving-maid.

After allowing due weight to the many disadvantages and trials of a new-country life, it would scarce be fair to pass without notice the com-pensating power of a feeling, inherent as I believe, in our universal nature, which rejoices in that freedom from the restraints of pride and ceremony which is found only in a new country. To borrow from a brilliant writer of our own, "I think we have an instinct, dulled by civilization, which is like the caged eaglet's, or the antelope's that is reared in the Arab's tent; an instinct of nature that scorns boundary and chain; that yearns to the free desert; that would have the earth like the sky, unappropriated and open; that rejoices in immeasurable liberty of foot and dwelling-place, and springs passionately back to its freedom, even after years of subduing method and spirit-breaking confinement!"

This "instinct," so beautifully noticed by Willis,[4] is what I would point to as the compensating power of the wilderness. Those who are "to the manor born" feel this most sensibly, and pity with all their simple hearts the walled-up denizens of the city. And the transplanted ones—those who have been used to no forests but "forests of chimneys," though "the parted bosom clings to wonted home," soon learn to think nature no step-mother, and to discover many redeeming points even in the half-wild state at first so uncongenial.

That this love of unbounded and *unceremonious* liberty is a natural and universal feeling, needs no argument to show; I am only applying it on a small scale to the novel condition in which I find myself in the woods of Michigan. I ascribe much of the placid contentment, which seems the heritage of rural life, to the constant familiarity with woods and waters—

> All that the genial ray of morning gilds,
> And all that echoes to the song of even;
> All that the mountain's sheltering bosom yields,
> And all the dread magnificence of heaven—

To the harmony which the Creator has instituted between the animate and inanimate works of His hands.

Authorities crowd upon me, and I must be allowed to close my chapter with a favourite paragraph from Hazlitt.[5]

"The heart reposes in greater security on the immensity of nature's works, expatiates freely there, and finds elbow-room and breathing-space. We are always at home with Nature. There is neither hypocrisy, caprice, nor mental reservation in her favours. Our intercourse with her is not liable to accident or change, suspicion or disappointment: she smiles on us still the same. ** In our love of Nature, there is all the force of individual attachment, combined with the most airy abstraction. It is this circumstance which gives that refinement, expansion and wild interest to feelings of this sort. ** Thus Nature is a sort of universal home, and every object it presents to us an old acquaintance, with unaltered looks; for there is that constant and mutual harmony among all her works—one undivided spirit pervading them throughout—that to him who has well acquainted himself with them, they speak always the same well-known language, striking on the heart amidst unquiet thoughts and the tumult of the world, like the music of one's native tongue, heard in some far-off country."

CHAPTER XXXVII

Per mezz' i boschi inospiti e selvaggi
Onde vanno a gran rischio uomini, ed arme
Vo secur' io; che non può spaventarme
Altri, che 'l Sol.—
E vo cantando—
Raro un silenzio, un solitario orrore
D' ombrosa selva mai tanto mi piacque.
    —Petrarca, Son. CXLII[1]

A BRIDLE-PATH through the deep woods which lie south-west of our village, had long been a favourite walk on those few days of our Boreal summer, when shade had seemed an essential element of comfort. The forest itself is so entirely cumbered with shrubs and tangled vines, that to effect even a narrow path through it, had been a work of no little time and labour; and as no money was likely to flow in upon us from that direction, I had no fears of a road, but considered the whole as a magnificent *pleasaunce* for the special delight of those who can discern glory and splendour in grass and wild-flowers.

We lacked not carpets, for there was the velvet sward, embroidered with blossoms, whose gemmy tints can never be equalled in Brussels or in Persia; nor canopy, for an emerald dome was over us, full of trembling light, and festooned and tasselled with the starry eglantine, the pride of our Western woods; nor pillars, nor aches; for, oh! beloved forests of my country, where can your far-sounding aisles be matched for grandeur, your "alleys green" for beauty? We had music too, fairy music, "gushes of wild song," soft, sighing murmurs, such as flow from

The convolutions of a smooth-lipped shell,[2]

And recalling, like those other murmurs, the summer swell of the distant ocean; and withal, the sound of a bubbling stream, which was ever and anon sweetly distinct amid the delicate harmony.

Many a dreamy hour have I wandered in this delicious solitude, not "book-bosomed;" for, at such times, my rule is *peu lire, penser beaucoup;*[3] nor yet moralizing, like the melancholy Jaques,[4] on the folly and inconstancy of the world; but just "daundering," to borrow an expression from Mr. Galt;[5] perhaps Fanny Kemble[6] would have said "dawdling;" so I leave the choice with my reader, and make an effort to get on with my story, which seems as much inclined to loiter in my favourite wood as I am myself.

I had never ventured far from Montacute in my strolls with the children, or with my female friends. To say nothing of my sad *pausse,*[7] I hate it in English; but "'tis not half so shocking in French:" not to mention that at all, there are other "lions in the way;" Massasaugas for instance, and Indians, and blue racers, six or eight feet long, and as thick as a man's arm; "harmless," say the initiated, but *j' en doute,*[8] and my prime and practical favourite among mottoes and maxims, is "'ware snakes!" Then toads; but if I once mount a toad, I shall not get back this great while.

It so happened that one morning when the atmosphere was particularly transparent, and the shower-laid earth in delicious order for a ride, I had an invitation from my husband for a stroll—a "splorification" on horseback; and right joyously did I endue myself with the gear proper to such wood-craft, losing not a moment, for once, that I might be ready for my "beautiful Orelio," old Jupiter, when he should come round. We mounted, and sought at once the dim wood of which I have been speaking.

We followed the bridle-path for miles, finding scarcely a trace of human life. We scared many a grey rabbit, and many a bevy of quails, and started at least one noble buck; *I* said two, but may be the same one was all around us, for so it seemed. I took the opportunity of trying old Jupiter's nerves and the woodland echoes, by practising poor Malibran's "Tourment d'Amour,"[9] at the expense of the deepest recess of my lungs, while my companion pretended to be afraid he could not manage Prince, and finally let him go off at half speed. Old Jupiter, he is deaf, I believe, jogged on as before, and I still amused myself by arousing the Dryads, and wondering whether they ever heard a Swiss *refrain* before, when I encountered a sportsman, belted, pouched, gunned, and dogged, quite *comme il faut,* and withal, wearing very much such a face as Adonis must have looked at when he arrayed himself at the fountain.

What an adventure for a sober village matron! I almost think I must have blushed. At least I am sure I must have done so had the affair happened only ten years earlier.

I thought seriously of apologizing to the stranger for singing in the woods, of which he seemed like the tutelar deity; but fortunately Mr. Clavers at this moment returned, and soon engaged him in conversation; and it was not long before he offered to show us a charming variety in the landscape, if we would ride on for a quarter of a mile.

We had been traversing a level tract, which we had supposed lay rather low than high. In a few minutes, we found ourselves on the very verge of a miniature precipice; a bluff which overhung what must certainly have been originally a lake, though it is now a long oval-shaped valley of several miles in extent, beautifully diversified with wood and prairie, and having a lazy, quiet stream winding through it, like—like—"like a snake in a bottle of spirits;" or like a long strip of apple-paring, when you have thrown it over your head to try what letter it will make on the carpet; or like the course of a certain great politician whom we all know. My third attempt hits it exactly, neither of the others was crooked enough.

The path turned short to the right, and began, not far from where we stood, to descend, as if to reach at some distance, and by a wide sweep, the green plain below us. This path looked quite rocky and broken, so much so, that I longed to try it, but my companion thought it time to return home.

"Let me first have the pleasure of shewing you my cottage," said our handsome guide, whose air had a curious mixture of good-breeding with that sort of rustic freedom and abruptness, which is the natural growth of the wilderness. As he spoke he pointed out a path in the wood, which we could not help following, and which brought us in a few minutes to a beautiful opening, looking on the basin below the bluff on one side, and on the deep woods on the other. And there was a long, low, irregularly-shaped house, built of rich brown tamarack logs, nearly new, and looking so rural and lovely that I longed to alight. Every thing about the house was just as handsome and picturesque-looking, as the owner; and still more attractive was the fair creature who was playing with a little girl under the tall oaks near the cottage. She came forward to welcome us with a grace which was evidently imported from some civilized region; and as she drew near, I recognized at once an old school-friend; the very Cora Mansfield who used to be my *daughter* at Mrs. ———'s; at least the dozenth old acquaintance I have met accidentally since we came to the new world.

Mutual introductions of our honoured spouses were now duly per-formed, and we of Montacute did not refuse to alight and make such short tarry with our ten-mile neighbours, as the lateness of the hour permitted. We found the house quite capacious and well-divided, and furnished as neatly though far less ostentatiously than a cottage *ornée* in the vicinity of some great metropolis. There was a great chintz-covered sofa—a very jewel for your siesta—and some well-placed lounges; and in an embayed window draperied with wild vines, a reading-chair of the most luxurious proportions, with its foot-cushion and its prolonged rockers. Neat, com-pact presses, filled with books, new as well as old, and a cabinet piano-forte, made up nearly all the plenishin', but there was enough. The whole was just like a young lady's dream, and Cora and her Thalaba[10] of a hus-band looked just fit to enjoy it.

The contrast was amusing enough when I recalled where I had last seen Cora. It was at a fancy ball at Mrs. L———'s, when she was a little, dimpled, pink-and-silver maid of honour to Mary of Scots, or some such great personage, flitting about like a humming-bird over a honey-suckle, and flirting most atrociously with the half-fledged little beaux who hung on her footsteps. She looked far lovelier in her woodland simplicity, to my simplified eyes at least. She had not, to be sure, a "sweet white dress," with straw-coloured kid-gloves, and a dog tied to a pink ribbon, like "the fair Curranjel," but she wore a rational, home-like, calico—"horrors!" I hear

my lady readers exclaim—aye, a calico, neatly fitted to her beautiful figure; and her darkly-bright eyes beamed not less archly beneath her waving
locks than they had done ———— years before. You did not think I was
going to tell, did you?

Two hundred and forty questions, at a moderate guess, and about
half as many answers, passed between us, while Mr. Hastings—did n't I
say his name was Hastings?—was shewing Mr. Clavers his place. Cora and
I had no leisure for statistics or economics on this our first rencontre. She
rocked the basket cradle with her foot, and told me all about her two little
daughters; and I had a good deal to say of the same sort; and at length,
when superior authority said we could not stay one moment longer, we
cantered off, with promises of reunion, which have since been amply re-
deemed on both sides. And now shall I tell, all in due form, what I have
gathered from Cora's many talks, touching a wild prank of hers? She said I
might, and I will, with the reader's good leave.

CHAPTER XXXVIII

Love sat on a Lotus-leaf afloat,
And saw old Time in his loaded boat;
Slowly he cross'd Life's narrow tide,
While love sat clapping his wings and cried,
                    Who will pass *Time?*

EVERARD HASTINGS, a tall, bright-haired, elegant-looking boy of nineteen, handsome as Antinous, and indolent as—any body on record, left
college with his head as full of romance and as far from any thing like plain,
practical, common-sense views of life and its wearisome cares and its
imperious duties, as any young New-Yorker of his standing; and he very
soon discovered that his charming cousin Cora Mansfield was just the
bewitching little beauty for such a hero to fall shockingly in love with. To
be freed from college restraints and to be deeply in love, were both so
delightful, that Everard "argued sair" to persuade his father not to be in
such haste to immure him in a law-office. He thought his health rather
delicate—exertion certainly did not agree with him. He passed his slender
fingers through the cherished love-locks which had been much his care of

late; looked in the glass and wished he was of age and had finished his studies; and then went and sat the evening with Cora. And though law did not get on very fast, love made up for it by growing wondrously.

His diary in those days, if he had found time to keep a diary, must have run somewhat on this wise:

"Monday morning. Rose at eight. Got to the office about ten, or pretty soon after. Mr. J. looked a little dry. Went with Cora at twelve to see ————'s pictures. Took us a long time. Dined at uncle Phil's—and found all in bed but Pa when I came home.

Tuesday. Overslept. Office at ten, or perhaps a little after. Mr. J. asked me if I was not well. Vexed to think how I coloured as I said "not very." Cora and I were engaged to make a bridal call with Mrs. L. Carriage called for me at the office. Dined at uncle Phil's and went to the theatre with aunt Charlotte and the girls. Cora grows prettier. Henry Tracy says she is handsomer than the great beauty Miss ———— of Boston.

Wednesday. All dined with us, and company in the evening. Did not get to the office at all.

Thursday. Rose early. Walked with the girls on the battery, and breakfasted at uncle Phil's. Felt quite ill. Rising early never did agree with me. Obliged to lie on the sofa and have my forehead bathed with Cologne till it was too late to go to the office. Dined at uncle Phil's, and rode with girls afterwards," &c. &c.

And what were uncle Phil and aunt Charlotte thinking of all this time? Why, that Everard and Cora were but children; and that by-and-bye, when the fitting time should come, a marriage would be just the very thing most agreeable to all concerned.

When spring came—delicious tempting days of warm sun and bright skies, both families prepared for their usual summer flight to their rural palaces on the North River, not far from town; and Everard pleaded so hard for one single summer, or part of a summer, that his father, who was too indulgent by half, gave way and suffered him to postpone his studies; hoping of course that Everard would gain studious habits by sauntering in the woods with his cousins. 'T is pity parents can so seldom stop at the *juste milieu* between weak compliance and severe requisition; but then I should have had no story to tell, so it is better as it is.

"How fond the children are of each other!" said Mrs. Hastings to Mrs. Mansfield.

What parent ever thought that a child had arrived at maturity?

I have heard of an octogenarian who declined staying two days with a relative because he was afraid "the boys" could not get along without him; one of the "boys" a bachelor of fifty, the other a grandfather. But to return.

Wandering one afternoon over the woody hills which make so charming a part of those elegant places on the Hudson, Cora and Everard, by one of those chances which *will* occur, spite of all one can do, were separated from their companions.

"Everard," said the fair girl, stopping short and looking around her with delight, "only see! it seems now as if we were in a lonely wilderness without a single trace of man but this little path. Would n't it be charming if it were really so? if there were nobody within, oh! ever so many miles, but just ourselves—" she stopped and blushed.

"Ah Cora!" said Everard, passionately, "if you only loved me half as well as—" but he had not time to finish, for the little hand which had lain quietly within his arm, was snatched away, leaving the glove behind it, and Cora, running away from her own blushes, was at the river-side quick as lightning.

Love had not blinded Everard's eyes when he called Cora a beauty. She was a beauty, and of the most bewitching style too; with eyes of all sorts of colours, just as she happened to feel, but the fringing lashes were always silky-black, and the eyes seemed so too, to the unconcerned spectator. She might have passed for one of "Spain's dark-glancing daughters," if one looked at her elastic form, and her tiny hands and feet, but her skin was too exquisitely white to warrant the supposition, and besides, she had mind enough in her face to have furnished forth a dozen Senoras.

Imagine such a being, graceful as a sylph, and withal,

Ruby-lipp'd and tooth'd with pearl—

And you have Cora Mansfield before you, as she stood on the beach, every charm heightened by the sudden exertion, and the confusion into which Everard's last speech, (of which I gave only an inkling,) had thrown her.

There had long been a tacit understanding between the young lovers; but after all, the first *words* of love will, whatever may have been the preparation, inevitably overset a woman's philosophy.

Cora was *almost* sixteen, reader, and *thought* herself a woman at least, though her mother—but that's quite another thing.

It was sunset before Everard and Cora found their way back to the house; but they did not stop on the lawn as usual, to talk about the western sky. Cora's little heart throbbed audibly, as a heroine's ought; and as for Everard, he walked with his eyes fixed on the earth, though he thought

155

only of the bright being beside him. Both looked most terribly conscious, but nobody thought of noticing them, and Mrs. Mansfield, whom they found in the parlour, only said, "Cora, child, you are very imprudent to be running about after sunset without your bonnet."

Now Cora did hate, above all other things, to be called "child," and it was quite a comfort to her that evening to reflect, "Mamma would not be always calling me child, if she knew——!"

It was not long before Mamma knew all about it, for there was no motive for concealment, except the extreme youth of the parties. Everard said three years would soon pass away, which is very true, though he did not think so.

I forgot, when I was describing Cora, to say she was even more deeply tinged with romance than Everard himself. She lived entirely in an ideal world. Her mind was her kingdom or her cottage—her ball-room or her dungeon—as the imaginary drama shifted the unities. Everard's reveries had in them nothing defined. There was always a beautiful creature, just like Cora, but the inferior parts of fancy's sketch were usually rather dim. With his fairy mistress the case was different. The first poem her Italian master, the Marquis ————, had put into her hands, had been the Pastor Fido;[1] and the "Care beate selve" of Amaryllis had been ever since the favourite theme of her musings. And then the sweet little enchanting "Isola Disabitata" of Metastasio,[2] proved, just as young ladies like to have things proved—that people, nay, women alone, can live in a wilderness, and even in a desert island; and oh! what a pretty variety of paradises she wove out of these slight materials. She was always herself the happy tenant of a cottage; so happy in herself that even Everard did not always find a place in the dream. She had her books, her needle-work, and her music; a harp of course, or a guitar at the very least; ever-smiling skies and ever-rippling rivulets; the distant murmur of a water-fall, or perhaps a boat upon a deep-shaded lake; and a fair hill-side with some picturesque sheep grazing upon it.

> "No sound of hammer or of saw was there,"[3]

no thought of dinner, no concern about "the wash," no setting of barrels to catch rain-water—oh, dear! only think of coming to Michigan to realize such a dream as that!

CHAPTER XXXIX

Go follow the breeze that flies over the sea,
　Go fasten the rainbow's dyes;
Go whistle the bird from yonder tree,
　Or catch on the wave the sparkles that rise:
This to do thou shalt easier find,
Than to know the thoughts of a woman's mind.

WITH A HEAD full of such fantastic notions, it is hardly surprising that the distant prospect of an old-fashioned wedding—all the aunts and uncles and fifteenth cousins duly invited—a great evening party, and then a stiff setting-up for company—had not many charms for our heroine, and that Everard, almost equally romantic, and *éperdument amoureux,*[1] should have learned to think with his pretty wilful cousin in this as in all other particulars.

He did not at all relish Cora's living so much in these home-made worlds of hers. He sometimes questioned her pretty closely as to particulars, and, I regret to say, was often more jealous than he cared to own, of certain cavaliers who played conspicuous parts in Cora's dramas. She declared they all meant Everard, but he thought some of them but poor likenesses.

He found her one day crying her pretty eyes red, over one of Barry Cornwall's[2] Dramatic Scenes, sweet and touching enough for any body to cry over. It ran thus:—

"There stiff and cold the dark-eyed Guido lay,
His pale face upward to the careless day,
That smiled as it was wont.
　　　　　　And he was found
His young limbs mangled on the rocky ground,
And 'mid the weltering weeds and shallows cold
His dark hair floated, as the phantom told:
And like the very dream, his glassy eye
Spoke of gone mortality!—"

And he took it quite hard of her to weep over a handsome boy, who was not a bit like him. Cora declared he was, and they made quite a pretty quarrel of it.

It must come out at last—I have put it off as long as I decently could, and I am sorry to be obliged to tell it—but this silly young couple in their dreamy folly, concluded that since all the papas and mammas were quite willing they should marry, it could be no great harm if they took the how and the when into their own hands, and carved out for themselves a home in the wilderness, far from law-offices and evening parties, plum-cake and white satin. Accordingly, on pretence of dining with an aunt in town, the imprudent pair were irrevocably joined by a certain reverend gentleman, who used to be very accommodating in that way and the very next evening set out clandestinely for ———, some hundreds of miles west of Albany.

Cora left, all in due form, a note of apology on her dressing-table; placed whatever money and valuables she possessed, in security about her person,—I believe she did not take any particular heroine for a model in these arrangements, but all;—and then prepared to leave her father's house.

Unfortunately nobody was watching. There was no possible excuse for jumping out of the window, but she waited till all were in bed, and then unlocked a door with much care, and let herself out. She felt a sort of pang as she looked back at the house, but the flurry of her spirits scarcely allowed her to be as sentimental as the occasion demanded.

Everard, whose purse had just been replenished by his father's bountiful half-yearly allowance, joined her before she had reached the highroad. He was a shade less thoughtless than his volatile companion, who had been ever a spoiled child, and his heart felt portentously heavy ere they had lost sight of their happy homes.

It was a beautiful moonlight night, somewhere near the middle of July, and a slight shower in the afternoon had rendered the walking delightful. Cora was enchanted: the hour, the scene, the excitement of her romance-ridden brain, conspired to raise her spirits to an extravagant pitch, and to make her forget all that ought to have deterred her from the mad step she was now taking. She only regretted that the whole journey could not be performed on foot; and it was with some difficulty that Everard convinced her of the impracticability of this, her first and darling scheme. It was to have been what my friend Mrs. ——— calls a "predestinarian tower." To be indebted to wheels and boilers for transportation, detracted terribly from the romance of the thing; but she was comforted by the thought that it was only by travelling as rapidly as possible, that they could hope to elude the search which she doubted not would be immediately commenced, by the astonished friends they had left behind.

Cora confessed herself a little weary when they reached the little Dutch tavern where they were to find the carriage which was to bear them to a landing on the river. By some mistake, the carriage had not yet arrived, and the hour which elapsed before it came, was one of feverish anxiety to both. A dreary unfurnished room, lighted by one forlorn little candle, was rather too much for Cora's philosophy. She began to feel terribly sleepy, and, if the truth must be told, wished herself safely in bed at home.

But she would not have lisped such a thing for the world; and to Everard's repeated inquiry, "My dearest Cora, what has become of all your charming spirits? Do you repent already?"—almost hoping she would say, yes,—she still replied,

"No, indeed! Do you think I have so little resolution?"

And she silenced the loud whispers of her better feelings, aided as they were by this temporary depression of spirits, by the consideration that it was now too late to recede; since, although she had found it easy to quit her father's house unnoticed, to re-enter it in the same manner would now be impossible, and to return in the morning was not to be thought of.

The rapid motion of the carriage, and the refreshing air of approaching morning, revived her flagging energies; and they had not proceeded many miles before her fancy had drawn for her one of its brightest pictures, and this soon after subsided into a most fantastically charming dream. In short, she fell asleep, and slept till day-break. At sunrise they found themselves at the landing, and, in the course of half an hour, on board the steamer.

The morning was express. No lovelier sunshine ever encouraged a naughty girl in her naughtiness. A cold rain would have sent her back probably, wilted and humble enough, but this enchanting morning was but too propitious. Cora felt her little heart dilate with pleasure as the boat shot through the foaming waters, and the bugles awakened the mountain echoes. She kept her green silk veil closely drawn, until she had ascertained that all on board were strangers to her; and Everard, who could not adopt the same means of masking his Apollo front, was much relieved at making the same discovery.

A few hours brought them to Albany, and here Everard would gladly have remained a few days; but there was now an anxious restlessness in Cora's heart, which sought relief in rapid motion; and she entreated him to proceed immediately. So he disposed of his watch—for who needs a time-piece in the woods, where there is nothing to do but watch the shadows all day?—and, with much reluctance, of a ring of Cora's; a rich diamond, a splendid birth-day gift from the grandmother who had done Cora the favour to spoil her by every possible indulgence. The jeweller, who, for-tunately for the headlong pair, proved very honest as times go, agreed to receive these articles only in pledge, on being allowed what he called moderate interest for one year, the time he engaged to retain them.

To our wise lovers, the sum now in their possession seemed in-exhaustible. All difficulties seemed at an end, and they set out with all sails filled by this happy raising of the wind. 'T is, after all, a humiliating truth that

Lips, though blooming, must still be fed.

To wander over the woody hills all the morning with—the poet or the novelist whom the reader loves best; to watch the sailing clouds till the sultry noon is past, then linger by the shadowy lake till its bosom begins to purple with day's dying tints, while it fills the soul with dreamy happiness, only makes the unsympathizing body prodigiously hungry; and then to go home, wondering what on earth we can have for dinner, strikes me as a specimen of pungent bathos. But to return.

Cora's desire to perform certain parts of the westward journey on foot, Everard himself bearing the two small valises which now enveloped all their earthly havings;—"some kinds of baseness are nobly under-gone;"—this wish had yielded to that feverish haste, that secret desire to fly from her own pursuing thoughts, to which I have before alluded. So they travelled like common people.

At Utica, Everard purchased a few books; for Cora had not been able to crowd into her travelling basket more than two mignon volumes of her darling Metastasio;[3] and to live in a wilderness without books, was not to be thought of. Robinson Crusoe would have been the most rational pur-chase, but I dare say he did not buy that. Perhaps Atala,[4] perhaps Gertrude of Wyoming,[5] perhaps—but these are only conjectures. For my own part, I should have recommended Buchan's Domestic Medicine, the Frugal Housewife, the Whole Duty of Man,[6] and the Almanac for 18—. But, counselled only by their own fantasies, these sober friends were, I doubt, omitted, in favour of some novels and poetry-books, idle gear at best.

With this reinforcement of "the stuff that dreams are made of," they proceeded; and, after some two or three days' travel, found themselves in a small village, in the south-western part of New-York. Here Cora was content to rest awhile; and Everard employed the time in sundry excursions for the purpose of reconnoitring the face of the country; wishing to ascertain whether it was rocky, and glenny, and streamy enough to suit Cora, whose soul disdained any thing like a level or a clearing.

Ere long he found a spot, so wild and mountainous and woody, as to be considered entirely impracticable by any common-sense settler; so that it seemed just the very place for a forest-home for a pair who had set out to live on other people's thoughts. Cora was so charmed with Everard's description of it, and—whispered be it—so tired of living at the ———— Hotel, that she would not hear of going first to look and judge for herself, but insisted on removing at once, and finding a place to live in afterwards.

CHAPTER XL

Love conceives
No paradise but such as Eden was,
With *two* hearts beating in it.
—Willis, *Bianca Visconti,* Act I. Sc. 1 [1]

ON THE CONFINES of this highland solitude stood a comfortable-looking farm-house, with only the usual complement of sheds and barns; but, on approaching near enough to peep within its belt of maples and elms, a splendid sign was revealed to the delighted eye of the weary traveller, promising "good entertainment for man and beast." Thus invited, Everard and Cora sought admission, and were received with a very civil nod from the portly host, who sat smoking his pipe by the window, "thinking of nothing at all;" at least so said his face, while his great dog lay just outside, ready to bark at customers.

The cognomen of this worthy transplanted Yankee,—the landlord, not the dog,—was, as the sign assured the world, Bildad Gridley; and the very tall, one-eyed "ottomy" who sat knitting by the other window, was addressed by him as "Miss Dart." Mr. Gridley, a widower, in the decline of life, and "Miss Dart," a poor widow, who, in return for a comfortable home, assisted his daughter Arethusa to do "the chores." There was yet another member of the family, Mr. Gridley's son Ahasuerus, but he had not yet appeared. Miss Arethusa was a strapping damsel, in a "two-blues" calico, and a buff gingham cape, with a towering horn comb stuck on the very pinnacle of her head, and a string of gold beads encircling her ample neck.

The arrival of our city travellers, at this secluded public, produced at first quite a sensation. Few passengers, save the weary pedlar, or the spruce retailer of books, clocks, or nutmegs, found their way to these penetralia of Nature. Now and then, indeed, some wandering sportsman, or some college student picturesquing during his fall vacation, or perhaps a party of surveyors, rested for a night at the Moon and Seven Stars; but usually, although those much bedaubed luminaries had given place to "an exact likeness," as said Mr. Gridley, "of Giner'l Lay-Fyette," with his name, as was most meet, in yellow letters below the portrait, the house was as silent as if it had not borne the ambitious title of an inn, and the farming business went on with scarcely an occasional interruption.

But now the aspect of things was materially changed. Everard had signified his desire to remain in so beautiful a spot for a week or two at least, provided Mr. Gridley could board—himself "and—and—this lady," he added, for he could not call Cora his wife, though he tried.

The landlord, with a scrutinizing glance at poor Cora, said he rather guessed he could accommodate them for a spell; and then went to consult the other powers. Our "happy pair," each tormented by an undefined sense of anxiety and conscious wrong, which neither was willing to acknowledge to the other, awaited the return of honest Bildad with a *tremblement de cœur*,[2] which they in vain endeavoured to overcome. At length his jolly visage reappeared, and they were much relieved to hear him say in a more decided tone than before, "Well, sir! I guess we can 'commodate ye."

And here, how I might moralize upon the humbling effects of being naughty, which could make these proud young citizens, who had felt so wondrously well-satisfied with their own dignity and consequence only a week before, now await, with fearful apprehension, the fiat of a plain old farmer, who, after all, was only to board and lodge them. The old gentleman had such a fatherly look, that both Everard and Cora thought of their own papas; and now began to reflect that may be these papas might not after all see the joke in its true light. But neither of them said such a word, and so I shall pass the occasion in silence.

They were shown to a small white-washed room on the second floor, possessing one window, guiltless of the paint brush, now supported by means of that curious notched fixture called a button, so different from the article to which the title of right belongs. A bed adorned with a covering on which the taste of the weaver had expatiated, in the production of innumerable squares and oblongs of blue and white; a very diminutive and exceedingly rickety table stained red; a looking-glass of some eight inches breadth, framed in a strip of gorgeous mahogany, and showing to the charmed gazer a visage curiously elongated cross-wise, with two nondescript chairs, and an old hair trunk, bearing the initials "B. G." described in brass nails on its arched top, constituted the furniture of the apartment.

Cora busied herself in arranging things as well as she could, Mr. Gridley called her "quite a handy young woman, considering she had n't been brought up to nothing;" and while this employment lasted, she managed to maintain a tolerable degree of cheerfulness; but when all was done, and she paused to look around her, such a tide of feelings rushed upon her, that her pride at length gave way, and sitting down on the old trunk, she buried her face in her lap, and burst into a passion of tears.

Everard tried to comfort her as well as he could, but his own heart was overcharged; and after a few ineffectual efforts, he threw himself on the floor at her side, and wept almost as heartily as she did. As soon as his feelings were relieved by this overflowing of nature, he felt heartily ashamed of himself, and lifting Cora to the window, insisted that she should look out upon the glorious prospect which it commanded. She struggled to regain her low seat, that she might indulge to the uttermost this paroxysm of remorse and misgiving; but he pursued his advantage, and held her before the window till the fresh breeze had changed the current of her sad thoughts, and thrown her rich curls into a most becoming confusion; and then, reaching the eight inch mirror, held it suddenly before her still streaming eyes. And now, like true boy and girl, they were both seized with incontrollable laughter, and sat down and enjoyed it to the uttermost.

"How foolish we look," said Cora at length. "Oh, Everard! if mamma—" but at that word her pretty eyes began to fill again, and Everard declared she should not say another word.

"Let us take a walk," said he, "one of your own long rambling walks. You know we have yet to find a spot lovely enough for you to live in." And the volatile girl was all gaiety in a moment.

They were on their return after a very long ramble, when they came to a dell deep enough to make one think of listening to the talkers in

Captain Symmes' world;[3] and this Cora declared to be the very home of her dreams. This and none other should be her "forest sanctuary;"—Qu. What was she flying from?—here should the cottage stand, under whose lowly roof was to be realized, all of bliss that poet ever painted.

> "Mighty shades,
> Weaving their gorgeous tracery over head,
> With the light melting through their high arcades,
> As through a pillar'd cloister's."

Oh? it was *too* delicious! and all the good thoughts took flight again.

CHAPTER XLI

Gon. Here is every thing advantageous to life.
Ant. True, save means to live.
                —*The Tempest* [1]

THAT EVENING after tea, Everard began his negotiations with Mr. Gridley, for the purchase of the much-admired glen.

"Glen!" said honest Bildad, who sat as usual, pipe in mouth, by the front window.

Everard explained.

"Why, Lord bless ye! yes, I own two hundred and seventy-odd acres jist round there; and that 'ere gulf is part on 't. Ahasuerus began to make a clearin' there, but it 's so plaguily lumber'd up with *stuns,* and so kind o' slantin' besides, that we thought it would never pay for ploughin'. So Hazzy has gone to work up north here, and gets along like smoke."

"Would you be willing to sell a small place there?" inquired Everard, who felt inexpressibly sheepish when he set about buying this "stunny" spot.

Mr. Gridley stared at him in unfeigned astonishment.

After a moment's pause, he answered, after the manner of his nation, by asking,

"Why, do you know any body that wants to buy?"

"I have some thoughts of settling here myself," said his guest.

Another stare, and the landlord fell to smoking with all his might, looking withal, full of meditation.

At length—"*You* settle here!" he said; "what for, in all nature?"

"I've taken a fancy to the place," said Everard; "and if you choose to sell, I may perhaps be a purchaser."

"Well!" said the landlord, laying his pipe on the window-sill, "if this aint the queerest—But I'll tell ye what, Mr.————I never can think o' your name; if you really want the place, why, I'll—" but here he stopt again. He fixed his eyes on Everard, as if he would look through his mortal coil.

"There's one thing," proceeded he again, "may I jist be so sa'acy as to ask you—I do n't know as you'd think it a very civil question; but I do n't know as we can get on without it. Are you sure," speaking very deliberately—"are you sure that you're married to this young gal?"

"Married!" said Everard, his fine eyes flashing lightning, while poor Cora, completely humbled, felt ready to sink through the floor, "Married!" he repeated, in high indignation, which an instant's pause served to calm. "I can assure you—I can assure you—"

And he was flying after Cora, who had slipped out of the room, but the good man called him back.

"No 'casion, no 'casion! you say you sartinly are, and that's enough; but ra'ly you and your wife both look so young, that we've been plaguily puzzled what to make on 't."

Everard, deeply mortified, reverted as speedily as possible to his desired purchase; and after a few observations as to the unprofitableness of the scheme, Mr. Gridley concluded, with an air of kindness, which soothed the feelings of his young auditor, "You know your own business best, I dare say; and if so be you are determined upon it, you may have it, and make use of it as long as you like; and I 'spose you wont think o' puttin' up *much* of a house upon sich a place as that, when you are tired on 't, we'll settle the matter one way or 'tother."

Everard readily agreed to this proposition, for he knew himself the avowed heir of the rich bachelor uncle whose name he bore, and he was little concerned about the pecuniary part of his affairs.

And there was a house to be built on a green hill-side in the deep woods; and this *grande opus* fully absorbed our friends until it was completed. In taking possession of it and in arranging the simple requisites which formed its furniture, Cora found herself happier than she had been since she left home. It must be confessed that every day brought its incon-veniences; one can't at first snuff the candle well with the tongs. Here were neither papa's side-boards nor mamma's dressing tables; but there was the charm of *housekeeping,* and every young wife knows what a charm that is, for a year or two at least; and then pride whispered, that whenever papa *did* find them out, he would acknowledge how very well they had managed to be happy in their own way.

After all, it must be confessed, that the fairy-footed Cora nourished in some unexplored nook of her warm little heart, a fund of something which *she* dignified by the names of resolution, firmness, perseverance, &c., but which ill-natured and severe people might perhaps have been disposed to call obstinacy, or self-will. But she was a spoiled child, and her boy-husband the most indulgent of human beings, so we must excuse her if she was a little naughty as well as very romantic. The world's harshness soon cures romance, as well as some other things that we set out with; but Cora had as yet made no acquaintance with the world, that most severe of all teachers.

But no word yet of inquiries from home. No advertisements, no rewards, "no afflicted parents." This was rather mortifying. At length Everard ventured to propose writing to his uncle, and though Cora pre-tended to be quite indifferent, she was right glad to have an excuse for opening a communication with home. But no answer came. The cold winds of autumn turned the maple leaves yellow, then scarlet, then brown, and no letter! The whole face of the earth presented to the appalled eye of the city-bred beauty, but one expanse of mud—deep, tenacious, hopeless mud. No walks either by day or evening; books all read and re-read; no sewing, for small change of dress suffices in the woods; no company but squire Bildad or Mrs. Dart, (the squire's "gal" was teaching school for the winter, and the interesting Hazzy thought Everard "a queer stick to set all day in the house a readin," and did not much affect his society.)

Deep winter, and no word from New-York.

Everard now wrote to his father, the most indulgent of fathers; but though he often saw the name of the well-known firm in a stray news-paper, no notice whatever was taken of his missives. This was a turn of affairs for which he was entirely unprepared. Cora tossed her pretty head, and then cried, and said she did not care, and cried again. But now a new interest arose. The prospect of becoming a mother awakened at once the most intense delight and a terror amounting almost to agony; and Cora at length wrote to her mother.

Spring came and with the flowers a little daughter; and Cora found in the one-eyed, odd-looking widow the kindest and most motherly of nurses, while Mr. Gridley and his family kindly interested in their inexperienced neighbours, were not lacking in aid of any sort. So Cora made out much better than she deserved.

When she was able to venture out, the good squire came with his waggon to fetch her to spend the day by way of change; and Cora most thankfully accepted this and the other kindnesses of her rustic friends. A short residence in the woods modifies most surprisingly one's views on certain points.

Some travellers emigrating to far Michigan, had been resting at Mr. Gridley's when Cora spent her day there, and it was to this unlucky encounter that we must ascribe the sickening of Cora's darling, who was after some days attacked with an alarming eruption. Mrs. Dart declared it the small-pox, and having unfortunately less judgment than kindness, she curtained its little bed from every breath of air, and fed it with herb-teas and other rustic stimulants, till the poor little thing seemed like to stifle; and just at this juncture Everard was taken ill, with the same symptoms.

Cora bore up wonderfully for a few days, but the baby grew worse, and Everard no better. Medical aid was sought, but the doctor proved quite as much of an old woman as Mrs. Dart.

The dear baby's strength was evidently diminishing, the spots in its little cheeks assumed a livid appearance; Mrs. Dart's pale face grew paler, and Cora awaited with an agony which might be read in her wild and vacant eye, the destruction of her hopes. The recollection of her own undutiful conduct towards her parents was at her heart, weighing it down like a mill-stone. Everard, who might have assisted and comforted her, was stretched helpless, and at times slightly delirious.

"I fear the baby is going," said the kind widow with trembling lips.

The wretched mother cast one look at its altered countenance, and with a wild cry sunk senseless on the floor. Her punishment was fulfilled.

CHAPTER XLII

On the breast
That rock'd her childhood, sinking in soft rest;—
Sweet mother—gentlest mother! can it be?
  —Mrs. Hemans

Pros. If I have too austerely punish'd you
    Your compensation makes amends; for I
    Have given you here a thread of mine own life—
        Here afore Heaven
  I ratify this my rich gift.
      —*The Tempest* [1]

Hath not old custom made this life more sweet
Than that of painted pomp?
  —*As You Like It* [2]

SHE became conscious of resting on a soft bosom—her hands were gently chafed, and a whispering voice whose thrilling sounds aroused her very soul, recalled her to a sense of her situation. She looked first at her infant's little bed. It was empty.

"My baby! my baby!" she shrieked in agony.

Her mother, her own dear mother, laid it on her bosom without a word, but she saw that it breathed in a soft sleep, and tears relieved her bursting heart.

"O mother, mother, can you forgive," was all that she could say, and it was enough. Her father too was there and he took her in his arms, and weeping blest her and forgave all.

The crisis or *turn* of the disease, had been so severe as to assume the aspect of approaching dissolution, and from that hour the precious baby, (the wilderness is the place to love children,) began to amend, and the young papa with it. And then came such long talks, about the past, the present, and the future; such minute explanations of all feelings and plans; Everard and Cora seemed to live a whole year extra in these few weeks which succeeded the time of this sore trial. And Cora was a new creature, a

What makes woman a rational being?

rational being, a mother, a matron, full of sorrow for the past and of sage plans for the future.

The silent disregard of the letters had been systematic. The flying pair had been recognized by some person on their journey westward; and the parents, indulgent as they were, felt that some atonement was due for this cruel disregard of their feelings, and forgetfulness of the common obligations. When months passed on without any evidence of repentance they felt still more deeply hurt, as well as seriously anxious; and though Everard's letters relieved in some measure their solicitude for the welfare of their undutiful children, it was not until Cora wrote to her mother, that the visit was resolved on which proved so opportune and so delightful.

And there was more to be told. Fortune had become weary of smiling on the long-established house of Hastings and Mansfield, and heavy losses had much impaired the worldly means of these worthy people. The summer-palaces on the Hudson were about to pass into other hands, and great changes were to be made in many particulars. And Everard must get his own living. This was a thing which Cora at least, had never included in her plans.

After much consultation it was conceded on all hands that it would be rather awkward returning to Mr. J.'s office after this little excursion. A frolic is a frolic to be sure, but people don't always take the view we wish them to take of our vagaries. Mr. Mansfield proposed his Michigan lands.

And Everard and his subdued and humbled but happy Cora, confessed that they had imbibed a taste for the wilderness, an unfashionable liking for early rising and *deshabille;* a yearning, common to those who have lived in the free woods,

To forsake
Earth's trouble waters for a purer spring.

Visionary still! says the reader. Perhaps so, but to Michigan they came, and with a fine large fertile tract, managed by a practical farmer and his family, they find it possible to exist, and are, I had almost said the happiest people of my acquaintance.

CHAPTER XLIII

On ne doit pas juger du merite d'un homme par ses grandes qualités, mais par l' usage qu'il en sait faire.—Rouchefoucault [1]

Des mots longs d' une toise,
De grands mots qui tiendroient d' ici jusqu' à Pontoise.
—Racine, *Les Plaideurs* [2]

But what he chiefly valued himself on, was his knowledge of metaphysics, in which, having once upon a time ventured too deeply, he came well nigh being smothered in a slough of unintelligible learning.—W. Irving, *Knickerbocker* [3]

MR. SIMEON JENKINS entered at an early stage of his career upon the arena of public life, having been employed by his honoured mother to dispose of a basket full of hard-boiled eggs, on election day, before he was eight years old. He often dwells with much unction upon this his debût; and declares that even at that dawning period, he had cut his eye-teeth.

"There was n't a feller there," Mr. Jenkins often says, "that could find out which side I was on, for all they tried hard enough. They thought I was soft, but I let 'em know I was as much baked as any on 'em. 'Be you a dimocrat?' says one. Buy some eggs and I'll tell ye, says I; and by the time he'd bought his eggs, I could tell well enough which side *he* belonged to, and I'd hand him out a ticket according, for I had blue ones in one end o' my basket, and white ones in the other, and when night come, and I got off the stump to go home, I had eighteen shillin' and four pence in my pocket."

From this auspicious commencement may be dated Mr. Jenkins' glowing desire to serve the public. Each successive election day saw him at his post. From eggs he advanced to pies, from pies to almanacs, whiskey, powder and shot, foot-balls, playing-cards, and at length, for ambition ever "did grow with what it fed on," he brought into the field a large turkey, which was tied to a post and stoned to death at twenty-five cents a throw. By this time the still youthful aspirant had become quite the man of the world; could smoke twenty four cigars per diem, if any body else would pay for them; play cards, in old Hurler's shop, from noon till day-break, and rise winner; and all this with suitable trimmings of gin and hard words. But he never lost sight of the main chance. He had made up his mind to serve his country, and he was all this time convincing his fellow-citizens of the disinterested purity of his sentiments.

"Patriotism," he would say, "patriotism is the thing! any man that's too proud to serve his country aint fit to live. Some thinks so much o' themselves, that if they can have jist what they think they 're fit for, they wont take nothing; but for my part, *I* call myself an American citizen; and any office that 's in the gift o' the people will suit *me*. I'm up to any thing. And as there aint no other man about here,—no suitable man, I mean— that's got a horse, why I'd be willing to be constable, if the people's a mind to, though it would be a dead loss to me in my business, to be sure; but I could do any thing for my country. Hurra for patriotism! them 's my sentiments."

It can scarcely be doubted that Mr. Jenkins became a very popular citizen, or that he usually played a conspicuous part at the polls. Offices began to fall to his share, and though they were generally such as brought more honour than profit, office is office, and Mr. Jenkins did not grumble. Things were going on admirably.

> The spoils of office glitter in his eyes,
> He climbs, he pants, he grasps them—[4]

Or thought he was just going to grasp them, when, presto! he found himself in the minority; the wheel of fortune turned, and Mr. Jenkins and his party were left undermost. Here was a dilemma! His zeal in the public service was ardent as ever, but how could he get a chance to show it unless his party was in power? His resolution was soon taken. He called his friends together, mounted a stump, which had fortunately been left standing not far from the door of his shop, and then and there gave "reasons for my ratting" in terms sublime enough for any meridian.

"My friends and feller-citizens," said this self-sacrificing patriot, "I find myself conglomerated in sich a way, that my feelin's suffers severely. I'm sitivated in a peculiar sitivation. O' one side, I see my dear friends, pussonal friends—friends, that 's stuck to me like wax, through thick and thin, never shinnyin' off and on, but up to the scratch, and no mistake. O' t' other side I behold my country, my bleedin' country, the land that fetch'd me into this world o' trouble. Now, sence things be as they be, and can't be no otherways as I see, I feel kind o' screwed into an auger-hole to know what to do. If I hunt over the history of the universal world from the creation of man to the present day, I see that men has always had difficulties; and that some has took one way to get shut of 'em, and some another. My candid and unrefragable opinion is, that rather than remain useless, buckled down to the shop, and indulging in selfishness, it is my solemn dooty to change my ticket. It is severe, my friends, but dooty is dooty. And now, if any man calls me a turn-coat," continued the orator, gently spitting in his hands, rubbing them together, and rolling his eyes round the assembly, "all I say is, let him say it so that I can hear him."

The last argument was irresistible, if even the others might have brooked discussion, for Mr. Jenkins stands six feet two in his stockings, when he wears any, and gesticulates with a pair of arms as long and muscular as Rob Roy's.⁵ So, though the audience did not cheer him, they contented themselves with dropping off one by one, without calling in question the patriotism of the rising statesman.

The very next election saw Mr. Jenkins justice of the peace, and it was in this honourable capacity that I have made most of my acquaintance with him, though we began with threatenings of a storm. He called to take the acknowledgement of a deed, and I, anxious for my country's honour, for I too am something of a patriot in my own way, took the liberty of pointing out to his notice a trifling slip of the pen; videlicet, "Justas of Piece," which manner of writing those words I informed him had gone out of fashion.

He reddened, looked at me very sharp for a moment, and then said he thanked me; but subjoined,

"Book-learning is a good thing enough where there aint too much of it. For my part, I've seen a good many that know'd books that did n't know much else. The proper cultivation and edication of the human intellect, has been the comprehen*sive* study of the human understanding from the original creation of the universal world to the present day, and there has been a good many ways tried besides book-learning. Not but what that's very well in its place."

And the justice took his leave with somewhat of a swelling air. But we are excellent friends, notwithstanding this hard rub; and Mr. Jenkins favours me now and then with half an hour's conversation, when he has had leisure to read up for the occasion in an odd volume of the Cyclopedia, which holds an honoured place in a corner of his shop. He ought, in fairness, to give me previous notice, that I might study the dictionary a little, for the hard words with which he arms himself for these "keen encounters," often push me to the very limits of my English.

I ought to add, that Mr. Jenkins has long since left off gambling, drinking, and all other vices of that class, except smoking; in this point he professes to be incorrigible. But as his wife, who is one of the nicest women in the world, and manages him admirably, pretends to like the smell of tobacco, and takes care never to look at him when he disfigures her well-scoured floor, I am not without hopes of his thorough reformation.

CHAPTER XLIV

🦋🦋🦋🦋🦋🦋

Dandin. Ta, ta, ta, ta. Voilà bien instruire une affaire!
A-t-on jamais plaidé d' une telle méthode?
Mais qu' en dit l' assemblée?

. . . .

Ma foi! je n' y conçois plus rien.
De monde, de chaos, j' ai la tête troublé.
Hé! concluez.
—Racine, *Les Plaiduers* [1]

IT WAS "an honour that I dreamed not of," to be called before this same squire Jenkins in his dignified capacity of "Justas." I had not even heard a murmur of the coming storm, when I was served with a *subpœna,* and learned at the same time the astounding fact, that at least half the Montacute Female Beneficent Society were about to receive a shilling's worth of law on the same occasion. A justice court!

My flesh did creep, and each particular hair
Did stand on end—

but there was no remedy.

The court was to be held at the Squire's, and as Mrs. Jenkins was a particular friend of mine, I went early, intending to make her a call before the awful hour should approach, and hoping that in the interval I might be able to learn something of the case in which I was expected to play the important part of witness.

But good Mrs. Jenkins, who was in her Sunday gown and looked very solemn, considered herself bound to maintain an official mysteriousness of deportment, and she therefore declined entering upon the subject which was so soon to come under the cognizance of "the good people of this state." All she would be persuaded to say was, that it was a slander suit, and that she believed "women-folks" were at the bottom of it.

But ere long the more prominent characters of the drama began to drop in. Mrs. Flyter and her "old man," and two babies were among the first, and the lady looked so prodigiously sulky, that I knew *she* was concerned in the fray at least. Then entered Squire Jenkins himself, clean shaved for once, and arrayed in his meetin' coat. He asked his wife where the pen and ink was, and said he should want some paper to write down the "dispositions."

And the next comer was the plaintiff, the Schneider [2] of our village, no Robin Starveling he, but a magnificent Hector-looking [3] fellow, tall enough to have commanded Frederick of Prussia's [4] crack regiment; and so elegantly made, that one finds it hard to believe his legs have ever been crossed on a shop-board. The beetle-brows of this stitching hero were puckered like the seams of his newest 'prentice, and he cast magnanimous glances round the assembly, as who should say—

> Come one, come all! this rock shall fly
> From its firm base as soon as I!

Though the rock was but slenderly represented by Mrs. Jenkins's bureau, against which he leaned.

The world now began to flock in. The chairs were soon filled, and then the outer edges of the two beds. Three young pickles occupied the summit of the bureau, to the imminent jeopardy of the mirrored clock which shone above it. Boards were laid to eke out the chairs, and when the room was packed so that not a chink remained, a sensation was created by the appearance of Mrs. Nippers and Miss Clinch. Much turning out and tumbling over was now to be done, although those active ladies appeared less than usually desirous of attracting attention.

All was at length ready, and the squire opened the court by blowing his nose without calling upon his pocket handkerchief.

What was my surprise when I learned that our "most magnanimous mouse," Mr. Shafton, the tailor, had been set down a thief; and that Mr. Flyter had been called on, by the majesty of law, to answer for the calumny; not that *he* had ever thought of bringing such a charge against his neighbour, for he was a silent man, who always had his mouth too full of tobacco to utter slander, or any thing else; but that his lady, on a certain occasion where women had convened in aid of one of the afflicted sisterhood, had, most "*un*-prudently," as she said herself, given vent to certain angry feelings towards Mr. Shafton, "in manner as aforesaid." To think of bringing a woman into trouble for what she happened to say after tea! I began to consider Mr. Shafton as no more than the ninth part of a man, after all.

Things went on very quietly for a while. The "dispositions" occupied a good deal of time, and a vast amount of paper; the scribe finding the pen less germane to his fingers than the plough, and making his lines bear no small resemblance to the furrows made by a "breaking-up team." But when the ladies began to figure on the stage, the aspect of affairs was altered. Each wished to tell "the truth, the whole truth, and nothing but the truth;" and to ask one question, elicited never less than one dozen answers; the said answers covering a much larger ground than the suit itself, and bringing forward the private affairs and opinions of half the village. In vain did Mr. Jenkins roar "silence!" his injunctions only made the ladies angry, and of course gave their tongues a fresh impetus.

"Cabbage! yes, you said he took a quarter of a yard of satinett, and that that was as bad as stealing!" "Yes! and then Miss Flyter said he *did* steal cloth, and thread and buttons too!" "Well, Miss Nippers told me so, and she said she see a chair-cushion at Miss Shafton's, that was made all out of great pieces of fulled cloth!" "Who? I? oh, mercy! I do n't believe I ever said such a word!" "Oh you did, you did! I'm willin' to take my afferdavy of it!" "Silence!" vociferated Squire Jenkins. "Ladies," began Mr. Phlatt, the plaintiff's counsel, "if you *would* wait a minute"—

In vain—alas! in vain, ye gallant few!

In vain do ye assay to control

The force of female lungs,
Sighs, sobs and passions, and the war of tongues.[5]

And Mr. Phlatt sat down in despair, looked out of the window, and drummed on the table with his fingers, as if to pass away the time till he could be heard.

Squire Jenkins, who was but newly dignified, and did not like to proceed to extremities, now adjourned the court for one hour, a recess much needed by the exhausted state of some of the witnesses. During this interval, and while the wordy war was waxing stronger and stronger, Mr. Flyter and Mr. Shafton very wisely withdrew, and in less than five minutes returned, and informed the company that they had "settled it." Mr. Flyter was to pay Mr. Shafton three dollars and fifty cents worth of lumber for his character, with costs of suit; and Mrs. Flyter was to unsay all she had said, and confess that three yards of satinett for a pair of pantaloons, would leave the tailor no more than his regular cabbage.

So here was four hours' time of something nearly thirty people spent to good purpose in chasing a Will-o'-the-wisp. And Montacute sees equally important suits at law every few weeks; expensive enough, if "settled" midway as they often are, between the parties themselves; still more so if left to pursue the regular course, and be decided by the Justice.

The intelligence of the "settlement" was received with various aspects by the persons concerned. The counsel on both sides were of course disappointed, for they had calculated largely upon the *spunk* of the splendid-looking son of the shears, and had counted on a jury-trial at least, if not an appeal. Mrs. Flyter was evidently much relieved to find that she had come off so easily; and sundry other ladies, who had been trembling under the consciousness of conversational "sins unwhipped of justice," shawled and India-rubbered with more than usual alacrity, and I doubt not, made vows, sincere, whether well-kept or not, to let their neighbours' business alone for some time.

Mr. Jenkins was evidently disappointed at the tame result of so much glorious preparation. He had made up his own mind on the first statement of the case, and had prepared his decision, with the addition of a concise view of the universe from chaos to the present day. But that will do for the next time, and he will not be obliged to reserve it long. Bartholine Saddletree himself would weary of the "never-ending, still-beginning" law-pleas of Montacute. Bad fences, missing dogs, unruly cattle, pigs' ears, and women's tongues, are among the most prolific sources of litigation; to say nothing of the satisfactory amount of business which is created by the collection of debts, a matter of "glorious uncertainty" in Michigan. These suits are so frequent, that they pass as part and parcel of the regular course of things; and you would find it impossible to persuade a thorough-bred Wolverine, that there was any thing unfriendly in suing his next door neighbour for a debt of however trifling amount.

Actions for trespass and for slander are rather more enjoyed, as being somewhat less frequent; but any thing like a trial, will always be enough to keep half a dozen unconcerned people idle for a day or more.

Mr. Shafton's spirited defence of his fair fame will, I see plainly, prove a lasting benefit to the talking sex of Montacute. It is perfectly incredible how much was done and how little said at the last week's meeting of the Female Beneficent Society. Mrs. Nippers to be sure had the ague, and did her chattering at home, and Miss Clinch staid to take care of her, as in duty bound. But I think that alone would not account for the difference. We shall see next week.

CHAPTER XLV

See! sae close as they're written down to the very seal! and a' to save postage!—*The Antiquary* [1]

Ant. We sent our school-master—
Is he come back?
            —*Antony and Cleopatra* [2]

I HAVE departed from all rule and precedent in these wandering sketches of mine. I believe I set out, a great many pages ago, to tell of the interesting changes, the progressive improvements in this model of a village of ours. My intention, as far as I had any, was to convey to the patient reader some general idea of our way of life in these remote and forgotten corners of creation. But I think I have discovered that the bent of my genius is altogether towards digression. Association leads me like a Will-o'-the-wisp. I can no more resist following a new train of thought, than a coquette the encouraging of a new lover, at the expense of all the old ones, though often equally conscious that the old are most valuable. This attempt to write one long coherent letter about Montacute, has at least been useful in convincing me that History is not my forte. I give up the account in despair, and lower my ambition to the collection of scattered materials for the use of the future compiler of Montacutian annals.

Yet it seems strange, even to my desultory self, how I could have passed in silence the establishment of a weekly mail, that sweetener of our long delicious winter evenings—that rich atonement for all that we lack of fresh scandal and new news. Since this treasure was ours, I have learned to pity most sincerely those who get their letters and papers at all sorts of unexpected and irregular times; a shower of scattering fire, feeble and ineffectual—a dropping in at all hours, seasonable and unseasonable, like some classes of visiters; coming often when one's mood is any thing but congenial; and sure to stay away when one longs for company—gay ones intruding when we had determined to be blue and miserable, and sad ones casting their long shadows on our few sunny hours.

But a weekly mail! a budget that one waits and gets ready for; a regularly-recurring delight, an unfailing pleasure, (how few such have we!) hours, nay days, of delicious anticipation—sure harvest of past care and toil, an inundation of happiness! Let no one think he has exhausted all the sources of enjoyment till he has lived in the back-woods and learned to expect a weekly mail with its lap-full of letters and its tumulus of papers; a feast enjoyed by anticipation for a whole week previous, and affording ample materials for *resumées* for that which succeeds.

This pleasure has become so sacred in my eyes, that nothing vexes me so intolerably as seeing our lanky mail-bags dangling over the bony sides of Major Bean's lame Canadian, and bestridden and over-shadowed by the portly form of the one-eyed Major himself, trotting or rather hobbling down Main-street on some intermediate and unpremeditated day. Men of business are so disagreeable and inconsiderate! To think of any body's sending fourteen interminable miles over bush and bog to B***, up hill both ways, as every one knows, just to learn the price of flour or salt three days sooner, and thereby spoiling the rest of the week, leaving an objectless blank where was before a delicious chaos of hopes; substituting dull certainty for the exquisite flutterings of that sort of doubt which leaves us after all quite sure of a happy result. I have often thought I would not open the treasures which reached me in this unauthorized, over-the-wall sort of way. I have declared that I would not have Saturday evening spoiled and the next week made ten days long. But this proper and becoming spirit has never proved quite strong enough to bear me through so keen a trial of all feminine qualities. One must be more or less than woman to endure the sight of unopened letters, longer than it takes to find the scissors. I doubt whether Griselidis[3] herself would not have blenched at such a requisition, especially if she had been transplanted to the wilderness, and left behind hosts of friends, as well as many other very comfortable things.

Another subject of the last interest which I have as yet wholly neglected, is the new school-house, a gigantic step in the march of improvement. This, in truth, I should have mentioned long ago, if I could have found any thing to say about it. It has caused an infinity of feuds, made mortal enemies of two brothers, and separated at least one pair of partners. But the subject has been exhausted, worn to shreds in my hearing; and whenever I have thought of searching for an end of the tangled clew, in order to open its mazes for the benefit of all future school-committees and their constituency, I have felt that every possible view of the case had been appropriated, and therefore must be borrowed or stolen for the occasion. I might indeed have given a description of the building as it now smiles upon me from the opposite side of the public square. But the reader may imagine St. Paul's, St. Peter's, the Parthenon, the mosque of St. Sophia, or any edifice of that character, and then think of the Montacute school-house as something inexpressibly different, and he will have as good an idea of it as I could give him in half a page. I think it resembles the Temple of the Winds more nearly than any other ancient structure I have read of; at least, I have often thought so in cold weather, when I have beguiled the hours of a long sermon by peeping through the cracks at the drifting snow; but it is built of unplaned oak-boards, and has no under-pinning; and the stove-pipe, sticking out of one window, looks rather modern; so the likeness might not strike every body.

The school-ma'am, Miss Cleora Jenkins, I have elsewhere introduced to the reader. From April till October, she sways "the rod of empire;" and truly may it be said,

> There through the summer-day
> Green boughs are waving,

though I believe she picks the leaves off, as tending to defeat the ends of justice. Even the noon-spell shines no holiday for the luckless subjects of her domination, for she carries her bread and pickles rolled up in her pocket-handkerchief, and lunches where she rules, reading the while "The Children of the Abbey,"[4]—which took her all summer,—and making one of the large girls comb her hair by the hour.

During the snowy, blowy, wheezy, and freezy months, the chair has been taken—not filled—by Mr. Cyrus Whicher,—not Switcher,—a dignitary who had "boarded round" till there was very little of him left. I have been told, that when he first bore the birch,—in his own hand I mean,—he was of a portly and rather stolid exterior; had good teeth and flowing locks; but he was, when I knew him, a mere cuticle—a "skellinton," as Mr. Weller would say—shaped like a starved greyhound in the collapsed stage, his very eyes faded to the colour of the skim-milk which has doubtless constituted his richest potation since he attained the empty honours of a district school.

When he came under my care, in the course of his unhappy gyrations, I did my best to fatten him; and, to do him justice, his efforts were not lacking: but one cannot make much progress in one week, even in cramming a turkey poult, and he went as ethereal as he came.

One additional reason for his "lean and hungry" looks I thought I discovered in his gnawing curiosity of soul—I suppose it would be more polite to say, his burning thirst for knowledge. When he first glided into my one and only parlour, I asked him to sit down, expecting to hear his bones rattle as he did so. To my astonishment he noticed not my civility, but, gazing on the wall as who should say—

"Look you, how pale he glares!"

he stood as one transfixed.

At length—"Whose profile is that?" he exclaimed, pointing to a portrait of my dear, cheerful-looking grand-mamma—a half-length, by Waldo.

I told all about it, as I thought, but left room for a dozen questions at least, as to her relationship—whether by father or mother's side—her age when the picture was taken, &c. &c. &c.; and Mr. Whicher's concluding remark, as he doubled up to sit down, was—

"Well! she's a dreadful sober-lookin' old critter, aint she now!" But ere he touched the chair, he opened again like a folded rule out of a case of instruments, and stood erect save head and shoulders.

"Is that a pi-anner?" he asked with sort of chuckle of delight. "Well! I heard you had one, but I did n't hardly believe it. And what's this thing?" twirling the music-stool with all his might, and getting down on his poor knees to look underneath both these curiosities.

"Jist play on it, will you?"

"Dinner is ready, Mr. Whicher: I will play afterwards."

He balanced for one moment between inanition and curiosity; then, "with his head over his shoulder turn'd," he concluded to defer pleasure to business. He finished his meal by the time others had fairly begun; and then, throwing himself back in his chair, said, "I'm ready whenever you be."

I could not do less than make all possible speed, and Mr. Whicher sat entranced until he was late for school: not so much listening to the tinkling magic, as prying into the nature and construction of the instrument, which he thought must have taken "a good bunch o' cypherin'."

That week's sojourn added a good deal to the school-master's stores of knowledge. He scraped a little of the chrystallized green off my inkstand to find out how it was put on; pulled up a corner of the parlour-carpet, to see whether it was "wove like a bed-spread;" whether it was "over-shot or under-shot;" and not content with ascertaining by personal inspection the construction of every article which was new to him, he pumped dry every member of the household, as to their past mode of life, future prospects, opinion of the country, religious views, and thoughts on every imaginable subject. I began to feel croupish before he left us, from having talked myself quite out.

One of his habits struck me as rather peculiar. He never saw a letter or a sealed paper of any kind that he did not deliberately try every possible method, by peeping, squeezing, and poking, to get at its contents. I at first set this down as something which denoted a more than usually mean and dishonest curiosity; but after I had seen the same operation performed in my presence without the least hesitation or apology, by a reverend gentleman of high reputation, I concluded that the poor schoolmaster had at least some excuse for his ill-breeding.

Mr. Whicher had his own troubles last winter. A scholar of very equivocal, or rather unequivocal character, claimed admission to the school, and, of all concerned, not one had courage or firmness to object to her reception. She was the daughter of a fierce, quarrelsome man, who had already injured, either by personal abuse, or by vexatious litigation, half the people in the place; and though all detested her, and dreaded contamination for their daughters, not a voice was raised—not a girl removed from the school. This cowardly submission to open and public wrong seems hardly credible; but I have observed it in many other instances, and it has, in most cases, appeared to arise from a distrust in the protecting power of the law, which has certainly been hitherto most imperfectly and irregularly administered in Michigan. People suppress their just indignation at many abuses, from a fear that they may "get into trouble;" i.e. be haled before an ignorant justice of the peace, who will be quite as likely to favour the wrong as the right, as interest or prejudice may chance to incline him. Thus a bad man, if he have only the requisite boldness, may trample on the feelings, and disturb the peace of a whole community.

When Hannah Parsons applied for admission to the district school, Mr. Whicher made such objections as he dared in his timidity. He thought she was too old—her mother said she was not nineteen, though she had a son of two years and upwards. And she did not wish to study anything but arithmetic and writing; so that there could be no objection as to classes. And the wretched girl forced herself into the ranks of the young and innocent, for what purpose or end I never could divine.

From this hour the unfortunate Wicher was her victim. She began by showing him the most deferential attention, watching his looks, and asking his aid in the most trivial matters; wanting her pen mended twenty times in the course of one copy, and insisting upon the schoolmaster's showing her again and again exactly how it should be held. She never went to school without carrying a tribute of some sort, a custard, or an apple,— apples are something with us,—or a geranium leaf at least. Now these offerings are so common among school-children, that the wretched master, though writhing with disgust, knew not how to refuse them, and his life wore away under the anguish inflicted by his tormentor.

At length it was whispered that Hannah Parsons would again bring to the eye of day a living evidence of her shame; and the unfortunate schoolmaster saw himself the victim of a conspiracy.

It needed but this to complete his distraction. He fled in imbecile despair; and after the wonder had died away, and the scandal had settled on the right head, we heard no word of the innocent pedagogue for a long time. But after that came news, that Cyrus Whicher, in the wretchedness of his poverty, had joined a gang of idlers and desperadoes, who had made a vow against honest industry; and it is not now very long since we learned that he had the honour of being hanged at Toronto as a "Patriot."

CHAPTER XLVI

> Go with speed
> To some forlorn and naked hermitage,
> Remote from all the pleasures of the world;
> There stay until the twelve celestial signs
> Have brought about their annual reckoning.
> If this austere, insociable life—
> If frosts and fasts, hard lodging and thin weeds
> Nip not the gaudy blossoms of your *pride*—
> —*Love's Labour's Lost* [1]

They wear themselves in the cap of time there; do muster true gait, eat, speak, and move, under the influence of the most received star; and though the devil lead the measure, such are to be followed—*All's Well That Ends Well* [2]

ONE MUST come quite away from the conveniences and refined indul-
gences of civilized life to know any thing about them. To be always inun-
dated with comforts, is but too apt to make us proud, selfish, and
ungrateful. The mind's health, as well as the body's, is promoted by occasional privation or abstinence. Many a sour-faced grumbler I wot of, would
be marvellously transformed by a year's residence in the woods, or even in
a Michigan village of as high pretensions as Montacute. If it were not for
casting a sort of dishonour on a country life, turning into a magnificent
"beterinhaus"[3] these

> "Haunts of deer,
> And lanes in which the primrose ere her time
> Peeps through the moss"[4]

I should be disposed to recommend a course of Michigan to the Sybarites,[5]
the puny exquisites, the world-worn and sated Epicureans of our cities. If I
mistake not, they would make surprising advances in philosophy in the
course of a few months' training. I should not be severe either. I should not
require them to come in their strictly natural condition as featherless
bipeds. I would allow them to bring many a comfort—nay, even some real
luxuries; books, for instance, and a reasonable supply of New-York Safety-
Fund notes, the most tempting form which "world's gear" can possibly
assume for our western, wild-cat wearied eyes. I would grant to each
Neophyte a ready-made loggery, a garden fenced with tamarack poles, and
every facility and convenience which is now enjoyed by the better class of
our settlers, yet I think I might after all hope to send home a reasonable
proportion of my subjects completely cured, sane for life.

I have in the course of these detached and desultory chapters, hinted
at various deficiencies and peculiarities, which strike, with rather unpleasant force, the new resident in the back-woods; but it would require volumes to enumerate all the cases in which the fastidiousness, the taste, the
pride, the self-esteem of the refined child of civilization, must be wounded
by a familiar intercourse with the persons among whom he will find himself thrown, in the ordinary course of rural life. He is continually reminded
in how great a variety of particulars his necessities, his materials for comfort, and his sources of pain, are precisely those of the humblest of his
neighbours. The humblest, did I say? He will find that he has no humble
neighbours. He will very soon discover, that in his new sphere, no act of
kindness, no offer of aid, will be considered as any thing short of insult, if
the least suspicion of *condescension* peep out. Equality, perfect and practical,

is the *sine qua non;* and any appearance of a desire to avoid this rather trying fraternization, is invariably met by a fierce and indignant resistance. The spirit in which was conceived the motto of the French revolution, "La fraternité ou la mort,"[6] exists in full force among us, though modified as to results. In cities we bestow charity—in the country we can only exchange kind offices, nominally at least. If you are perfectly well aware that your nearest neighbour has not tasted meat in a month, nor found in his pocket the semblance of a shilling to purchase it, you must not be surprised, when you have sent him a piece, to receive for reply,

"Oh! your pa wants to *change,* does he? Well, you may put it down." And this without the remotest idea that the time for repayment ever will arrive, but merely to avoid saying, "I thank you," a phrase especially eschewed, so far as I have had opportunity to observe.

This same republican spirit is evinced rather amusingly, in the reluctance to admire, or even to approve, any thing like luxury or convenience which is not in common use among the settlers. Your carpets are spoken of as "*one* way to hide dirt;" your mahogany tables as "dreadful plaguy to scour;" your kitchen conveniences as "lumberin' up the house for nothin';" and so on to the end of the chapter. One lady informed me, that if she had such a pantry full of "dishes," under which general term is included every variety of china, glass and earthenware, she should set up store, and "sell them off pretty quick," for she would not "be plagued with them." Another, giving a slighting glance at a French mirror of rather unusual dimensions, larger by two-thirds, I verily believe, than she had ever seen, remarked, "that would be quite a nice glass, if the frame was done over."

Others take up the matter reprovingly. They "do n't think it right to spend money so;" they think too, that "pride never did nobody no good;" and some will go so far as to suggest modes of disposing of your superfluities.

"Any body that 's got so many dresses, might afford to give away half on 'em;" or, "I should think you 'd got so much land, you might give a poor man a lot, and never miss it." A store of any thing, however simple or necessary, is, as I have elsewhere observed, a subject of reproach, if you decline supplying whomsoever may be deficient.

This simplification of life, this bringing down the transactions of daily intercourse to the original principles of society, is neither very eagerly adopted, nor very keenly relished, by those who have been accustomed to the politer atmospheres. They rebel most determinedly, at first. They perceive that the operation of the golden rule, in circumstances where it is all *give* on one side, and all *take* on the other, must necessarily be rather severe; and they declare manfully against all impertinent intrusiveness. But, sooth to say, there are in the country so many ways of being made uncomfortable by one's most insignificant enemy, that it is soon discovered that warfare is even more costly than submission.

And all this forms part of the schooling which I propose for my spoiled child of refined civilization. And although many of these remarks and requisitions of our unpolished neighbours are unreasonable and absurd enough, yet some of them commend themselves to our better feelings in such a sort, that we find ourselves ashamed to refuse what it seemed at first impertinent to ask; and after the barriers of pride and prejudice are once broken, we discover a certain satisfaction in this homely fellowship with our kind, which goes far towards repaying whatever sacrifices or concessions we may have been induced to make. This has its limits of course; and one cannot help observing that "levelling upwards" is much more congenial to "human natur'," than levelling downwards. The man who thinks you ought to spare him a piece of ground for a garden, because you have more than he thinks you need, would be far from sharing with his poorer neighbour the superior advantages of his lot. He would tell him to work for them as *he* had done.

But then there are, in the one case, some absolute and evident superfluities, according to the primitive estimate of these regions; in the other, none. The doll of Fortune, who may cast a languid eye on this homely page, from the luxurious depths of a velvet-cushioned library-chair, can scarce be expected to conceive how natural it may be, for those who possess nothing beyond the absolute requisites of existence, to look with a certain degree of envy on the extra comforts which seem to cluster round the path of another; and to feel as if a little might well be spared, where so much would still be left. To the tenant of a log-cabin whose family, whatever be its numbers, must burrow in a single room, while a bed or two, a chest, a table, and a wretched handful of cooking utensils, form the chief materials of comfort, an ordinary house, small and plain it may be, yet amply supplied, looks like the very home of luxury. The woman who owns but a suit a-piece for herself and her children, considers the possession of an abundant though simple and inexpensive wardrobe, as needless extravagance; and we must scarcely blame her too severely, if she should be disposed to condemn as penurious, any reluctance to supply her pressing need, though she may have no shadow of claim on us beyond that which arises from her

185

being a daughter of Eve. We look at the matter from opposite points of view. *Her* light shows her very plainly, as she thinks, what is *our* Christian duty; we must take care that ours does not exhibit too exclusively her envy and her impertinence.

The inequalities in the distribution of the gifts of fortune are not greater in the country than in town, but the contrary; yet circumstances render them more offensive to the less-favoured class. The denizens of the crowded alleys and swarming lofts of our great cities see, it is true, the lofty mansions, the splendid equipages of the wealthy—but they are seldom or never brought into contact or collision with the owners of these glittering advantages. And the extreme width of the great gulf between, is almost a barrier, even to all-reaching envy. But in the ruder stages of society, where no one has yet begun to expend any thing for show, the difference lies chiefly in the ordinary requisites of comfort; and this comes home at once "to men's business and bosoms." [7] The keenness of their appreciation, and the strength of their envy, bear a direct proportion to the *real* value of the objects of their desire; and when they are in habits of entire equality and daily familiarity with those who own ten or twenty times as much of the *matériel* of earthly enjoyment as themselves, it is surely natural, however provoking, that they should not be studious to veil their longings after a share of the good, which has been so bounteously showered upon their neighbours.

I am only making a sort of apology for the foibles of my rustic friends. I cannot say that I feel much respect for any thing which looks like a willingness to live at others' cost, save as a matter of the last necessity.

I was adverting to a certain unreservedness of communication on these points, as often bringing wholesome and much-needed instruction home to those whom prosperity and indulgence may have rendered un-sympathizing, or neglectful of the kindly feelings which are among the best ornaments of our nature.

But I am aware that I have already been adventurous, far beyond the bounds of prudence. To hint that it may be better not to cultivate *too* far that haughty spirit of exclusiveness which is the glory of the fashionable world, is, I know, hazardous in the extreme. I have not so far forgotten the rules of the sublime *clique* as not to realize, that in acknowledging even a leaning toward the "vulgar" side, I place myself forever beyond its pale. But I am now a denizen of the wild woods—in my view, "no mean city" to own as one's home; and I feel no ambition to aid in the formation of a Montacute aristocracy, for which an ample field is now open, and all the proper materials are at hand. What lack we? Several of us have as many as three cows; some few, carpets and shanty-kitchens; and one or two, piano-fortes and silver tea-sets. I myself, as *dame de la seigneurie*,[8] have had secret thoughts of an astral lamp! but even if I should go so far, I am resolved not to be either vain-glorious or over-bearing, although this kind of superiority forms the usual ground for exclusiveness. I shall visit my neighbours just as usual, and take care not to say a single word about dipped candles, if I can possibly help it.

CHAPTER XLVII

> Why, then, a final note prolong,
> Or lengthen out a closing song?

THE GROWTH of our little secluded village has been so gradual, its pros-perity so moderate, and its attempts so unambitious, that during the whole three years which have flown since it knew "the magic of a name," not a single event has occurred which would have been deemed worthy of record by any one but a midge-fancier like myself. Our brief annals boast not yet one page, enlivened by those attractive words, "prodigious under-taking!" "brilliant success!" "splendid fortune!" "race of enterprise!" "march of improvement!" "cultivation of taste!" "triumph of art!" "design by Vitruvius!" "unequalled dome!" "pinnacle of glory!" Alas! the mere enumeration of these magnificent expressions, makes our insignificance seem doubly insignificant! like the joke of our schooldays—"Soared aloft on eagles' wings—then fell flat down, on father's wood-pile." Irredeem-ably little are we; unless, which Heaven forefend! a rail-road stray our way. We must content ourselves with grinding the grists, trimming the bonnets, mending the ploughs, and schooling the children, of a goodly expanse of wheat-fields, with such other odd jobs as may come within the abilities of our various Jacks-of-all trades. We cannot be metropolitan, even in our dreams; for Turnipdale has secured the County honours. We cannot hope to be literary; for all the colleges which are to be tolerated in Michigan, are already located. The State-Prison favours Jacksonburg; the Salt-works some undistinguished place at the north-east; what is left for Montacute?

Alas for Tinkerville! less happy under the cruel blight of her towering hopes, than we in our humble notelessness. She rose like a rocket, only to fall like its stick; and baleful were the stars that signalized her explosion. Mournful indeed are the closed windows of her porticoed edifices. The only pleasurable thought which arises in my mind at the mention of her name, is that connected with her whilome president. Mrs. Rivers is coming to spend the summer with Mrs. Daker, while Mr. Rivers departs for Texas with two or three *semblables,*[1] to attempt the carving out of a new home, where he need not "work." I shall have my gentle friend again; and her life will not lack interest, for she brings with her a drooping, delicate baby, to borrow health from the sunny skies and soft breezes of Michigan.

The Female Beneficent Society grows, by dire experience, chary of news. The only novel idea broached at our last meeting, was that of a nascent *tendresse* between Mrs. Nippers and Mr. Phlatt, a young lawyer, whose resplendent "tin" graces, within the last month, the side-post of Squire Jenkins' door. I have my doubts. This is one of the cases wherein much may be said on both sides. Mr. Phlatt is certainly a constant visitor at Mrs. Nippers', but the knowing widow does not live alone. He praises with great fervour, Mrs. Nippers' tea and biscuits, but then who could do less? they are so unequivocally perfect—and besides, Mr. Phlatt has not access to many such comfortable tea-tables—and moreover, when he praises he gazes, but not invariably on Mrs. Nippers. I am not convinced yet. Miss Clinch has a new French calico, *couleur de rose,* and a pink lining to her Tuscan.[2] And she is young and rather pretty. But then, she has no money! and Mrs. Nippers has quite a pretty little income—the half-pay of her deceased Mr. Nippers, who died of a fever at Sackett's Harbour—and Mrs. Nippers has been getting a new dress, just the colour of blue-pill, Dr. Teeny says. I waver, but time will bring all things to light.

Mr. Hastings goes to the Legislature, next winter; and he is beginning to collect materials for a house, which will be as nearly as may be, like his father's summer-palace on the Hudson. But he is in another county, so we do not feel envious. Cora will never be less lovely, nor more elegant, nor (whispered be it!) more happy than she is in her pretty log-house. And the new house will be within the same belt of maples and walnuts which now encircles the picturesque cottage; so that the roses and honey-suckles will tell well; like their fair mistress, graceful and exquisite any-where.

Many new buildings are springing up in Montacute. Mr. Doubleday has ensconced himself and his wife and baby, in a white and green tenement, neat enough even for that queen of housewives; and Betsy, having grown stout, scours the new white-wood floors, *à merveille.* Loggeries are becoming scarce within our limits, and many of our ladies wear silk dresses on Sunday. We have two physicians, and two lawyers, or rather one and a half. Squire Jenkins being only an adopted son of Themis.[3] He thought it a pity his gift in the talking line should not be duly useful to the public, so he acts as advocate, whenever he is not on duty as judge, and thereby ekes out his bread and butter, as well as adds to his reputation. And in addition to all the improvements which I have recorded, I may mention that we are building a new meeting-house, and are soon to have a settled minister.

And now, why do I linger? As some rustic damsel who has, in her simplicity, accepted the hurried "Do call when you come to town," of a fine city guest, finds that she has already outstaid the fashionable limit, yet hesitates in her awkwardness, when and how to take leave; so I— conscious that I have said forth my little say, yet scarce knowing in what style best to make my parting reverence, have prolonged this closing chapter—a "conclusion wherein nothing is concluded." But such simple and sauntering stories are like Scotch reels, which have no natural ending, save the fatigue of those engaged. So I may as well cut short my mazy dance and resume at once my proper position as a "wall-flower," with an unceremonious adieu to the kind and courteous reader.

LITERARY WOMEN

LET IT NOT BE for a moment supposed that we are about to attempt a crusade in defence of blue-stockings! Better undertake, single-handed, to lay a T rail to the Pacific, tunnelling the Rocky Mountains. Whether the prejudice entertained against this class—is it numerous enough to claim the title of a class?—be just or not, it is most potent; and, like the deaf adder, it stoppeth its ears. We hardly know of one more obstinate, unless it be that against old maids,—or that other, perhaps worse one, against stepmothers.

Now, prejudices are very respectable things. They have antiquity and ancestry in their favour. They enjoy unflinching allegiance from many very dignified and important people. They partake of the nature of faith, the most consolatory and consonant of all the tendencies of the human mind. They save the trouble of argument and reflection, and all the discomfort of doubt. Who, then, will rashly quarrel with prejudices?

To be sure they may be occasionally the cause of injustice; even the epithet cruel has been from time to time applied to them by precise and over-conscientious people. They often sweep into one category instances the most obviously incongruous, forcing into a single class individuals of all sizes, till the array is like that of the army in Bombastes Furioso,[1] which consists of 'three-foot drummer, six-foot fifer, two very odd privates, and the general.' Prejudice never wastes time in sifting or weighing, measuring or comparing. It glories at once in the promptitude and the irrevocable-ness of its decisions. It is fond of whirling a sword horizontally, and feels quite clear of any guilt when heads are sliced off. The only thing that makes it at all nervous, is the head's venturing to talk afterwards. This is *lèse majesté*[2]—'most tolerable and not to be borne.'

Therefore, we shall not attempt it,—least of all when literary women are in question. It is many a long year, many a dusty century, since this would have been safe. In the days of Miriam or Deborah,[3] perhaps— but that was in the world's callow time, before lordship had become so much an object of desire among the stronger part of creation, and before education had been brought to offer its all-potent arm in aid of this design. Now-a-days, to be betrayed into the quixotism of defending blue- stockings, is to allow one's self to be suspected of wearing them. The utmost extent to which our courage will carry us is some little examina- tion, after the natural-history fashion; some search into growth and prop- erties, aims, destiny, and uses, or no-uses. And to keep very clear of all ungenerous imputations of sympathy, we shall take care to deal with the subject after the desultory, unsystematic, and feminine manner. We re- pudiate learning; we disclaim accuracy; we abjure logic. We shall aim only at the pretty prattle which is conceded to our sex as a right, and admired as a charm.

How many literary women has any one person ever seen? How many has the world seen? How would the list compare in length with that of the pretty triflers who never in the whole course of their mortal lives took up a book with the least intention of obtaining any information from it? The spite which is generally nourished against these unhappy ladies implies great respect; for their numbers are too insignificant to attract notice, if the individuals were not of consequence. And it may be noticed here, as being particularly curious, that the man who declaims loudest against the idea of a writing woman, is sure to be the most vain-glorious of the smallest literary performance on the part of his wife or daughter. The gift of a place does not sooner silence a vehement patriot, than the first essay or magazine story produced by a lady of his family does the indignant definer of 'woman's sphere,' with a pudding and a shirt for its two poles.

But as to the comparative scarcity of literary ladies. It seems strange to a simple looker-on that they should not be prized, at least on the principle of the Queen Anne's farthing, which, valueless in itself, became precious because there were but four struck. There is not even yet a 'mob of gentle[*women*] that write with ease.' Women are said to be peculiarly favoured in the possession of the quality called 'passive courage,' (for- titude?) one of the benevolent provisions of nature for need—but they have always, as a body, shown a good deal of cowardice in this matter. The risks are too fearful. So that really the number is kept down as low as prudence can desire. It would require no Briareus[4] to count on his fingers all that have dabbled in ink during the last century. No fear of usurpation; no danger that the pen will be snatched from strong hands and wielded in defiance, or even in self-defence. A handful of chimney swallows might as well be suspected of erecting their quills against the eagles—or owls. Swallows! literary ladies are hardly more abundant than dodos.

Now let us ask what is the distinguishing mark of the literary woman of our day. Is it inky fingers—corrugated brows—unkempt locks—unrighteous stockings—towering talk—disdain of dinner—aspirations after garments symbolical of authority—any or all of these? Who pretends anything of the kind? One could almost wish there were some startling peculiarities, even though exhibited by only a few individuals, to break up the uniformity of society. What a treat it would be to see a blue enter a party with the suitable airs, and cross the awful space of carpet which sometimes intervenes between the door and the hostess, with gown pinned up from the mud, or one black slipper and one white one, the unconscious head all the while nodding graciously on either side, secure of the due effect of the *entrée!* But alas! no literary lady, since Mrs. Anne Royall,[5] has borne about with her the least outward token of the dreaded power within. Curls, ribbons, bracelets, bouquets, fans—not an item lacking; all correct, to the very shoe-tie. Here surely is a title to respect—a claim to the feminine character, though a loss to society. Lady Mary Wortley Montagu[6] did better when she received her English visitors at Venice in a mask and domino, as a reproof to their curiosity.

And as in dress, so in other matters. Whether from the increased facilities of life, or because the world has grown older, and so more cunning and commonplace, there is no telling a bookish woman any more, even in her housekeeping. There are no more cobwebs in literary parlours than elsewhere. The presence of 'books that are books' does not necessarily now imply the absence of books which are principally covers and 'illustrations.' All sorts of unmanageable and worse than useless bindings may be found intermixed with plain, serviceable duodecimos, and the blue, and yellow, and gray paper of the Reviews and Magazines. Even an inkstand does not take the place of nick-nacks and pretty lumber, though these generally drive the more suspicious article into a by-corner.

'There is a general notion,' says Sydney Smith,[7] 'that if you once suffer women to eat of the tree of knowledge, the rest of the family will soon be reduced to the same aerial and unsatisfactory diet.' But the children of literary mammas seem to be nearly as well cared for, as if their mothers did not, or could not read—which is probably in some minds the criterion of a thoroughly admirable wife and mother. They are even found in some cases to entertain the profoundest and most tender affection for her whom society agrees to consider a deluded female. This would seem as if a love of books did not quite extinguish the affections, or the qualities which inspire affection. 'Would a mother desert her infant for a quadratic equation?' says the satirist just quoted. And it remains to be proved that there is greater complaint of missing buttons, or more neglect of the 'stitch in time,' in consequence of some use of the pen as well as the thimble, than in houses where the only amusement is dressing, and the only serious employment scolding the servants.

With regard to domestic government, the point on which the sensitive wisdom of the world is most alarmed—fearing lest the staff of authority should be wrested from the grasp of the legal ruler by hands that were long ago decided to be too weak to wield it, even if peaceably accorded—does it not seem as if the want of interest in home affairs, which is charged as a natural fault in the literary lady, should set at rest any dread of her usurping too large a share of direction in home arrangements? Is it the absent-minded, absorbed, wool-gathering, star-gazing dame that will quarrel to have the bacon fried instead of boiled? Will she recall the eyes ever 'in fine frenzy rolling,' to the dull earth long enough or with interest enough to insist upon new carpets? It seems as if one fear or the other must be unfounded. Either literary women care about domestic matters or they do not. If they do, their employments cannot be objected against as interfering with exclusively feminine duties; if not, surely their husbands need not fear improper interference.

But we have hitherto neglected to inquire what it is that entitles a woman to the appellation of literary; or perhaps we should express the matter better, if we should say, what fastens upon her that imputation. Must she have written a book? Phœbus Apollo! how few then have claims upon a _tabouret_[8] at thy court! And must the size of the book be taken into account? Then those who dilate most unscrupulously will sit highest. Or will the number of volumes settle precedence? There will, in that case, be little room for any but Mrs. Ellis, Mrs. Gore,[9] and their immediate sisterhood. But to the point. If not a book, will a poem be sufficient? or an essay? or a magazine article? Then more of us are included in the glory or odium of female authorship. Or does writing letters make one literary? In these Californian days it is to be hoped not, lest some of our fair friends should be tempted to neglect their absent brothers rather than be liable to mis-construction, in so important a particular. Writing letters sometimes ends in writing books, as more than Madame de Sévigné[10] can testify. How is it with keeping a journal? Does that come within the canon? Might it not be maliciously interpreted into writing a book in disguise?

Does the toleration for which a female writer may hope depend in any degree upon the class of subjects which may engage her pen? We have an idea that some gentlemen would award a palm (no pun, positively,) to her who writes a Cook's Oracle, where a rod or a fool's cap would be the doom of a lady who should presume to touch political economy. Next to a family receipt-book, one would suppose books of instruction for children would be most popular in female hands; but there is no doubt that some men think Mrs. Barbauld[11] wore, or should have worn, a beard, and would be surprised to see a picture of Mrs. Trimmer[12] in petticoats. The novel of fashionable life, provided it have no suspicion of a moral, and make no pretension to teach anything whatever, may pass as feminine, without detracting from the fame of its author; but a novel with the least bit of bone in it is 'mannish'—a very different term from 'manly.' Poetry, provided it be of the sigh-away, die-away cast, does not injure a lady's reputation; acrostic-making is considered quite an accomplishment, and so are watch-paper verses; but poetry which some unthinking, out-of-the-world critics praise as 'masculine' for vigour and freshness, is insufferable. If we could show to some objectors the delicate Elizabeth Barrett Browning[13]—the minutest, most fragile, most ethereal creature the sun ever shone upon, with a voice like a ring-dove's, we might swear in vain to her identity as the author of some of the strongest and bravest poetry that has appeared in our day; so obstinate a conviction exists in some minds of the close connexion between mental power and masculine coarseness.

It seems a little inconsistent that anybody should venture in our day to put such dangerous weapons as the *ologies* into the hands of a sex to whose peculiar charms too much mind is known to be so fatal. Why not leave a girl in the hands of the nurse until she is fit to be transferred to those of the seamstress, the pastry-cook, the dancing-master, the teacher of music, in succession? Why occupy precious hours and risk fine eyes over even French and Italian, which could be learned in colloquy with these artists? Why not adapt means to ends? Is it certain that school-knowledge will pass in at one ear and out at the other? If not, how far safer not to impart it! Considering the advantage that may be taken of it, the unsexing and unsphering that may ensue upon an indiscreet use of it, surely it were best to send Grammar and History, Philosophy and Mathematics, to the limbo of forgotten things, as far as females are concerned. If Madame de Staël[14] had been brought up only to sing and dance, regulate household affairs, and tend children, would she have written the books which pro- voked Napoleon to banish her from Paris? If Mrs. Somerville[15] had spent years sitting with her feet in the stocks and her arms pinioned in a back- board to make her genteel, while her eyes were employed in counting bead-work, or devising stitches in crochet, could she ever have lowered herself by writing about the geography of the heavens? Prevention is cer- tainly better than cure. Choke the fountain rather than have to dam the river (no pun will be suspected here). Shut up our schools for young ladies; bid the teachers 'go spin!' Use the copy-books for recipes or papillottes; the learned treatises popularized 'for the use of schools' to kindle fires less to be dreaded than those of literary ambition: and if our daughters should not thereafter be 'like polished stones at the corners of the temple,' they will at least make kitchen-hearths, which we all know to be a far more obviously useful part of the social edifice.

One great duty of woman, if not the greatest, is to be agreeable. Now, if teaching her to think for herself, and so putting her upon the temptation of expressing her thoughts, imperil in the least degree this her high avoca- tion, we vote for the instant abandonment of female cultivation, and would advocate a heavier fine on selling to a female under forty, unaccompanied by parent or guardian, a card of Joseph Gillott's pens,[16] than for allowing a paper of poison to go from the shop unlabelled. We would be the very Jack Cade[17] of legislators for such offenders. To be sure there may be question as to the universality of the feeling on which our zeal is predicated. Some men openly profess to like intelligent women, and there are doubtless others who in secret do not altogether reprobate the use of the pen in female hands, although they may for harmony's sake refrain from the avowal of such liberality, except, as we have hinted, the case fall within the limits of their own family circle, when they usually go beyond mere tolera- tion. It is very desirable that unanimity be obtained in this matter. The natural desire to be agreeable will be quite strong enough to set things right after they are fully understood. To stand well with all men will far outweigh the penurious and timid praise of a few. So true is this that Madame de Staël herself confessed that she would gladly give her intellect and her fame for beauty!

But is beauty always the alternative? Ah, there is an important ques- tion. Many scandals have been uttered against the outward charms of literary ladies. 'Ugly!' said a celebrated poet in our own hearing, on this very topic; 'ugly, yes—they *all* are!' Which must mean that lines of thought are disadvantages to the peculiar charm of the female face—an equivocal compliment, rather. But waiving this delicate point, is the face which has no lines of thought, on that account beautiful? If not, how fearful the risk of leaving the head unfurnished! If the face may be vacant, yet not lovely—if we may neglect the brain without securing the beauty, how difficult becomes the decision of the parent. In old times—happy times!—when fairies attended at the birth of daughters, and offered choice of gifts, the balance between beauty and good sense was easily struck. It was understood that to select the one, precluded all chance of obtaining the other without a new and more compulsive spell. Now, without any great insight into futurity, and with only a little fat beginning of a face, with a button nose and twinkling eyes to guide our estimate of proba-bilities of comeliness, while on the other hand frowns the fear lest furnish-ing the brain may, by giving a superabundance of meaning to the face, mar the promise of beauty, how anxious must be the deliberation! A critical survey of society might lead one to suppose that with some parents a decision proves impossible, the poor child being left to grow up without either beauty or brains.

Our own convictions on this subject were rendered unalterable some years since, in the course of a lecture by a young gentleman before a debating society, at whose sitting we were so happy as to assist. The ques-tion was one not unfrequently discussed on those occasions—the com-parative education of the sexes. Our friend was warm against sharing the sciences with women. His picture of the ideal blue-stocking, a hideous man-woman, with high-crowned cap and spectacles, hoarse voice and masculine stride, still haunts our imagination, and has ever proved an effectual scare-crow in that field. On the other hand, his fancy's sketch of a charming young person, was such as to leave in one's mind a somewhat confused mass of roses, lilies, smiles, blushes, pearls, snow, raven's wings, and Aurora's fingers,[18] very fascinating, though suggestive of despair to most of the sex. But what made the most distinct impression on our memory was the question, repeated in various forms as different branches of knowledge were examined with reference to their fitness for female use—'Will it render her more *alluring?*' Here lay the key—far more po-tent than Blue Beard's, which locked up only women literally headless—to the whole popular philosophy of female claims on the score of intellect. This hint as to the object of woman's being, solved a world of doubts. Here was a touchstone by which to try any pursuit—a test to determine the value of any talent. Whatever does not conduce to the grand aim must be, if not noxious, at best indifferent. Whoever contends that an education regulated by this principle would leave woman insignificant and unhappy, shows only his ignorance of the world; for do we not see every day splendid people who avow it, consciously or unconsciously? and can splendid people be unhappy or insignificant?

There is one potent argument against allowing women in habits of literary employment—the injury that would arise to the great cause of public amusements. Our theatres would be worse filled even than they are at present, and the opera would cease its languishing existence at once, if the fair eyes that now are fain to let down their "fringed curtains" as a veil against the intensity of floods of gas-light, should learn to prefer the shaded study-lamp at home, and the singing of the quiet fire to the louder efforts of the cantatrice. Dancing, except in horrible sobriety, after the piano, would become obsolete; waltzing might be studied in the abstract, or as an illustration of the revolution of the heavenly bodies; but 'certain stars' would no longer 'shoot madly from their spheres,' to join the giddy round in person. Parties would break up at eleven; for eyes and nerves would so rise in value if put to serious use, that any wilful expenditure of their powers would soon be voted *mauvais ton;* [19] and if that should ever happen, adieu to suppers and champagne! There is really no end to the overturn that might result from an innovation of this sort. Imagination pictures the splendid fabric of Fashion tottering to its fall—undermined by that seemingly impotent instrument, the pen, wielded by female hands. We shrink from our own picture of so mournful a reversal of the present happy state of things. It is one of the perversities of the imagination to torment itself with delineations of what can never by any possibility occur; and this is truly a case in point.

The truth being conceded that no women but those who are ugly and unattractive should or do write, a thought suggests itself with respect to the limited duration of the beauty which is so justly considered the most desirable of female possessions, and the most natural and proper bar to any extensive cultivation of the mind. As none but very robust beauty lasts beyond forty, would it not be advisable to establish schools, specially fitted for that age, in which the remains of a lovely woman might have an opportunity of some education suited to the thirty years which may be supposed still to lie before her? It would be irksome to pass so long a period in silence, and mortifying to continue to talk nonsense without rosy lips to set it off. Here a certain amount of knowledge might be communicated by those whom inexorable plainness of person had condemned to intellectual exercises in early life; and the circumstance might prove mutually beneficial, since the husbands of the once beautiful would undoubtedly be willing to pay liberally for having some ideas infused into their minds, as provision for the conversation of old age. The face could no longer be injured, while the head, and perhaps the heart too, might gain materially.

> 'Teeth for the toothless, ringlets for the bald,
> And roses for the cheeks of faded age—'

would be valueless, compared with this more potent elixir of life. The practice of the old surgeons, who sometimes filled the shrunken veins of decreptitude with the rich blood of bounding youth, might be considered a precedent for such efforts as we propose. Scruples were sometimes entertained as to the lawfulness of that mode of repairing the decay of Nature; but to the attempt to make education the substitute for beauty, we are sure society will not object, even though the result should be that 'dim horror'—a literary woman.

EXPLANATORY NOTES

A NEW HOME

TITLE PAGE

1. William Shakespeare (1564–1616), *A Midsummer's Night's Dream* (1600) III.i.39–41.
2. Sir Philip Sidney (1554–86). This line does not appear in the *Arcadia*.

PREFACE

1. Parthia was an ancient kingdom of western Asia. Parthian horsemen were supposedly very skilled in battle, using tricks to baffle their opponents such as throwing missiles backward while in real or pretended flight.

2. Mary Russell Mitford (1787–1855), author of *Our Village,* a collection of sketches about British provincial and country life (1819–32). Written in a realistic and humorous style, they were popular in the United States as well as England.

CHAPTER I

1. William Cullen Bryant (1794–1878).
2. Alexander Pope (1688–1744), "Epistle to Miss Blount" (1712)18.
3. See Preface, n. 2.
4. François de La Rochefoucauld (1613–80), *Maximes* (1665)132. "It is easier to be wise for others than to be so for oneself."
5. John Milton (1608–74), *Paradise Lost* (1667) 9.445.
6. Percy Bysshe Shelley (1792–1822), "The Sensitive Plant" 7.
7. Charles Lamb (1775–1834), British poet and writer in the romantic style.
8. Edward George Bulwer-Lytton (1803–73), novelist and poet, whose earliest published verse was the Byronic tale *Ismael* (1820).
9. Milton *L'Allegro* (1631)140.
10. Charles Fenno Hoffman (1806–84). The reference is to Hoffman's book *Winter in the West* (1835), which describes his horseback trip through sparsely settled Michigan and Illinois.
11. Probably James Hall (1793–1868), editor in frontier Illinois and author of many books about pioneer life including *Letters from the West* (1828) and *The Sketches of History, Life and Manners in the West* (1834).

12. Hoffman, *A Winter in the West*, refers to the settlers' curious habit of not building their houses in the "tempting looking oak-openings" (154).

13. Pope, *Dunciad* (1728) 2.191.

14. To purge or cleanse.

CHAPTER II

1. Shakespeare, *Cymbeline* (1611) III.xi.64–65.

2. Shakespeare, *Julius Caesar* (1598–1600) II.i.230.

3. Eblis is a jinn (demon) of Arabian mythology, the ruler of fallen angels.

4. Edmund Spenser (c. 1552–99), *The Faerie Queene* (1590) 2.7.29.6.

5. Milton, *Paradise Lost* 4.162–63.

6. Don Quixote's dilapidated horse in Miguel de Cervantes' *Don Quixote* (1605, 1615).

CHAPTER III

1. Sir Francis Bacon (1561–1626).

2. In *The Antiquary* (1816) by Sir Walter Scott (1771–1832), Herman Dousterswivel is a German adventurer who tricks Sir Arthur Wardour by a pretended discovery of a treasure, and is himself similarly tricked by Ochiltree.

3. A wandering eye (Lat.).

4. Sylvester Graham (1794–1851), American dietician, best known as an advocate of unbolted (Graham) flour.

5. Montacute is an English surname of a line of nobles in the position of earl of Salisbury.

CHAPTER IV

1. Washington Irving (1783–1859). Diedrich Knickerbocker is the fictitious chronicler of Irving's humorous *History of New York* (1809).

2. Abraham Cowley (1618–67).

3. Isaac A. VanAmburgh is credited with pioneering wild animal acts sometime between 1820 and 1835 when he first entered a cage containing a lion, a tiger, a leopard, and a panther.

4. Roderick Dhu is a character in Sir Walter Scott's novel *The Lady of the Lake* (1810). A rebel Scottish Highland chief, he was known for his ruthless military tactics.

5. A houri is a nymph of the Mohammedan Paradise, hence a name applied allusively to a voluptuously beautiful woman.

Explanatory Notes

CHAPTER V

1. Shakespeare, *Romeo and Juliet* (1595) V.i.60–61.
2. George Withers (1588–1667), British poet and pampleteer.
3. The substance obtained by rasping, slicing, or calcining the horns of harts, formerly the chief source of ammonia, to be used as smelling salts. (OED)
4. Mischieviousness (Fr.).
5. One who openly acknowledges—professes—his or her religious belief.

1. Spenser, *The Faerie Queene* 1.1.41.2–5.
2. Joseph Warton (1722–1800), British poet and critic.
3. Idleness (It.).

1. Shakespeare, *The Winter's Tale* (1611) IV.iii.82 and IV.iv.315–20.

1. La Rochefoucauld, *Maximes* 134. "Our wisdom is not less or no more at the mercy of fortune than our possessions."
2. Sir Walter Scott, source unidentified.
3. Johann Nepomuk Maelzel (1772–1838). German inventor of mechanical instruments, whose other inventions include the metronome and an automatic chess player. Mechanician (1808) to the court at Vienna.
4. Someone who is not married (Fr.).
5. To divert attention from being bored, to seek diversion (Fr.).
6. Esau and Jacob were the biblical sons of Isaac, and were the fathers of the rival nations Edom and Israel. Esau sold his birthright to Jacob for a bowl of lentils once when he was hungry (Gen. 2.5–33).
7. An inopportune event, a tiresome or mortifying mischance (Fr.).

CHAPTER IX

1. Thomas Campbell (1777–1844), British poet.
2. Shakespeare, *Timon of Athens* (1607) IV.iii.328–29.
3. Tadmor is the biblical name of the ancient city Palmyra, an important commercial center of the ancient world which is now mere ruins in the desert.

4. In English folk materials, Tom is a general name for dullards or fools of various kinds (Tom o'Bedlam, a lunatic, for example).

5. A game played around the fire. A piece of stick is set on fire and whirled around rapidly in the hand of the first player, who says, "Robin's alight, and if he goes out I will saddle your back." It is then passed on to the next player, who says the same thing, and so on. The person who lets the spark die must pay a forfeit.

CHAPTER X

1. Oliver Goldsmith (1728–74), *She Stoops to Conquer* (1773), V.ii.
2. William Cowper (1731–1800), "John Gilprin" (1782) 16.
3. Robert Burns (1759–96), *Epistle to a Young Friend* (1786), 87–88.

CHAPTER XI

1. Pope, *Dunciad* (1728) 4.493, 627–28.
2. Jewelry (Fr.).
3. Harriet Martineau (1802–76), English philosophical and religious writer. In 1834 she visited America and assisted the Abolitionists. The work referred to is either *Society in America* (1836) or *Retrospect of Western Travel* (1838).
4. A cat fight to the finish.

CHAPTER XII

1. Sir Francis Bacon, source unidentified.
2. Pope, *Essay on Criticism* (1711) 213–14.
3. Since the Roman poet Virgil (70–19 BC) celebrated human courage and wisdom in his works, he came to be represented in the Middle Ages as a magician and enchanter with the power to outwit the devil. Much Italian folklore represents him in this manner, and in one story Virgil is said to have tricked the devil into a glass bottle, keeping him there until he had learned the devil's magic. The text to which Kirkland refers is possibly the *Gesta romanorum*, a collection of popular tales in Latin, each with a moral attached, compiled at the end of the thirteenth century or beginning of the fourteenth. Shakespeare, Chaucer, and Rossetti, among others, use tales and plots from it.
4. Phillida may be a generic term for shepherdess; the reference could also be to an anonymous poem, "Phillada Flouts Me."

Explanatory Notes

1. La Rochefoucauld, *Maximes,* 270 in 1st ed. (1665). "In all professions and in all arts, everyone creates a look and an exterior that he puts in place of the thing whose quality he wants to have; in such a way everybody is composed only of masks; and it is useless for us to try to find anything real there."

2. Sir Francis Bacon, source unidentified.

3. According to biblical tradition, Shinar is the land of Nimrod, including Babel, Erech, and Accad. Hence the reference is to the Tower of Babel (Gen. 11.2).

4. Edwin Forrest (1806−72), American actor. The play referred to is probably a translation of Friedrich Schiller's drama *Wilhelm Tell* (1804).

5. Romance by François-Auguste-René de Chateaubriand (1768−1848) which first appeared in France in 1801. *Atala* is the story of an American Indian girl who became converted to Christianity, and is a highly romantic evocation of the American wilderness.

6. Cowper, *The Task* (1783−84) 1 ("The Sofa") 560−56.

CHAPTER XIV

1. Shakespeare, *The Tempest* (1611) I.i.34.

2. Shakespeare, *Hamlet* (1600−1601) II.ii.549−50.

3. Thomas Gray (1716−71) "Elegy Written in a Country Churchyard" (1750), stanza 8.

4. Touchstone is a shrewd, honest goldsmith in *Eastward, Ho* (1605) by Ben Jonson (1572−1637), George Chapman (1559−1634), and John Marston (1575−1634).

CHAPTER XV

1. Scott, *The Antiquary.*

2. Shakespeare, *The Tempest* II.ii.27−30.

3. An unauthorized anthology of poems by various authors, published by William Jaggard in 1599, and attributed on the title page to Shakespeare but containing only a few authentic poems by him.

4. The original poem reads: "Revolving in his alter'd soul / The various turns of chance below," Dryden, *Alexander's Feast,* 85−86.

5. Pan was the Greek god of pastures and flocks. He played a group of pipes (syrinx) made up of reeds.

6. In *The Critic* (1799) by Richard Brinsley Sheridan (1751−1816), Lord

Burleigh is a character in Mr. Puff's play within a play, *The Spanish Armada*. The character has no lines, only the memorable nod which, according to Mr. Puff, expresses a great deal.

CHAPTER XVI

1. Shakespeare, *All's Well That Ends Well* (1603–04) II.i.159–60.

2. Philip Dormer Stanhope, fourth earl of Chesterfield (1694–1773), known for his worldliness and elegant manner.

3. Galen (130–200), Greek physician and philosophical writer whose works in physiology remained the standard until the Renaissance.

4. Shepherd in Virgil's seventh ecologue, the *Idylls* of Theocritus (c. 310–250 BC), and Spenser's *Faerie Queene*. A conventional name in pastoral poetry for a shepherd or a rustic swain.

5. The science of medicine as practiced by a "professional" doctor: Kirkland refers to the prejudice against doctors.

CHAPTER XVII

1. Spenser, *The Faerie Queene* 2.7.28.1–3, 7–10.

2. Sir Francis Bacon, source unidentified.

3. Nominative case of Latin declension of "this"; Kirkland probably refers to the Clavers' son's delight in having a room of his own in which to study.

4. Poem in *Irish Melodies* (1817) by Thomas Moore (1779–1852).

5. Lady Mary Wortley Montague (1689–1762), English writer.

6. To excess, to a shocking extreme (Fr.).

CHAPTER XVIII

1. Shakespeare, *Julius Caesar* III.ii.73.

2. Charles Colton (1780–1832), British clergyman. *Lacon: or many things in few words: addressed to those who think* is a collection of aphorisms (1822).

3. Whoever it may be (Fr.).

4. Robert Burns, "On the Late Captain Grose's Peregrinations thro' Scotland, Collecting the Antiquities of that Kingdom" (1789), 2. In Burns's text the line reads, "Frae Maidenkirk to Johny Groats."

5. Samuel Johnson (1709–84), English essayist and poet.

Explanatory Notes

1. La Rouchefoucauld, *Maximes* 61. "The happiness and unhappiness of men depends less on their temperament than on chance."

2. George Gordon, Lord Byron (1788–1824), "Werner" (1822) 1.134–37, 139–41.

3. Shakespeare, *A Midsummer's Night Dream* II.i.2.

4. Half-Swiss (Fr.).

5. Hab. (2.2). The full biblical quote is: "Write the vision; make it plain upon tablets, so he who runs may read it."

6. Shakespeare, *Hamlet* I.ii.11.

CHAPTER XX

1. Felicia Hemans (1793–1835), British poet.

2. Sir Francis Bacon, source unidentified.

3. Either *The American Gardner: A treatise on the situation, soil, fencing, and laying out of garden's; on the making and managing of hot-beds and green-houses; and on propagation and cultivation* (1819) by William Cobbett or *The American Gardner: containing ample directions for working a kitchen garden every month in the year; and copious instructions for the cultivation of flower gardens, vineyards, nurseries, hop-yards, green-houses, and hot houses* (1804) by John Ralph Gardiner. Both works were in multiple editions when Kirkland's book was published.

4. A rotating bar bristling with spikes set on the top of a wall to discourage entry; a line of fixed spikes or fragments of broken glass on top of a wall.

5. This word does not actually exist in French: *potager* or *potagère* are used to mean vegetables to be used for culinary purposes.

6. Recasting (It.).

7. As few others do (Fr.).

8. Bellows mender from Shakespeare's *A Midsummer's Nights' Dream*. He is referred to only as Flute in the play.

9. Cardinal de Retz (1613–79), French politician and author. Probably a reference to his *Mémoires*, which detail court life of his day.

10. Middle English word meaning the stems or tops of cultivated plants, especially after the crop has been gathered.

11. In the Spanish mode, legs to the side of the horse (Fr.).

12. Dutch governor of New Netherland (New York), 1633–37.

Explanatory Notes

CHAPTER XXI

1. La Rochefoucauld, *Maximes* 137. "Men would not live long in society if they were not the dupes of one another."

2. George Colman the Younger (1762–1836), *Sylvester Daggerwood: or New Hay at the Old Market* (1808) sc. 1.

CHAPTER XXII

1. Colton, *Lacon*.

2. Title and heroine of a romance by Baron de la Motte Fouqué (1777–1843) published in German in 1811. A water spirit, Undine is endowed with a soul by her marriage with a mortal.

CHAPTER XXIII

1. Thomas Campbell (1567–1620), British author. Source unidentified.

2. Jets of water, a fountain (Fr.).

3. Frances Trollope (1780–1863), English novelist and writer of travel works, most notably about the American frontier.

4. By chance. The correct French is *par hasard*.

CHAPTER XXIV

1. Byron, *Childe Harold* (1816) 3.212–15.

CHAPTER XXV

1. Shakespeare, *The Tempest* III.iii.21–26.

2. Overseas (Fr.).

CHAPTER XXVI

1. Thomas Moore, source unidentified.

2. The refinements of social life, courtesies (Fr.).

3. Very happy (Fr.).

CHAPTER XXVII

1. Shakespeare, *The Merry Wives of Windsor* (1602) II.ii.66–67.

2. Shakespeare, *Romeo and Juliet* II.ii.60.

3. Miss Biddy Fudge is a character in Thomas Moore's satirical novel *The Fudge Family in Paris,* published in 1818.

4. Literally "no vice" in French. Perfect, without blemish.

5. James Crichton (1560–82), Scottish scholar and adventurer, celebrated for his extraordinary accomplishments and attainments in languages, the sciences, and the arts.

6. Affectedly dainty. Probably a variation of *mimpsy pimsy,* an English vernacular expression for fastidious or excessively dainty.

7. The Della-Cruscans were a group of English poets living in Italy at the end of the 18th century who wrote sentimental verse.

8. Hero, Ursula, and Beatrice are all characters in Shakespeare's *Much Ado about Nothing* (1600). "Pleached bower" is from III.i.7, "like a lapwing" from III.i.24.

9. Battle-dore and shuttlecock, the game that evolved into badminton.

10. William Harrison Ainsworth (1805–82), British author of historical and criminal romances, and George Payne Rainsford James (1799–1860), English novelist and historical writer. Both wrote in the tradition of Sir Walter Scott.

11. Bulwer–Lytton, British novelist, poet, dramatist, politician.

12. James Fenimore Cooper (1789–1851), American novelist best known for his *Leather-Stocking Tales,* a group of romantic historical action novels of the American wilderness.

13. Catharine Maria Sedgwick (1789–1867), popular American novelist. Her characters include Native Americans and the poor, who often speak in dialect.

14. Patron saints of shoemakers, tanners, and saddlers, Crispin and Crispinian were martyrs of the early Christian church who had supported themselves by mending and making shoes.

15. "Pour passer le temps" (Fr.), to pass time.

16. Novel by Benjamin Disraeli (1804–81), published in 1831.

CHAPTER XXVIII

1. Goldsmith, *The Traveller* (1764), 153–58.

2. Shakespeare, *2 Henry VI* (1585) III.ii.161–62.

CHAPTER XXIX

1. Felicia Hemans. Reference unknown.

2. Hyson is a species of green tea from China.

Explanatory Notes

CHAPTER XXX

1. Shakespeare, *The Merry Wives of Windsor* I.iv.62–64, and I.i.34, 42–44, 146–47.
2. Shakespeare, *Julius Caesar* (1599) I. ii.120, 121–22.
3. Castle in Blarney, Ireland. The fame of the castle is due to the Blarney stone, a block bearing the name of the builder and the date it was built (1446). Legend has it that whoever kisses the stone is endowed with powers of cajolery.

CHAPTER XXXI

1. Scott, *The Antiquary.*
2. Character in *The Review* (1800), a play by Colman. Quotem is an extremely talkative jack-of-all-trades.
3. Pope, "The Basset-Table," 81.

CHAPTER XXXII

1. Scott, *The Antiquary.*
2. La Rochefoucauld, *Maximes* 194. "One can be more clever than another but not more clever than all the others."
3. Gray, "Elegy Written in a Country Churchyard," stanza 19.
4. Sir David Wilkie (1785–1841), Scottish genre painter, appointed royal painter in 1830.
5. In later Jewish demonology, a destructive demon gifted with the power to look inside houses as he flies over them.

CHAPTER XXXIII

1. Cowper, *The Task* 2 ("The Time Piece") 326–28.
2. *Ibid.* 338.
3. Jam. 3.5.
4. Cowper, *The Task* 2.395–96.
5. Philip Dormer Stanhope, earl of Chesterfield (1694–1773), *Letters to His Son* (1772), letter of 5. Sept. 1748. The full quote reads, "Women, then, are only children of a larger growth."
6. There's a good time coming (Fr.).

Explanatory Notes

CHAPTER XXXIV

1. A device whereby a colored image is projected through a small hole or a lens onto a suitable surface in a dark room.

2. Character in Sheridan's *The School for Scandal* (1777).

3. Goldsmith, *The Deserted Village* (1770) 211.

CHAPTER XXXV

1. Samuel Taylor Coleridge (1772–1834), "Christabel" (1816) 408–09, 422, 423.

CHAPTER XXXVI

1. Byron, *Childe Harold* 3.406–08, 707–10.

2. Cowper, *The Task* 1 ("The Sofa") 71. The line reads correctly, "The ladies first 'Gan murmur—as becomes the softer sex."

3. The deformed half-human slave of Prospero in Shakespeare's *Tempest*.

4. Nathaniel P. Willis (1806–67), American man of letters and friend of Kirkland.

5. William Hazlitt (1778–1830), British critic and essayist.

CHAPTER XXXVII

1. Kirkland condensed this sonnet by Petrarch (1304–1374) considerably. The complete English translation is:

> The time and scene where I a slave became
> When I remember, and the knot so dear
> Which Love's own hand so firmly fasten'd here,
> Which made my bitter sweet, my grief a game;
> My heart, with fuel stored, is, as a flame
> Of those soft sighs familiar to mine ear,
> So lit within, its very sufferings cheer;
> On these I live, and other aid disclaim.
> That sun, alone which beameth for my sight,
> With his strong rays my ruin'd bosom burns
> Now in the eve of life as in its prime,
> And from afar, so gives me warmth and light,
> Fresh and entire, at every hour, returns
> On memory the knot, the scene, the time.

In the English translation of the Sonnets arranged by Marsand, this sonnet is numbered CXLII. In the Italian edition by Giosue Carducci and Severino Ferrari (G. C. Sansoni, 1946), however, it is numbered CLXXVI.

2. William Wordsworth (1770–1850), *The Excursion* (1814) 4.1127.

3. Read a little, think a lot (Fr.).

4. Character in Shakespeare's *As You Like It* (1599). Jaques is part of the Duke's court and specializes in melancholy philosophizing.

5. John Galt (1779–1839), Scottish fiction writer.

6. Fanny Kemble (1809–93), Anglo-American actress who made her first public appearance in 1829.

7. Laziness. The correct spelling is "paresse."

8. I doubt that (Fr.).

9. Madame Maria Felicia Malibran (1808–36), French opera star. Kirkland is commenting that this artist's life was tragically cut short at the height of her career.

10. Narrative poem (1801) by Robert Southey (1774–1843). Thalaba is a young Muslim who sets out to destroy an undersea kingdom of magicians. He dies while doing so, but is reunited in paradise with his wife.

CHAPTER XXXVIII

1. *Il pastor fido*, "The Faithful Shepherd" (1590), pastoral drama by Giovanni Battista Guarini (1538–1612). Amaryllis is the shepherdess.

2. Pietro Metastasio (1698–1782), Italian poet, court poet at Vienna. He provided opera librettos for various composers, including Glück Handel, and Mozart.

3. Cowper, *The Task* 5 ("The Winter Morning Walk") 144.

CHAPTER XXXIX

1. Distractedly or madly in love (Fr.).

2. Pseudonym of Bryan Waller Proctor (1787–1874), English poet whose *Dramatic Scenes and Other Poems* was published in 1819.

3. See ch. XXXVIII, n. 2.

4. See ch. XIII, n. 5.

5. Poem by Campbell, published in 1809.

6. *The New Domestic Medicine: or Universal Family Physician* (1802), by William Buchan (1729–1805). *The Frugal Housewife* is either by Susannah Carter or a book by the same title by Lydia Maria Child (ca. 1829); multiple editions of both existed

Explanatory Notes

at the time Kirkland was writing. *The Whole Duty of Man; laid down in a plain and familiar way for the use of all, but especially the meanest reader* (ca. 1716) by Richard Allestree.

CHAPTER XL

1. Nathaniel P. Willis, *Bianca Visconti* (1837) I.i.
2. Heart that is being overcome by emotion, "trembling heart" (Fr.).
3. May refer to Colonel John Symmes (1742–1814), pioneer and colonizer of the Northwest Territory.

CHAPTER XLI

1. Shakespeare, *The Tempest* II.i.50–51.

CHAPTER XLII

1. Shakespeare, *The Tempest* IV.i.1–8.
2. Shakespeare, *As You Like It* II.i.2–3.

CHAPTER XLIII

1. La Rochefoucauld, *Maximes* 437, "One must not judge the merit of a man by his great qualities, but by how he uses them."
2. Jean Racine (1639–99) *Les Plaideurs,* (1688) III.i. "Words, long as your arm; big words, which would go from here to Pontoise."
3. See ch. IV, n. 1.
4. William Cowper, *The Task* 4 ("The Winter Evening") 59–60.
5. Nickname of Robert M'Gregor (1671–1734), Scottish patriot. According to Scott, "his shoulders were so broad . . . as . . . gave him something the air of being too square in respect to his stature; and his arms, tough, round, sinewy, and strong, were so very long as to be rather a deformity" (*Rob Roy,* 1817, ch. xxiii).

CHAPTER XLIV

1. Racine, *Les Plaideurs* III.iii.

Dandin: Ta, ta, ta, ta. That will instruct this affair! . . . Has one ever pleaded with such a method? But what is the jury saying about it?

. . . .

215

My, my! I no longer understand anything about it. About the world, about chaos, I have a mixed-up mind. Hey! Conclude!

2. Tailor (Ger.).

3. The principal character of the *Iliad* on the Trojan side; the greatest warrior of the Trojans.

4. Frederick the Great (1712–86) king of Prussia from 1740 until his death. A military genius, who raised Prussia to the rank of a powerful state.

5. Pope, *The Rape of the Lock* (1712) 4.83–84.

CHAPTER XLV

1. Scott, *The Antiquary.*

2. Shakespeare, *Anthony and Cleopatra* (1606–07) III.ix.71.

3. The model of enduring patience and wifely obedience. One heroine of the last tale of *The Decameron* (1349–50) by Giovanni Boccaccio (1313–75). The tale concerns a man who marries a woman of great beauty and subjects her to almost unendurable trials until he is convinced of her patience and devotion.

4. Romance story by Irish novelist Regina Maria Roche (1764–1845), published in 1798.

CHAPTER XLVI

1. Shakespeare, *Love's Labour's Lost* (1595), V.ii.794–802.

2. Shakespeare, *All's Well That Ends Well* II.i.53–56.

3. House of prayer (Ger.).

4. Cowper, *The Task* 6 ("The Winter Walk at Noon") 112–14.

5. Epithet concerning luxury, originating from the ancient Italian city of Sybaris, founded 720 BC and celebrated for its wealth.

6. Fraternity or death (Fr.).

7. Sir Francis Bacon, *Essays* (1625), ded.

8. An aristocrat, a noble woman, literally, lady of the manor (Fr.).

CHAPTER XLVII

1. One who resembles another in class or character (Fr.).

2. Tuscan is a term applied to a method of plaiting the fine wheaten straw grown in Tuscany for hats, bonnets, etc. (OED)

3. Ancient Greek goddess, originally a sort of earth goddess. Prophecy was one of her attributes. She became a personification of law, custom, and justice.

EXPLANATORY NOTES

LITERARY WOMEN

1. A farce by the British writer W. B. Rhodes (1772–1826), published in 1810.

2. High treason, an offense against the majesty of a sovereign or a nation (Fr.).

3. Hebrew prophetess and sister of Moses and Aaron, Miriam is represented as giving a response to the song of Moses sung by the Israelites at the Red Sea (Exod. 15.20). Deborah, biblical prophetess and judge of Israel, sang a famous song of triumph after a victory over the Canaanites (Judg. 5).

4. In Greek mythology, a monster with a hundred arms, a son of Uranus and Ge.

5. American writer (1769–1854), who began writing to support herself after a nephew challenged the inheritance left her by her husband. In 1824 Royall went to Washington in near rags to lobby Congress to gain an income for her husband's military service.

6. English writer (1689–1762), eldest daughter of fifth earl of Kingston, she settled in Venice in 1758.

7. Scottish satirist and essayist. (1721–71)

8. A low stool without back or arms.

9. Sarah Stickney Ellis (1812–72) was a prolific British author of advice books for women. Catherine Grace Frances Gore (1799–1861), British writer, published about seventy novels between 1824 and 1862. Her novels, with their marked predilection for titled ladies and fashionable life, were parodied by Thackeray.

10. Marie de Rabutin-Chantal, Marquise de Sévigné (1626–96). Her reputation rests on her lifelong correspondence with her daughter, published posthumously in 1725.

11. Anna Laetitia Barbauld (1743–1824), British writer, published several volumes of prose for children with her brother John Aikin.

12. Sarah Trimmer (1741–1810), British author of children's prose and textbooks.

13. Elizabeth Barrett Browning (1806–61), noted British poet; she was ill and frail for much of her life.

14. Anne-Louise-Germaine de Staël (1766–1817), French writer who occupied a central place in French intellectual life for over three decades. The work

referred to is *De l'Allemagne* (1810), which opened French literature to the influence of the German writers and thinkers at the end of the eighteenth century.

15. Mary Somerville (1780–1872), British mathematician and scientific writer.

16. Joseph Gillott (1799–1873), British manufacturer of pens.

17. Leader of rebellion in 1450 against English royal forces, he is represented by Shakespeare in *2 Henry VI* as reckless, ferocious, and vulgar.

18. Roman goddess of the dawn, represented by poets as rising out of the ocean in a chariot, her rosy fingers dripping gentle dew.

19. Bad fashion (Fr.).